In the Service of
the Sultan

Happy Birthday, Robert!
With kind salaams and very best wishes.

In the Service of
the Sultan

A First Hand Account of the Dhofar Insurgency

Ian Gardiner

January 2022

Pen & Sword
MILITARY

First published in Great Britain in 2006
and reprinted in 2007, 2008, 2009, 2011, 2014, 2015 and 2017
by Pen & Sword Military
An imprint of Pen & Sword Books Limited
47 Church Street
Barnsley
South Yorkshire
S70 2AS

ISBN 978 1 84415 467 8

Typeset in 10/12pt Palatino
by Concept, Huddersfield

Printed and bound in the UK
by CPI Group (UK) Ltd, Croydon, CRO 4YY

Pen & Sword Books Limited incorporates the imprints of Atlas,
Archaeology, Aviation, Discovery, Family History, Fiction, History, Maritime,
Military, Military Classics, Politics, Select, Transport, True Crime, Air World,
Frontline Publishing, Leo Cooper, Remember When, Seaforth Publishing,
The Praetorian Press, Wharncliffe Local History, Wharncliffe Transport,
Wharncliffe True Crime and White Owl.

For a complete list of Pen & Sword titles please contact
PEN & SWORD BOOKS LIMITED
47 Church Street, Barnsley, South Yorkshire S70 2AS, United Kingdom
E-mail: enquiries@pen-and-sword.co.uk
Website: www.pen-and-sword.co.uk

Dedicated to the soldiers sailors and airmen of the many nations who fought in the Dhofar War 1965–1975, and remembering especially

Corporal Hamed Khamis
killed in action on 13 March 1974
and
Major Johnny Braddell-Smith
killed in action on 25 December 1974.

Contents

Maps

Foreword

On a typically sunny Dhofar day in 2004 I drove out of the gates of Salalah airfield with my good friend and colleague, Air Vice-Marshal Yahyah bin Rashid al Juma, Commander of the Royal Air Force of Oman. Immediately we found ourselves in the streets of a busy, bustling town. As I gazed around at the people thronging the byways, and at the burgeoning prosperity that was so much in evidence, my thoughts slipped back some thirty years, to a time when both I and my surroundings looked very different.

I first set foot in Salalah towards the end of 1973, as a newly arrived loan service officer in the Sultan of Oman's Air Force. It was my first experience of the country and the region where I was to spend the better part of the next two years. In those days it was a drive of some distance, along dirt tracks and potholed roads, from the airfield to the small and impoverished fishing village of Salalah. My colleagues and I used to take this route on our sporadic days off, driving our minimokes in pursuit of a little beach solitude as a break from the intense environment of an airbase in the middle of a war zone. The few houses in the village were strung along the shore, and looked as they might have done for the past couple of hundred years. There were few vehicles; donkeys were a far more common sight. There was little of the 20th century apparent in this scene, and while it might have been picturesque for the visitor, it did not seem to hold great prospects for the inhabitants.

And yet – and yet there I was in 2004 looking at a modern Omani town with a strong economy and underpinning infrastructure, and at lively, friendly people who clearly faced the future with confidence. What a change over the intervening decades. As I took in the scene, I thought of those who had fought in this region in the 1970s – of the colleagues who were now 'full of years', and of those who never had the chance to grow older, and for whom Dhofar was the last battle – and it seemed to me that the people of Salalah in the 21st century were our justification and our vindication. The lives that they were able to lead, and the promise the future held for them and their children, followed on from our success in the Dhofar War.

Military action on its own could not achieve this success. Yes, it was essential in achieving the conditions within which the other elements of state power could be brought to bear. But without the political initiatives and civil aid programmes set in hand by His Majesty The Sultan, the efforts of the Armed Forces would, at the last, have been in vain. The successful coordination of the military campaign with the many other strands of activity was the real secret of our victory; an approach which we continue to build on today.

So this book is more than just a fascinating tale about a little known war – a conflict that, to those who noticed it at all, seemed a marginal affair on the fringes of the Cold War that overshadowed all else. The picture that it paints and the incidents that it relates certainly provide us with a marvellous insight into the location and period; but it is not just of historical interest. It is the story of people who had to deal with the kinds of problems that are only too relevant to us today. And it is the story of how they, great and small, solved those problems and helped to create a future for a nation.

JOCK STIRRUP
Air Chief Marshal, GCB, AFC, ADC, FRAeS, FCMI, RAF,
Chief of the United Kingdom Defence Staff

Acknowledgements

Memories – mine and others – have been the principal sources for this book, but I have been fortunate to have a number of handrails to lean on for accurate factual and chronological background.

I have drawn on the unpublished dissertation, *Britain and Oman: the Dhofar War and its Significance,* written by Lieutenant Colonel John McKeowen, Royal Engineers for his Master of Philosophy degree from Cambridge University. *Oman before 1970* by Ian Skeet was also a most useful reference.

For overall context, and in particular the course of the war from November 1974 until its conclusion in December 1975, General Sir John Akehurst's book *We Won a War* has been invaluable.

The late General Sir Timothy Creasey delivered a presentation on the Dhofar War to the Army Staff College at Camberley each year for a number of years after the war. I am grateful to Major General Angus Ramsay who supplied me with a copy of the script of that presentation and other associated papers.

One memory on its own is an unreliable witness. It is debatable whether twenty memories are much better, but at least through consulting some of my brother officers in the Northern Frontier Regiment and others who served in Oman at the same time, the book is more complete than it otherwise might have been. It would be a poor anorexic thing if I had relied solely on what I alone remembered. I am therefore grateful to Bryan Ray, Angus Ramsay, Viv Rowe, Nick Knollys, Chris Barnes, Charlie Daniel, Tony Willis, Mike Kingscote and the late David Nicholls, all of the Northern Frontier Regiment, for jogging my brain cells; and for the loan of theirs.

I am also indebted to Ian Gordon of the Muscat Regiment, and Roger Jones, David Sayers, Mike Austen and David Daniels of the Jebel Regiment and Jonathan Salusbury-Trelawney of the Frontier

Force for their efforts in support of my accuracy. Gordon Gillies kept me straight on naval matters; Bob Mason, Dick Forsythe, Dick Allan, Nick Holbrook and Barry West on matters of the air. Ian Ventham of the Oman Artillery, Mike Lobb of the Firqat, Donal Douglas and Peter Isaacs of the Frontier Force, and Peter Sincock of Dhofar Brigade Headquarters all contributed important insights which enriched the book. The wise advice of Air Vice Marshal Yahya Rashid Al Jummah was invaluable. I thank all these gentlemen, furthermore, for the lie detector service that they performed on the parts of the book which they read during its gestation.

My thanks are also due to Air Chief Marshal Sir Jock Stirrup for kindly writing the foreword.

What more engaged and concerned auditors of one's work can one have than one's own family? Mine scrutinized this book and offered many valuable suggestions. With all its imperfections, it would have been a deal more imperfect without the help of my wife Louise and our children, Catriona and Angus.

I don't like reading a book without pictures and even less would I enjoy writing one. Hardly any of us took photographs of this most beautiful of countries with its photogenic people at this dramatic period of their history. I don't know why not. Perhaps we were discouraged by the natural disinclination of the older fashioned Arab to be photographed and thereby let us steal part of his soul. It wouldn't happen now. We laughed at Nick Knollys who, exceptionally, never went anywhere without photographing something. We are not laughing now. He very kindly let me have free rein of his unique photographic record to make this book more interesting and I am especially grateful to him. Bryan Ray too, supplied copies of pictures of officers and men that we never knew he had taken. Some of these also have enriched this book.

I thank Henry Wilson and all at Pen & Sword for humouring me gently and effectively and George Chamier, my copy editor, who has given freely of his detached wisdom and skill.

It was Major General Julian Thompson who encouraged me to turn some private notes into something that might withstand the light of day. I am grateful to him for his faith in the project throughout its development.

Perhaps most importantly, my understanding of Omani history and culture, the background to the war and its early stages, owes much to my recollection of long conversations with the late Arthur Brocklehurst who had a deep and abiding interest in Oman, and who fought in the war at company and regimental level throughout its ten long years. I learned much from him then. I used some of what he taught me in my daily life in Oman and on the *jebel*. As I wrote this book I used more and I found myself, not for the first time, wishing I had listened more carefully to him.

Finally dear Reader, I am grateful to you for picking up this book and reading thus far. I hope very much that you will read further, and that you may even get to the end. If you do, then I hope you will have enjoyed discovering something about the war in the Frankincense Mountains, and the mostly inexperienced but willing young men from widely differing countries and backgrounds who fought it, and the contribution they made to our world today, however imperfect that world may be. That world would have been worse without their effort and sacrifice.

Introduction

If you have ever heard of the Dhofar War, the chances are that you have either served or worked in the Sultanate of Oman at sometime in the last thirty years, or you know someone else who has done so. If neither of these applies, yet still you know something of what happened in that part of the world over thirty years ago, then you are unusually well informed.

It is one of the curiosities of history that this war, which was possibly of greater strategic significance to the industrialized Western world than the concurrent Vietnam War, was then and remains now largely unheard of. Even when mentioning Oman now, one has to pronounce the word carefully with the emphasis on the first syllable otherwise people tend to think you are talking about the capital of Jordan. And in a military context, the Sultan of Oman's Armed Forces are frequently confused with the neighbouring Trucial Oman Scouts with whom they had no connection whatsoever. Paradoxically, one reason for this obscurity is that from the Western point of view the war was highly successful. Although great change took place in Oman at this time, British support was given to try to maintain the status quo. A friendly, more or less stable regime governed Oman before the war. A friendly stable regime has governed Oman since. Where is the news story in that?

But there is a story and it is as exciting and dramatic as any fictional thriller. The Omani victory was hard won. Indeed, the war was nearly lost, and defeat would almost certainly have condemned the Gulf to years of instability and anarchy, and would probably have drawn other countries, possibly including the superpowers, into a greater and more destructive conflict. In the end, a model counter-insurgency campaign brought about a rare, unambiguous and enduring victory over Communism. The war involved on one side soldiers from Oman,

1

Jordan, Iran, India, Pakistan and Britain, and on the other men and women from Yemen, Russia, China, Cuba and Libya – and, because it was a civil war, also from Oman. This was no colonial adventure for prestige or territory. The stability of the Gulf region of the Middle East hinged on the outcome and therefore at the heart of the *casus belli* was oil – oil without which we would barely be able to turn on so much as a light bulb, let alone enjoy the many other material benefits of our developed world.

If you wish to join that body of well informed people who know something of the Dhofar war, and to discover one reason why we are still able to enjoy those benefits – and to follow an exciting story – then read on.

This is a personal portrait of events that took place more than thirty years ago. It is not, and does not pretend to be, a definitive record. I have relied on my own recollections and the memories of my friends to a great degree. We somehow did not find the time, nor did we have the inclination, to write much down at the time.

When describing action, I have tried to confine myself to writing about events that I saw or was involved in to a greater or lesser degree, or events that were experienced by those who were there with me and who have been able to give me their first-hand accounts. The temptation to write more was strong, but I have tried to be mindful of Disraeli, who when describing a colleague, once said: 'He has increasingly vivid memories of things that did not happen at all.' If at any stage the reader feels Disraeli might also have been describing me, then I'm sorry. All errors of fact and omission are mine alone.

But it seemed important to me that before memories fade into oblivion altogether something was written down. History is the story so far. We are all part of a continuum which stretches as far back as you care to look, and what we do now will influence the history of the future. We all made history then, and the Omanis whom we helped to make it are still making it, developing and shaping their country, themselves shaped by what they saw and did in their salad days. But history lasts only as long as the last person who remembers it, unless it is recorded. It depletes exponentially with the passage of time. If one doesn't know the story so far, how is one supposed to know where one stands now?

At a time when new tensions, or perhaps simply the resurrection of old ones, have emerged between the Christian and the Muslim worlds, it also seems appropriate to describe a time and place when men of both faiths found common cause against men of no faith at all. Respect, inclusivity, outreach, compromise, understanding, ungrudging tolerance; these are neither the discovery nor the sole preserve of enlightened liberal modernity. All these were present in Oman thirty years ago and Omanis are enjoying their legacy now.

Churchill once said of the United Nations that it would never take us to Heaven but it might help to keep us from Hell. So it is with most wars. They are not always about winning something; they are mostly about not losing something. And if you are not prepared to fight for what you hold dear, sooner or later someone will take it away. If you value peace over freedom, you will lose them both. And if you value comfort, prosperity and peace over justice and freedom, you will lose them all.

Communism is history now. However, for much of my working life it threatened to engulf in a new serfdom all who did not success-fully resist it. It was especially difficult to fight because unlike the demonstrable wickedness of Fascism, Communism and its ideals had an attractive lure for many people of goodwill who chose not to see the tyranny, brutality and unaccountability with which it was invariably applied. Liberation theory, workers' ownership of the means of production, power to the people – how seductively they trip off the tongue. Yet, was there ever an ideology which so comprehensively denied human nature and induced so many people to be imprisoned by so few?

This short book is about a small, little-known war which was fought quite a long time ago, by people from very diverse backgrounds, in a very old fashioned country, so that some big important things might not be lost; and it has a happy ending. With luck, this small part of the story so far will also not now be lost.

Ian Ritchie Gardiner
Edinburgh 2006

Chapter One

The Trailer

The 'scramble' alarm bell went off with penetrating urgency in the dining room of the Officers' Mess at the RAF air base in Salalah. No one would ever hear that bell without a quickening of the heart and a thrill of anticipation. During the day, there was always the possibility that the call might be for a jet strike in support of the ground troops in the mountains. At night, it could only be for helicopters. Abandoning their curries, the two duty helicopter pilots threw back their chairs, ran out of the room, jumped into the standby vehicle and sped down the airfield to the waiting Wessex helicopter. They had to be airborne within five minutes, but professional pride demanded much less than that. The pre-flight checks had all been done two hours before when the crew had clocked in on shift.

The Wessex is like a double-decker bus, except that the pilots sit in the front of the top deck, while the crewman sits down below in the cabin behind them. For the pilots, the crewman remains a disembodied voice on the intercom throughout the flight.

The captain climbed up the outside round the engine exhausts and into the right-hand seat. Both pilots were equally well qualified to fly her, but flying up into the Dhofar mountains at night on an operational mission during the monsoon, the man in the left-hand seat was never merely a passenger. As navigator and radio man, he took the brief from the Brigade Operations Officer, then he too climbed up as the captain started the engines. All the wits and knowledge of two experienced men, and the crewman who had been scrambled at the same time, were going to be needed.

Between June and September, the south-west monsoon touches the Dhofar coast and shrouds much of the landscape in a drizzling mist. There are often gaps in the mist, and on this night it seemed to be clear around the airfield. But there was every chance that their destination in

4

the mountains would be obscured. Moreover, there was no moon and it was a black, black night. Any flying in the mountains to which they must surely be headed would be fraught with hazard. The Wessex had a compass, a radar altimeter and the usual set of instruments, and it was routinely flown at night. But the mist and lack of moonlight in the difficult terrain to which they were heading meant that the stopwatch, the 'Mark One Eyeball' and the seats of their pants would be their chief flying aids.

All this they knew or guessed as they went through their final procedures. As the sound of the twin Gnome jet engines increased in pitch and the rotors engaged, the second pilot briefed the captain and the crewman on the mission ahead of them. There had been a contact on the ground with the Communist guerrillas in the mountains. Some of our soldiers had been killed and some wounded and they were to pick them up and bring them back to the Field Surgical Team in Salalah. The Wessex was to fly westwards to a waiting point east of Ashawq, the troop base in the mountains from which the patrol had set off earlier that afternoon. They should then call the ground troops for further instructions.

The helicopter lifted off from the airfield into the darkness and the pilot brought her round on to a westerly heading. The lights of the airfield and the town of Salalah faded behind them and their night vision started to improve. In spite of the blackness of the night, the beach line, made clearer by the rollers from the Indian Ocean that break incessantly on the coast at that time of year, stretched out faintly in front of them and to the left. There was high level cloud with patches settling on the mountain tops. Ahead, it was pitch black, with no horizon to distinguish land from sky. Even the most modern night vision goggles, which amplify the ambient light, would not have helped them.

The flight to the holding point some twenty miles away would take about fifteen minutes. The likely landing would be on the ground just west of Ashawq. This was around 2,000 ft above sea level so they slowly climbed to 2,500 ft as they headed westwards. The cloud base gave them about 400 ft clearance above the ground in the area of their target, but large patches of cloud were swirling intermittently in off the sea. Climbing steadily, they struggled to stay clear of cloud and in sight of the surface. However, they knew that if they flew into cloud, they would be able to let down over the sea to the south until they could see the surface once more. Some lights at the headquarters of the army regiment based on the coast gave them an occasional reference point as they pulled into an orbit east of their target, dodging in and out of the cloud. The radio crackled and burst into life. They could not hear all that was going on but it was clear from the tone and intensity of the radio transmissions that there was still a battle taking place on the ground. 'Hold off! Wait out!'

Bit by bit, the situation became clearer. A patrol had gone out into enemy-dominated territory west of Ashawq, one of the army strong points in the mountains. This patrol had encountered a group of Communist guerrillas in the mist and fading light. The firefight had continued into darkness, and they were now attempting to break contact and withdraw with their wounded and dead. There was one dead reported and six wounded. The Wessex was to land and evacuate the casualties as soon as the patrol had withdrawn to a point secure enough to bring the helicopter in. They were hoping to set up a landing site, but our artillery was still engaging enemy locations and covering the withdrawal of the patrol. Once the landing site was known, an approach which avoided the possibility of the helicopter being hit by our own artillery shells would be indicated. 'Wait out.'

The cockpit of a helicopter at night is bathed in orange light and gives an illusion of safety. Concentration was vital as the orbit seemed to go on for ever – round and round for fifty minutes while the drama unfolded below. It was not clear to the pilots how they were going to pull this one off. Flying into an operational landing site was always something of an act of faith on behalf of the aircrew. During the day, the pilots could judge whether the site was technically suitable. At night this was not so easy, and in the mist it was nearly impossible. Were there any trees? Were there any lightweight obstacles like empty plastic water drums that might get blown up into the rotors? Most importantly of all, were there any enemy around who might take the chance to shoot this lumbering bird at its most vulnerable moment? On numerous occasions helicopters had returned to base from evacuating casualties with bullet holes in them. Some hadn't been that lucky and had become casualties themselves. And if hit by an RPG 7 rocket-propelled grenade, the helicopter would have no chance. Normal night landing procedures call for lights in a T shape on the ground, giving the pilots an indication of aspect and direction of approach. As the helicopter approaches the ground, a swivelling landing light under-neath the machine can be used to check the ground for obstacles. For a more tactical approach, a downward identification light can be switched on at the last moment. None of these options were to be available that night.

There was, however, a certain geometry about a Wessex helicopter descent. At night, a descent started at about 500 ft at 50 knots and reduced thereafter by 10 knots per 100 ft. The key was to avoid letting the rate of descent build up – if this happened, there was a risk that the enemy's job would be done for him. So, if the patrol was west of Ashawq at the same altitude as Ashawq, then the helicopter could head west from over Ashawq for thirty seconds before beginning to descend. The patrol on the ground would have to use a torch facing east to show the crew where they were waiting. Much depended on the troops on the ground for the safety and success of the mission; but faith and trust in each other is an essential element between all men at war.

The two pilots, Flight Lieutenants Dick Forsythe and Brian Mansfield, knew the regiment on the ground well. For the previous two months they and their fellow Wessex pilots had transported barbed wire, land mines and all the associated personnel, engineers' stores and equipment to build a twenty-mile-long wire and mine obstacle from the sea into the mountains. In the course of this operation they had placed underslung loads on the sides of ravines, flown men and stores down into the bottom of valleys, and then flown them back up to their mountain-top forts. It had been an extraordinary two months and the flying experience they had gained could not have been achieved in several lifetimes flying in the UK and Germany, their normal habitat.

They had also formed some unusually strong friendships with the soldiers on the ground. In the UK and Germany they rarely even spoke to the men they carried around in the back of their machine, let alone developed any kind of relationship with them. In Dhofar, day after day, they saw the same faces and heard the same voices. Moreover, and unusually, they had taken the time and trouble to spend a night with the troops on the ground in the mountains to discuss with the officers the sort of problems that might arise should they find themselves flying in support of operations at night. They observed at close quarters with awe and respect the job that the men on the ground were doing. Omani, British and Baluchi soldiers lived for months at a time in remote hill-top dugouts. From there they patrolled the mountains and ambushed Communist guerrillas by day and night. They had also built the barbed wire and mine obstacle across this extraordinarily rugged country with the stores flown in by the Wessex helicopters. Endurance, physical toughness, patience and resilience were all in high demand, not to mention the courage required to face a ruthless, hardy and determined enemy. Although by world standards the scale of this war was small, it was a vicious, hard-fought conflict; the dead, and the wounded men anxiously waiting up in the black, misty mountains for the sound of helicopter rotors, were testimony enough to that.

The helicopter had sufficient fuel to stay on station for at least two hours. Should they run short, they could either land at the regimental headquarters and take a suck from the stock of drums which they knew waited there for them, or they could alert another machine to come out from Salalah to take over.

More artillery fire missions were being called for on the ground. It looked as if things were getting worse, and the pilots were not encouraged by the fact that it seemed as if nobody really knew what was going on. Then at last a call came through on the radio: 'stand by for extraction in ten minutes.' Forsythe and Mansfield made sure that they were due east of Ashawq at the correct height, ready to fly westwards when called. The clouds drifted clear of Ashawq at just the right time.

From the ground came: 'clear to go in'. Now they were in business. Flight Sergeant John Mayes, the crewman in the back of the helicopter, lying on the floor of the cabin with his head out of the door, reported them 'overhead Ashawq'. Start the stopwatch: sixty knots, 2,600 ft, heading 270 degrees; nothing ahead but inky blackness; slowing down to fifty knots; commencing descent after thirty seconds. The reassuring patter from John Mayes in the back, leaning out and clearing the aircraft's immediate path forward, steadied Forsythe and Mansfield in the cockpit. Judging by his voice this could have been a routine training sortie on Salisbury Plain.

There is an innate reluctance in pilots to move forward and down into a black void, but encouraged by Mayes they pressed on, Forsythe at the controls, and Mansfield softly calling out the altitude from the radar altimeter: 400 ft, 300 ft ... a flash of light down to the left. It must be the patrol. The helicopter eased left and lined up with the light: 200 ft, 100 ft. Still absolutely nothing visible on the ground. Forsythe stared out of the right hand window through the engine exhaust, willing his eyes to get some reference on the ground. As the helicopter approached, the light went out. The radar altimeter was now reading only 150 ft. Still no reference point on the ground. Overshoot, overshoot! Entirely focussed on the instruments, Forsythe threw a left hand clearing turn to climb away over a safe area.

A few deep breaths to calm down, fly back over Ashawq, and start again. This time Brian Mansfield took the controls. Once more John Mayes' matter-of-fact patter from down in the back steadied the two pilots above him. Over Ashawq now; start the stopwatch, thirty seconds passed, start the descent. There was the torch again, this time on the nose, 400 ft, 300, 200, this time it was Forsythe calling out the heights, 50 ft. Once again, the light disappeared, and the pilots could see absolutely no reference to land on. Overshoot again! Then, just as they piled on the power, the sidelights of a Land Rover flickered on. What on earth was that doing here? The lights were on Forsythe's side and briefly illuminated a level patch of ground. The helicopter was sliding left about 10 ft over the top of the Land Rover. Forsythe, since he could see the Land Rover, took the controls again, corrected the drift and landed all in one fluid movement. A huge sigh of relief, but there could be better places to spend your time!

On the ground, the scene became a surreal and macabre vision: men with bandages round their heads, bodies and limbs; some being carried, some walking assisted; all being manhandled as quickly as possible, together with the corpse, into the soft red gloom of the interior of Mayes' helicopter cab. The company medic who had accompanied them during the battle, and who had applied first aid, finally jumped in to attend them on the journey to hospital. Mayes once more described what was happening on the ground in his calm and methodical way. Soon he declared that all were aboard and they were clear to take off. A take-off at night with no reference point on the ground was not a straightforward matter. The Wessex tended to hang left wheel low in the hover. However, power was applied smoothly if a little vigorously, then after a climbing left turn they headed for base to get the wounded men to the Field Surgical Team in Salalah as soon as possible.

On the flight home the pressures of the previous hour caught up with Dick Forsythe. For the first and only time in his flying career he briefly suffered tunnel vision – apparently a by-product of nervous tension. The instruments on the dashboard of the helicopter suddenly appeared to him as if he was looking at them through the wrong end of a pair of binoculars. Brian Mansfield took the controls and brought the machine into the landing pad of the Field Surgical Team next to the RAF base in Salalah. Twenty-five minutes after being extracted from the mountains, the wounded men were receiving expert surgical care.

The crew stood down on return to base, and another crew took over the standby duty. Mansfield and Forsythe returned to the Officers' Mess bar and did what countless aircrew have done before and since: they set about curing Forsythe's tunnel vision with the aid of several cans of beer.

Map 1 – South East Arabia

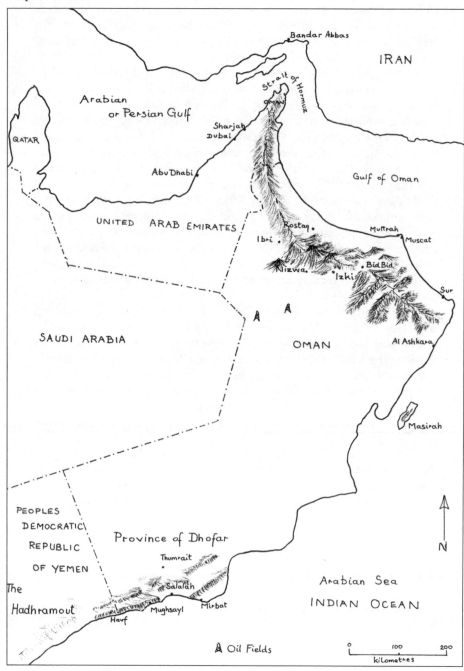

IRAN

Bandar Abbas

Arabian
or Persian Gulf

Strait of Hormuz

QATAR

Sharjah
Dubai

OMAN

Gulf of Oman

Abu Dhabi

UNITED   ARAB EMIRATES

Rostaq

Muttrah

Muscat

Ibri

SAUDI ARABIA

Nizwa

Izki

Bid Bid

OMAN

Sur

Al Ashkara

Masirah

PEOPLES
DEMOCRATIC
REPUBLIC
OF YEMEN

Province of Dhofar

The
Hadhramout

Thumrait

Salalah

Mughsayl

Hauf

Mirbat

Arabian Sea

INDIAN OCEAN

N

Oil Fields

0   100   200

kilometres

10

Chapter Two

The Stage

The Gulf – the Arabian Gulf if you're talking to an Arab, the Persian Gulf if to a Persian – is a place of world strategic importance. Authorities disagree on just how much oil comes from the region and who uses it. What is certainly true, and has been true ever since the Second World War, is that the industrialized world depends significantly on the free passage of tankers through the Strait of Hormuz, that narrow neck of water which is the gateway to and from the Indian Ocean. On the north side of the strait is Iran and on the south Oman. However much the Iranians or the Omanis might want it otherwise, neither can avoid the interest and concern of those powers whose lifeblood flows through this artery within sight of their coasts.

It was this waterway which, although most of the players in this story never set eyes on it, was at the heart of the war which they fought, and which is described in the following chapters. Their war was ultimately a struggle for control of the Strait of Hormuz and the free passage of oil through it. The democratic industrialized West held it; the Chinese and Soviet Communist East wanted it and saw an opportunity to take it. It was therefore a struggle at the very heart of the Cold War, the outcome of which mattered deeply to the West. So the stakes were high indeed.

In the late 1960s, Oman was remote, undeveloped and poor. It had been ruled since the 1930s by a very traditional, and by then rather elderly gentleman called Sultan Said bin Taimur bin Faisal bin Turki bin Said bin Sultan bin Ahmed bin Said Al Busaidi, and he governed his people in much the same way as his father, his grandfather and their forefathers had done for many generations.

It was not an isolated country in spite of its backward ways. Omani history goes back to Old Testament times. Sheba, the land of the queen who allegedly visited Solomon, was in the south-west corner of the Arabian Peninsula and possibly included Dhofar. Some scholars link Ophir, the biblical source of apes, gold and frankincense with the south-eastern corner of the Arabian Peninsula. What is certain is that frankincense trees grow in profusion on the Qara and Qamar Mountains in Dhofar, and their resinous product was traded by the inhabitants to the rest of the known world over two thousand years ago. The seafaring Portuguese had held sway there for a hundred and fifty years in the sixteenth and seventeenth centuries and had left their mark in the form of a number of forts perched precipitously on the crags around the capital, Muscat. One of these forts was still being used as the state gaol and the 'Ave Maria' could still be seen inscribed on the stone walls of these relics.

In the early nineteenth century, Muscat itself had been the centre of its own empire extending in a great arc from the north-western coast of the Indian subcontinent to the east coast of Africa. The title of the old sultans, Sultan of Muscat and Oman, Dhofar, Gwadur, Socotra and Zanzibar, reflected the maritime sweep of their domain. It had been a trading empire, exchanging goods and slaves between coastal India and coastal Africa. Such a disparate political union becomes more understandable when one realizes that the sea was then a highway, not a barrier. Transporting goods and people in significant quantities was much easier by ship than by camel, and the Omanis had been great sailors. Indeed, legend claimed Sinbad himself to be one of their own.

The British had never made Oman part of their empire in the way that many of her neighbouring states had been coloured pink on the map. Arm twisting, threats, subsidies, and the occasional gunboat had secured stability on terms to the Imperial satisfaction without actually taking possession, and Oman remained nominally an independent state. But the Imperial power could not be ignored, and successive sultans had come to a more or less friendly accord with Britain over the years.

The people are mainly Arabs. The population in the 1960s was about one million souls. They are Muslims, chiefly of the Ibadhi persuasion. The Ibadhi movement was founded within fifty years of the death of Muhammad and is therefore one of the very earliest divisions within Islam. The founder of the Ibadhis, Jabir bin Zaid Al Azdi, who actually came from Nizwa, the largest Omani town outside Muscat, sought to preserve most faithfully the example of the Prophet. As a result, Ibadhis tend to be traditional and conservative. But their conservatism should not be mistaken for fundamentalism. Ibadhis also have a reputation for moderation. Oman is unique in the Muslim world in having an Ibadhi majority, and to this day a high degree of religious tolerance is a salient feature of Omani society.

Oman's international past was also reflected in the diversity of its population. As well as the established Omani Arabs in the interior, the

Sharqiya, many coastal Arabs hailed from other Gulf Arab states. There were also Baluchis from Gwadur and Makran in what is now Pakistan. The association with Baluchistan was strong in the army: as well as individual Baluchis in Arab regiments, there were two complete regiments manned by Baluchi soldiers and British and Baluchi officers. In Dhofar, the southern province of Oman, the Dhofaris with their dark skins and high cheekbones looked part African and part Afghani.

South-east of Muscat was the small isolated town of Sur. It was something of a surprise to find so many black faces in this rather remote place, until one remembered its position on the wider map. Near Ra's Al Hadd, it was at a key point on the sea route connecting Oman's African and Indian territories. The black faces belonged to the descendants of the many slaves who had been part of the trade that had passed through here. Since slavery of a kind existed in Oman until well into the twentieth century, the older ones may well have been born slaves themselves.

Then there were Zanzibaris. The island of Zanzibar became part of the British East African Empire in the late nineteenth century but before that it had briefly been the capital of the Sultan's empire. Many Zanzibaris became citizens of both Zanzibar and Oman, but Sultan Said bin Taimur did not like Zanzibaris. Their relatively high level of education meant that they had aspirations for modernity that he felt Oman could not fulfil. He thought they were subversive and would destabilize the country. They were not made welcome and many were exiled back to their island.

By the time this story begins, Said bin Taimur had been gathered to his fathers, and 'development' was no longer a dirty word, so many Zanzibari Omanis had returned from exile. Because of their education, many were strong candidates for promotion – and thereby attracted a certain jealousy from the more traditional Omanis who had been denied the opportunity so to equip themselves. Perversely, education, the thing that many Omanis wanted most, was the thing Sultan Said had sought hardest to deny them.

The southern province of Dhofar is mountainous, and most Dhofaris lived in the mountains. The Arabic word for hill or mountain is *jebel* and so Dhofaris were often known as *Jebalis* – Highlanders. They are partly Ethiopian in origin. Omanis from the North who are Arabs regarded the Dhofaris with a caution varying from puzzled curiosity to suspicious hostility. For one Omani to call another Omani a *Jebali* was mildly pejorative, usually in fun, but not always so.

There are some curious parallels between the *Jebali* highlanders of Dhofar and the Gaelic highlanders of Scotland in the eighteenth and nineteenth centuries. The Dhofari highlanders, like the Scottish ones, are nearer to the aboriginal people and have their own language, customs and culture. With their high cheekbones and dark skin they are ethnically and visually distinctive. Even the wraparound garment that many men wear, the *wizar*, is based on the same idea as the kilt. Like the Gaels, they remained largely unaffected by the successive waves of immigrants who changed the population elsewhere in the country. Dhofar, like the Highlands, was often the seat of rebellion, and the sovereign power in the form of Sultan Said bin Taimur felt the need to suppress the highlanders to teach them a lesson. Eventual reconciliation was assisted by recruiting Dhofaris in large numbers into the armed forces where, like the Gaels in the British army, they were able to make a unique contribution at the same time as acquiring a stake in the Sovereign's peace. While the parallel can be drawn too far, it is generally true that Dhofaris regarded Northern Omanis as arrogant, complacent and soft, while many Omanis saw somewhere in every Dhofari an idle, wily, ungrateful thief – a juxtaposition which would have struck a chord with my Scottish Lowland forefathers.

Notwithstanding such prejudices and preconceptions, it was from these people that our enemy sprang: mountain men – and some women – who could carry large loads long distances across the most rugged terrain imaginable, often in bare feet and surviving on hardly any food or water; and who, like their Gaelic counterparts, fired by ideology and a sense of injustice, would fight to the death.

Sultan Said, in spite of his distrust of the people from his southern province, had serendipitously married a Dhofari. The mixed blood of his son Qaboos was a happy coincidence when the son came to try and win back the hearts and minds of the Dhofari people which the father had so palpably lost.

The people of Oman, although from a variety of ethnic backgrounds, lived together peacefully enough. Racial prejudice, however, was not entirely absent. Those of African slave stock were sometimes known as 'sambos'. I have already referred to the somewhat loaded Dhofari-Omani relationship. Moreover, many shopkeepers and merchants were Indian and were looked down upon by those of pure Arab stock, although the valuable service they provided tended to take the edge off any resentment that they might have engendered. Others from the Indian subcontinent such as the Baluch and other Pakistanis were seen and sometimes treated as outsiders. Towards the end of the war, a civil aid vehicle carrying a water tank and four people was ambushed by the enemy. The driver was killed in the initial fire, but the three surviving passengers were shot in cold blood in the back of the head. It seems likely that the fact that they were all Pakistanis contributed to the enemy's readiness to murder them. Perhaps because the *Jebalis* had been exposed less to the comings and goings of peoples than the rest of the population, racial differences were more keenly felt in Dhofar.

There is a story about an incident which took place one night while the film *Zulu* was being shown to all and sundry at an improvised outdoor cinema inside the military base in Salalah. At the moment in the film when the beleaguered British garrison at Rorke's Drift is attacked by thousands of black Zulu warriors, a fusillade of real rifle shots went ripping through the screen. The Dhofari tribesmen, known as Firqat and now working for the Sultan, unable to contain themselves had entered into the spirit of the film, taking the part of the British against the hordes of despised black men. One version of this story says that the screen was a sheet fixed to the canvas side of an army lorry, which had some soldiers asleep in the back as the bullets tore over them – an early and convincing example of reality cinema. Whether this story is true or not, for anyone who knew the Firqat it is certainly believable.

But in the Army, where all these peoples served alongside each other together with British, Jordanian, and Iranian soldiers, a remarkably high degree of tolerance and harmony existed. The common cause, the opportunity for each to demonstrate their worth, the shared risk, the shared hardship, the shared service to the Sultan; all no doubt contributed. Racial divisions existed in Oman as they do in almost every other country, but 'live and let live' seemed happily to be the prevailing sentiment.

Oman is one of the hottest countries in the world. It is about the size of the United Kingdom and it is a country of three geographical parts. In the North, the high, barren, precipitous Al Hajar mountain range runs parallel to the sea, with a fertile strip, the Batinah Plain, between the mountains and the coast of the Gulf of Oman, the body of water which lies just outside the Gulf itself. The highest of these features is the Jebel Akhdar, the Green Mountain, with its peak the Jebel As Shams – the Mountain of the Sun – which rises to over 10,000 ft. The capital, Muscat, is on the coast, together with its port of Muttrah. The hinterland was remote and mysterious, and regarded as wild and woolly by the coastal Arabs. In the past, the remote inland centres of habitation, Izki, Nizwa, and Ibri unsurprisingly had separatist tendencies, encouraged by Saudi Arabia, and it was this area and Akhdar itself which was the scene of a civil war in the 1950s, when Sultan Said and the Imam Ghalib bin Ali bin Hini, the leader of the separatist tribes, battled for supremacy.

Projecting into the Strait of Hormuz is the Musandam Peninsula. Physically separated from the rest of Oman by the United Arab Emirates, this rocky barren promontory dominates the Strait. There is rarely a moment when a large oil tanker is not visible sailing through the deep-water channel which is in Omani territorial waters adjacent to the Musandam Peninsula. Omani possession of this vital piece of real estate is not disputed in spite of its peculiar disjointed position, and by holding it Oman holds the very handle to the door of the Gulf.

The second geographical part, the land to the south of the Jebel Akhdar hinterland, flattens out to a long wide gravel plain where only the occasional *bedu* might live. It is here where such oil as Oman possesses is to be found. This plain is dry and featureless and stretches some 400 miles to the south-west and, even though it covers the greater part of the Omani land area, it plays no significant part in our story.

To the south-west of this plain is the province of Dhofar, the third part of Oman. Dhofar is about the size of Wales. On the coast, and flanked by a flat and potentially fertile plain is the main town of Salalah, mentioned by Marco Polo as a prosperous city in the thirteenth century. This plain was the bread basket for the British campaign in Mesopotamia in the Great War, but the area under cultivation in the 1970s was much reduced. Behind the plain, and visible from Salalah, rise the Qamar, the Qara, and the Samhan Mountains. These limestone highlands come down to the sea at either end of the Salalah plain. The Samhan are to the east, the Qara in the middle, and the Qamar to the west, and they are the scene for this story. They rise to over 4,000 ft. They are crenellated by deep sharp-sided gorges and honeycombed with caves. There are towering escarpments and cliffs which would have been sea cliffs in earlier geological times; sea shells can be found in profusion buried in the sand at 4,000 ft.

From the coast of the Indian Ocean the mountains stretch inland to the north for about thirty miles and then peter out into the Negd Desert and the Empty Quarter. For nine months of the year, they are arid and hot. Water is to be found only in isolated water holes. But it is not all a true desert. From mid-June to mid-September, a thick drizzling mist known as the *khareef* envelops much of Dhofar from sea level up to 2,000 ft. At the same time, large rollers sweep on to the many beautiful beaches. The mist forms a veil over the mountains for these three months, and when the veil lifts, the magic it has worked is revealed. The unpromising arid landscape is transformed and for several weeks in September and October every year, it looks as verdant and fertile as Somerset. This strange phenomenon is a result of the south-west monsoon which touches this otherwise barren corner of Arabia. At the same time the *khareef* is also working another magic, unseen: water trickles down through the permeable limestone rock and supplies subterranean aquifers perhaps 3,000 ft below the surface. This feature was to be of immense value to us when the time came to drill wells to supply the inhabitants of Dhofar with water, an essential element in the process of winning their hearts and minds.

The Dhofari people live either in villages by the coast or in small communities on the *jebel* in the same way as their countrymen to the north. Many lead a nomadic life on the *jebel*, herding their small hardy cattle from water hole to water hole – holes that might pass for small puddles in a more temperate climate. Large areas of the *jebel* are covered by frankincense trees. The resin from these trees provided the tradeable commodity which gave Dhofar the name of the Frankincense Coast in ancient times. It can still be bought in small quantities in the markets.

With its distinctive jagged mountains and gorges, its rugged coasts and its pristine beaches washed by the Indian Ocean, Oman is one of the most starkly beautiful places in the world.

Oman was poor and remained at peace as long as all her neighbours were poor too. The majority of Omani people lived chiefly by growing date palms, and herding goats, sheep and some cattle. The discovery of oil in the other Gulf States in the 1950s did not of itself destabilize Oman, because the Omanis knew they had no oil, and so they accepted their poverty with equanimity. Then oil was discovered in Oman in the late 1950s and early 1960s; not a lot, just enough to raise expectations, but Sultan Said was not willing to move with the times. He perceived nothing but turbulence and decadence destroying the culture and values of his neighbours. He believed it would corrupt his people to be exposed to all the manifestations of wealth that were evident in the newly rich Gulf States, so he held them in a repressive thrall. Having spent a lifetime tiptoeing the line between subsistence and bankruptcy, he was ill-equipped to ease the purse strings when his financial position started to improve. Since the end of the Jebel Akhdar War in 1959, he had received a small annual subsidy for development projects from the United Kingdom. It was the hope, if not the specified intention, that he would match this sum or even increase development resources from his own revenues. Not a chance. The certainty of future oil revenues did nothing to change his attitude. The idea of debt was an anathema to him. He was frugal beyond prudence. The oil revenues which eventually started to flow in the late 1960s he hoarded – some said literally – under his bed.

No hard-topped roads existed in Oman until the very early 1970s; there was but one hospital, one school up to primary level, no telephones, no infrastructure of any kind worthy of the name – other than ancient water distribution channels. It was illegal to listen to music in public or wear sunglasses. The gates of the walled town of Muscat, Sultan Said's capital city, were closed at night, and if you were outside

17

wanting to get in, too bad. To move around inside the town at night one had to carry a lantern. Dominated by two medieval Portuguese forts and protected on the landward side by a crescent of formidable jagged peaks, the superficial impression of the town from the sea was of an unspoilt, alluring, fascinating relic of ancient Arabia. The two most prominent buildings on the sea front were the Sultan's palace and the British embassy. On closer examination, one found a depressing degree of decrepitude in the buildings and a near total absence of any useful facilities, ancient or modern. The market or *suq*, when one could find it, sold very little of value or interest. And notwithstanding the seafront location, the surrounding hills trapped the air and fended off any sea breezes. The heat was therefore especially oppressive. This capital city was a warren of dusty, dirty, broken down buildings with very little to compensate in the way of things to see, buy or do. To all but the most hardened aficionado of ancient Arabia, Muscat was a dump.

By 1973, things had begun to change a little. There were now shops which sold modern electrical goods, although these would only be bought by those who had generators because there was not yet any mains electrical supply outside Muscat. There was also a shop run by an American Protestant Christian pastor which sold English language books. The range was not great, but in the circumstances, one might say he was indeed a Godsend. In Muttrah, the neighbouring town with its brand new harbour, there were signs of nascent modernity. A cold food store, a larger more diverse *suq*, a fair number of shops selling imported goods and a power station were all in evidence, and more and more entrepreneurs were starting up small businesses to take advantage of the freeing of commerce. Here, blood was at last beginning to flow through Oman's commercial veins.

Sultan Said had refused to delegate any substantial matters of government. Even the insubstantial ones he kept to himself. The ministries which might take the innumerable daily decisions necessary for the satisfactory functioning of any state, if they existed at all, did so only in name. And even where they did exist, they were run merely by secretaries rather than by ministers. This would have mattered less if Sultan Said had been good at taking decisions, but he wasn't. There were restrictions on owning any kind of motor vehicle. The Sultan vetted all applications to own a vehicle – personally. If they were replied to at all, such applications were almost always refused. The brake that this operated on any development of trade or commerce can be imagined. Similarly, the absence of any tractors in the country did nothing to raise the level of agricultural production. In Dhofar, the dead hand of time and history lay particularly heavy. There were no hospitals at all. People were not allowed to use electric pumps in their wells. Anybody who left the country, for whatever reason, was not allowed back in, and if they tried to re-enter, they risked imprisonment. Prison or exile – take your choice.

Government was haphazard and whimsical. One day the local governor or *wali* of the Sur area, who was out travelling in his large and remote area of responsibility, received an urgent message calling him to the capital at Muscat. He returned at best speed on his donkey to Sur and arranged an immediate sea trip up the coast to Muscat where he waited for three days before being asked why he had allowed a football team to sail from Sur to Muscat on a dhow. Baffled, he waited a further twenty-three days before being permitted to return to Sur. Meanwhile the secretary of the Muscat football club was thrown into gaol for a few days. Neither he nor the governor could discover why they had been treated this way.

Sultan Said bin Taimur no doubt had his reasons for what appears to be such peculiar behaviour. This, and the restrictions he imposed upon them, had long been tolerated by his patient, peaceable, traditional people, but arriving concurrently with the discovery of oil came the catalyst for revolution: the cheap, widely available Japanese transistor radio.

With this development, Sultan Said lost the means whereby he was able to retain near absolute power: sole possession of information. He could no longer rely upon the ignorance of his people to hold them in a medieval time warp. It became impossible to suppress them when they knew what others were enjoying and what could be available to them if he would just get off their backs. Rebellion started in Dhofar, the southern province, in 1965.

The Sultan's Army, which had been formed with British help at the end of the Jebel Akhdar War, was small and poorly equipped. However, it was efficient within the constraints of its capabilities and well led by British officers, either on loan from the British Government, or on contract direct to the Sultan. Indeed, it was virtually the only organ of state which had any recognizable structure or procedures. It was able to contain the Dhofari rebels for a while. For eighteen months, an active and hard-fought campaign was waged on the *jebel* with very limited resources and was remarkably successful. About twenty men were killed on either side. I read and heard about operations conducted by these men, our predecessors on the *jebel*, and could not help but be impressed. Lacking resources, helicopters or jets, and under rotten and gimcrack political leadership, the armed forces commanded firstly by Brigadier Corin Purdon and then Brigadier John Graham still held important areas and conducted bold aggressive operations all over the *jebel*.

But they could never win. They might be able to hold some kind of military equilibrium – for a time. But without effective, relevant, inspiring political leadership, their efforts were futile, and in the end they would have been defeated. There was a moment in 1967 when peace might have been secured if Sultan Said had been enlightened enough to reach out and offer some hope for the future to the Dhofaris. But there could be no question of amnesty or concession. The Sultan did not treat with rebels. The moment was lost.

The south-west corner of the Arabian Peninsula had undergone significant political change in recent years. What is now Yemen was then two states: North Yemen, with its capital at San'a and its coastline along the Red Sea, and South Yemen with its coastline along the Indian Ocean and its capital at Aden. The whole region had been subject to the imperial activities of the Egyptians, the Turks, and latterly the British, for many years. The Egyptians and Ottoman Turks held the region alternately until the British occupied Aden and its environs in 1839. San'a and North Yemen achieved independence from the Turks at the end of the First World War. Meanwhile, the British consolidated their control of Aden and the neighbouring area, the Hadhramout, which became a British crown colony and a protectorate in 1937.

The British retreated from their empire in the decades following the Second World War. In preparation for granting independence to this region, they had formed the Federation of South Arabia out of the Hadhramout and the other tribal areas based on Aden in 1963, finally departing in 1967.

In the latter part of the Cold War, Soviet Communism, as well as keeping up a strong military front in Europe, sought to achieve its aim of world domination by alternative means. It was clear that out-and-out violent confrontation with America and the West implied the possibility of a vastly destructive nuclear war. This would serve nobody's purpose. So both sides sought to buttress their positions around the world by developing allies and creating spheres of influence. Some states were seen to be pro-West, some were pro-Communist, and others declared themselves to be non-aligned. The Communist world saw the retreating empires of the West as an opportunity to strengthen their position by developing a group of client states, some of whom would become surrogate adversaries of the West. Vietnam was the best known of these; Angola and Mozambique were others. Some, like Cuba, proved more durable than the home of Communism itself. In other cases, like Malaya, the attempt was made but failed.

The Federation that the British put together in South Yemen based on Aden was riven with tribal and political fissures and very quickly became easy prey for the Marxist-orientated National Liberation Front which, backed by the Soviet Union, imposed its will without scruple. The Communist state of the People's Republic of South Yemen was formed in 1967, and was renamed the People's Democratic Republic of Yemen – the PDRY – in 1970.

Dhofar shared a southern border with this new secular Communist state. The People's Front for the Liberation of the Occupied Arab Gulf (PFLOAG) was the movement which the Communists formed as a vehicle to advance their aims. PDRY, PFLOAG: the enemy may have the best tunes, but perhaps not the best acronyms. After the Communists took over in what had been Aden and the Hadhramout, and was now the PDRY, they started taking an interest in their poor but strategically sited neighbour. The opportunity to piggy-back on the insurrection there was irresistible. The PDRY had no oil but with Dhofar in their possession they could take direct control of the oil fields that were now being developed in the gravel plains between Dhofar and the north of Oman. Infiltration and insurrection in the North could take place concurrently with revolutionary war in the South. Cells would be established and networks formed to foment trouble in the Army and other critical organs of government.

From 1967 onwards, the Dhofari rebellion was an ideal opportunity for the PDRY to make trouble and destabilize Oman. The ultimate prize, of course, was domination of the entrance to the Gulf, through which forty per cent of the oil used by Western Europe passed. The Communist movement, PFLOAG, jumped on the Dhofari bandwagon with a vengeance and things started to go badly for Sultan Said's Army. By 1970 it was perfectly plain that if Sultan Said were not removed from power, there was every chance that first Dhofar, and then the north of Oman, would eventually fall to the Communists.

Islam was something of a bulwark against Communism, but it was not immoveable. Those rebels who were not prepared to switch to the Marxist-Leninist doctrine were simply tortured or murdered. Some brave, devout people were prepared to be martyrs; but as those who have been subjected to a regime of terror understand only too well, there were plenty more who, with families to consider, felt obliged to support, outwardly at least, the alien creed. Moreover, success tends to breed success. If the Communists had been able to demonstrate their power with a successful guerrilla campaign and assassinate leading establishment figures, they might well have been able to supplant religion, the 'opium of the masses', with Marxist-Leninist liberation theory. Eventually the whole of Oman would have fallen under Communist control and called the shots in the southern Gulf. Who knows where it might have ended? Thus went the 'domino theory', that Western concern which influenced much strategic thinking during the Cold War.

Sultan Said could at least see that he was not able to defeat this new type of rebellion with his own resources. There were no schools or universities and so there were very few educated people in Oman. In any case, Sultan Said did not trust educated people. But he trusted the British. They had helped him win his war against separatists and rebels in the 1950s, and so he again turned to them to lead his Army.

It is impossible not to feel some sympathy for Said bin Taimur. He had ruled his country more or less successfully by the lights of his time and place for many years. He had only recently achieved undisputed suzerainty over the whole country through his hard won victory in the Jebel Akhdar War against the separatist Imam Ghalib bin Ali, and in the course of his reign he had faced his fair share of conflict. However daft or outrageous the restrictions he imposed upon his people might appear to us, he was not an inhumane man, and he always had his reasons. Somewhere underneath many of his more peculiar diktats can be discerned a wish to sustain his nation's resources or culture; he simply ruled in much the same way as his forefathers had done for centuries, guided by the strictures of Islam and Sharia Law.

Oman had been a backwater, and the currents which had driven change in other parts of the world had passed her by. We in the early twenty-first century with our instantaneous communications and global markets may find it strange that such a strategically important part of the world could be left behind in this way. But measured against the wide sweep of history it is not quite so strange: remember that Americans were still watching public hangings in 1937 – the year my parents were married and shortly before my own brother was born. Universal suffrage and votes for women in Britain were finally achieved in the lifetime of my parents, only thirty years before I was born. Slavery was abolished in Oman in the 1920s, only a short sixty years behind the United States where it had been abolished in the lifetime of my grandfather. It was only in the lifetime of his father that slavery was abolished in the British Empire. And while the great Provost George Drummond was conceiving the brilliant masterpiece that became Edinburgh New Town, his fellow Scottish countrymen were still burning witches. Even today, there are parts of Africa which owe very little to the twenty-first century, remaining imprisoned in a poverty and backwardness that would make old Oman look positively pleasant in comparison.

Now, in the evening of its ruler's years, Oman was swept into mainstream world politics and Sultan Said was beset with yet another war. His reign had been punctuated by revolts of unruly tribes and he had suppressed them all. So in the face of this new uprising he set about doing what he and his fathers had always done before, in the expectation that success would again attend his endeavours. How was he to know that the rules had changed?

But changed they had. At the root of all insurgent wars is bad government and Sultan Said was completely out of touch with the aspirations of his people. His government was ossified, ramshackle, arbitrary and repressive. He was unwilling and unable to change and had outlived his time. He was monumentally ill-equipped to lead his country in a modern war against Communist-inspired guerrillas. The British could see that there was only one likely conclusion to the Dhofar War unless modern, relevant political leadership was put in place. That leadership was there, ready in the wings in the form of the Sultan's son, Qaboos. Moreover, there had increasingly been concern that Britain was supporting a regime which was imprisoning its people in disease, squalor, hunger and ignorance. It was high time for a change.

Qaboos, watching his country and his inheritance crumble to destruction before his eyes, chose his moment in July 1970. He overthrew his father in a palace coup, actively supported by the British Government. When it came, it may have been a relief for the old man, and probably was not a surprise. Said himself had ousted his father many years before. The habit seems to have been in the family.

However, it seems that the old man put up quite a fight at the end. In an article in *The Mail on Sunday* published on 7 July 2002, Ray Kane, a British officer who, on orders from his British commanding officer forced his way into the palace in Salalah with his company of Omani soldiers, described what happened.

Kane burst into a large meeting room where, around the carpet's perimeter, were piled stacks of banknotes. Scattering the cash in the process, he rushed through the room to a darkened exit passage at the far side where he came under fire from the Sultan himself. Kane fired about twenty rounds back into the darkness, to which the Sultan responded in kind. Kane fired a machine-gun into the black space, and again fire was returned. Kane threw a hand grenade at where the fire was coming from. Again the Sultan fired back. Kane then climbed on to the palace roof to find an alternative approach. As he crossed the roof, bullets from the Sultan's weapon thudded into the surface beneath his feet. Jumping down onto a patio, Kane found he was facing a locked glass door. The Sultan was very probably in the room behind it. A burst from a machine-gun at the door had no effect. The door was made of armoured glass. While this protected the Sultan from fire from the outside, at least it also meant that those outside could not be shot by the Sultan inside. However, by continually firing a machine-gun at the same spot on the door, Kane managed to create a hole wide enough for him to speak through. He threatened to push an incendiary phosphorous grenade through the aperture into the room and explained to the Sultan precisely what the results would be if he did this. In the newspaper article Kane says he had no intention of actually carrying out the threat, but hoped the prospect of incineration and suffocation would be enough. Fortunately it was. In perfect English, the Sultan finally agreed to surrender to Kane's commanding officer.

Kane then goes on to describe how the door was opened from the inside revealing a bullet-scarred room with the Sultan and a couple of slaves with bloodied dishdashes, all armed with pistols. There were several casualties. While his palace was being forcibly entered, Sultan Said had shot and wounded in the stomach a man who was soon to become the governor of Dhofar. Another was killed in a firefight nearby. A third casualty was the Sultan himself. He seems to have received superficial flesh wounds to his body as well as a wound in the foot. Some say he shot his own foot by accident. Ray Kane himself was wounded in the leg after the fighting was over by a ricochet off the floor from an accidentally fired pistol. As he hobbled down the stairs, he was passed by the Sultan's son Qaboos going up, on his own, with a pistol in his hand.

Sultan Said bin Taimur bin Faisal Al Busaidi was forced to abdicate and eventually died in his sleep in his suite at the Dorchester Hotel in London the following year. Whatever his shortcomings as a modern ruler may have been, he certainly did not want for physical courage.

Qaboos took his father's place as Sultan. He was then twenty-nine. He had been educated initially by tutors in Salalah, and then at a private school in Suffolk. After completing the standard two year officers' training course at the Royal Military Academy at Sandhurst, he had spent six months with the Cameronians (Scottish Rifles) serving then in Germany. Sultan Said, having had his son Qaboos educated in the United Kingdom, had then somewhat perversely refused to trust him or give him any responsibility. It was as if Qaboos had been tainted by his modern education. Qaboos had suggested a number of areas where improvements might be made in the government of the country and had spent the better part of the next seven years under virtual house arrest at Mamoora in Dhofar for his pains. But his time had now come. With strong leadership qualities and a readiness to take wise counsel, he was well qualified to govern.

Qaboos had little difficulty in winning the loyalty of those who had served his father. There may have been some diehards who, having sworn loyalty to the old man, found it difficult to accept the young man's shilling, but they were few and far between. On a point of principle, Colonel Colin Maxwell, the senior contract officer in the country and a widely respected figure, offered his resignation on behalf of himself and all the contract officers. This was not accepted but the air was cleared. To any with eyes to see, the country was on a straight road to perdition unless new political leadership was found. Qaboos was the only agent whereby disaster might be averted.

Government troops received an immediate cash bounty. New and better equipment quickly began to appear, and a medal – the Accession Medal – was struck, to be worn by all who were serving when he came to power. Arthur Brocklehurst, with a wry smile, described it as his 'treachery medal' but he and almost all those who received it wore it with pride and set to their duties with a new sense of hope and purpose.

Qaboos immediately set about reforming his country, liberalising government and removing the grievances that had driven his people to rise up, however reluctantly, against his father. But by now, what had been a bona fide rebellion against a despotic ruler had become a Communist insurgency. It was not going to be a simple matter of building schools, clinics and community centres, patting the Dhofaris on their heads and then sending them back to their cattle and their goats on the *jebel*. Political forces far greater than the grievances of a few thousand tribes people had been let loose. The Communist genie was out of its bottle and the Sultan's Armed Forces needed help. The British had hitherto been content to provide limited assistance to Sultan Said in return for the continued use of Salalah and the island of Masirah as airbases. As the tribal rebellion was transformed into a Communist insurgency which threatened the security of the Gulf, so it became a cause of urgent strategic concern. Thus the British felt impelled to provide more proactive assistance.

An artillery battery, a squadron of the Special Air Service Regiment and some RAF Regiment forces to protect Salalah airfield were sent to Oman. They were joined by an engineer squadron in due course. Better aircraft, some helicopters and some coastal vessels were bought. The British officers already there, who were mainly ex-Army officers under contract to the Sultan – mercenaries in another word – were supplemented by more serving officers on loan service seconded from the regular British armed forces.

The Royal Marines filled a number of these posts and so it was that, in June 1973, as a lieutenant Royal Marines at the age of twenty-three, I assumed the local rank of captain and became the second-in-command of A Company, *Al Firqat Al Hudood Ashimaleeya*, the Northern Frontier Regiment, as a loan service officer in the Sultan's Armed Forces.

Chapter Three

Learning the Words

Arabic is a beautiful language. It is sonorous, mellifluous and poetic, and being idiomatically not greatly dissimilar to English, I found it surprisingly easy to learn. Having a Scottish accent, I had no trouble at all getting my tongue round the tighter corners, and I found I had a memory for sounds. It must also be said that I had the best possible incentive to learn: my survival depended on it. For ten weeks in the Spring of 1973 at the Army School of Languages at Beaconsfield, my fellow loan service officers and I were immersed in Arabic.

We were given twenty words to learn each day, and soon we were conversing. Our instructors were Arabs, and we took them out with us in the evenings to pubs and restaurants where the instruction continued. Each word was written down on a little card – English on one side, Arabic on the other – and we amassed pockets full of these, held together in piles with rubber bands. We would flick through them testing our memory, then turn them over and go through them again in the opposite direction. The beauty of this system is that you can do it almost anywhere: in a train, in bed, at a bus stop; and the pubs around Beaconsfield were frequented by small groups of officers shuffling decks of little cards and uttering strange sounds. It was great fun but we never forgot the serious purpose behind it all: we were going to war, and from time to time news would come through of a battle in Dhofar with names of men wounded or killed.

There was therefore something of a light-headed Epicurean atmosphere to our studies – 'eat drink and be merry for tomorrow you die.' There was nothing morbid about this and I would not want to exaggerate it. None of us expected to die, of course, but we certainly ate, drank and were merry with the purposeful vigour of young men who didn't want to let a perhaps unrepeatable opportunity pass them by, and the loaded nature of our circumstances added a certain piquancy to our revels.

The staff at the language school put up with our high spirits with remarkable patience, although occasionally we overstepped the mark. On return to the officers' mess after an evening's entertainment (always with our little language cards, of course) we would sometimes find that we were hungry, and an expedition to the mess kitchens would be organized.

Leftovers from dinner might be found in the fridge, or perhaps some bread and jam could be unearthed in an unlocked cupboard. One evening, when we turned the lights on in the kitchen, we were greeted by the sound of hundreds of cockroaches all scuttling for cover across the kitchen floor. After raiding the fridge, we decided to have a competition to see who could kill the most cockroaches – 'Bombay runners' we called them. The rules were agreed upon. Each person would get a minute to stamp on as many as possible. So we switched off the lights, poured some more beers, and waited a quarter of an hour. Then on went the lights and in went the first man to stamp on as many 'runners' as he could in the sixty seconds allowed. The corpses were then counted and marked with chalk (this was after all the home of the Army Education Corps) and after an appropriate interval to allow the targets to reassemble – during which time a few more beers were consumed – the process was repeated.

The state of the kitchen floor after a few rounds of this can be imagined. The following morning we were summoned by somebody rather senior and given a severe bollocking for our lack of consideration to the mess staff, who had not only been confronted with the results of our attempts at genocide, but also had to clear up the mess. We did feel sorry for the cleaners and gave them a genuine apology, but in our beery hilarity we had thought that we might in a rather oblique way be doing the authorities a favour by pointing out that they had an infestation problem. Perhaps we might deserve an apology for being forced to pay to eat food from a kitchen which was so manifestly unhygienic? Fat chance.

But our revels were the very acme of respectability compared to those of some of our predecessors who had gone through the school some months earlier. They had taken to 'BASE jumping'. BASE (Bridges, Antennae, Structures, Earth) jumping is the sport of parachuting not from an aeroplane, but from objects affixed to *terra firma*, such as a cliff, a radio tower, or a high building. This group had used the officers' mess accommodation, a fifteen storey tower, as their jumping base. It goes without saying that this is a highly dangerous activity, and the authorities at the language school were nervous that we might do something similar. They needn't have worried. Although I jumped a few times – from an aeroplane of course – parachuting is not a sport that I took to and, even in our most alcoholically irresponsible moments, none of us felt at all tempted by BASE jumping.

I passed the colloquial Arabic exam and went on to use the language extensively in Oman because very few of the soldiers spoke anything else. I never learned to write it. While the Sultan's Armed Forces went to some pains to teach their soldiers to read and write, most were still illiterate while I was serving there. I suppose I was eventually fluent in Omani Army Arabic. Sadly this skill has almost entirely evaporated because to retain it you need to use it, which I have not, except perhaps to startle the occasional innocent and unsuspecting Arab in restaurants or on the London Underground. But I believe if I had the same incentive that I had then, and were immersed in the language once more, it would come back again pretty quickly.

Chapter Four

The Set

I arrived in Oman in June 1973. There were four Omani infantry regiments, and they rotated through the war zone, Dhofar, two at a time, every nine or ten months. When they were not in Dhofar, they were based in the northern part of Oman, which was at comparative peace. The Northern Frontier Regiment was halfway through its time in the North, based at Bid Bid about two hours drive inland from Muscat. The regiment was due to go back to Dhofar in November 1973.

The barracks at Bid Bid were conventional military barracks for one battalion, and had most of the facilities that one would expect. All the buildings were single storey, there were barrack blocks for the soldiers, a rifle range, motor transport park, headquarters, medical centre, and sergeants' and officers' messes. The barrack blocks were new and had squat lavatories for the soldiers. There was no paper of course, but each loo had a tap positioned in the right place for subsequent washing. For many of the soldiers, this was one modern convenience too far. Those willing to use them persisted in using stones and putting them down the loo. The unwilling continued to take a short walk into the wadi to drop their trousers at a discreet spot. Change did not come overnight, but in due course the loos superseded the wadi and the stones stayed out of the loos.

All the officers, wherever they came from, lived together in the officers' mess. Each officer had his own room. This mess had a small swimming pool and the mess ante-room was air conditioned, as were a very few of the officers' rooms. Food was cooked by Goanese chefs and although the meals were European in format menus were heavily influenced by Arabic and Eastern cooking practices. Curries and exotic spices were part of the daily fare. Bacon was available for non-Muslims.

Alcohol was available in much the same way as in a British officers' mess, and the routine of daily life would have been familiar to British officers serving in a hot climate at any time in the past hundred years or so. Most Omanis did not drink alcohol, but a few did, and the Indian and Pakistani officers enjoyed it as much as we did. Eight or ten of the twenty or so officers who lived there would be British. Everybody, including the officers from the Indian subcontinent, spoke Arabic with varying degrees of fluency but most found it convenient to use English as their working language in the mess. However, none of the soldiers, either Baluch or Arab, spoke English so the lingua franca when working with them was Arabic. We spoke little or no Urdu, a language that some of our Baluch soldiers understood (although it was not their native tongue) and the few Baluch soldiers in our regiment spoke Arabic too. When talking to an Arab officer, you usually started in Arabic if you could. If your Arabic was good enough, or if he could bear you murdering his language, you might continue in Arabic, but often he would switch to English. They were as keen to learn our language as we were to learn theirs. Those who had come from Zanzibar were fluent in English.

I enjoyed the atmosphere and particularly enjoyed learning about Oman from the Arabs, but also from Arthur Brocklehurst. Arthur had started as a seconded officer from the Parachute Regiment in the mid 1960s and then left the British Army to become a contract officer with the Omani Army. He had been a company commander in the Muscat Regiment in the early years of the war and was now the second-in-command of the Northern Frontier Regiment. He was a fount of interest and knowledge.

We worked for six days a week. Our Friday was the Muslim *Jummah*, the day of rest. When not on exercise or otherwise out in the country, we worked from six in the morning and broke for an hour at nine for breakfast. By one o'clock the day was seriously hot and a light lunch might be followed by relaxation under a fan or in the swimming pool. Any further work that needed to be done that day started again at around four in the afternoon and went on as long as necessary. In the evening, once one was acclimatised, the temperature was not at all unpleasant and we would often sit out after dinner. Entertainment was pretty simple although I never recall being bored. Newspapers were rarely less than a week old. Mess magazines were well thumbed. Most people had a radio and some means of making music.

There was an acknowledged risk of overindulgence in alcohol. This did happen from time to time, and one was discouraged from taking booze back to one's room and drinking on one's own. However, the officers' mess was a civilised club and all who lived there were part of it. Life at Bid Bid was pleasant, but there was work to be done. The Regiment had returned from a very active and successful tour in Dhofar at the beginning of 1973 and would be going back down there again in November of that year.

The main military activities in the North were training and recruiting in preparation for the forthcoming Dhofar tour. On my arrival, I went on exercise almost immediately in the Wadi Mansah, a flat wide bowl of a *wadi* near Bid Bid. A *wadi* is simply a water course or valley, usually dry, but not always so. I had thought that having served in the Far East I might not find the heat so unusual, but never had I imagined heat like this. Hard physical labour was avoided during the middle of the day if at all possible. The lesson offered by 'mad dogs and Englishmen' had been taken on board in Oman. We tried to confine physical exertions to the cooler hours, but we did not always have that luxury.

Simply existing, even in the shade in the completely still air at the heat of the day almost drove me to faint. I can still remember each barely perceptible waft of wind, so rare and so welcome they were. Temperatures are traditionally recorded 'in the shade', but we had to operate frequently in the sun where, even on a thermometer measuring up to 50°C, the mercury would go off the scale.

I found myself trying to remember the lyrics of Flanders and Swann's song on the law of thermodynamics. 'Heat won't pass from a cooler to a hotter/You can try it if you like but you'd far better notter/'Cos the cold in the cooler will get hotter as a ruler,/'Cos the hotter body's heat will pass to the cooler'. I puzzled at the physics of it. With the air temperature in the shade being up to ten degrees higher than my body temperature of 36.4°C, would I not cook eventually? Then I also tried to remember the facts about latent heat and evaporation. I was drinking about two gallons of water a day but peeing about a tenth of that. It was this principle from which stemmed the miracle of cool water inside a *chargul* – a wet canvas bag or goat skin left in the hot sun. So perhaps I would live after all.

One became accustomed to the heat. The body can get accustomed to many things. After a month or so living outside like wild animals in the Falklands in midwinter nine years later, without tents, buildings, vehicles or cover of any kind other than groundsheets, and even sometimes without sleeping bags, my Marines and I became almost like wild animals: completely in harmony with our surroundings, not caring whether it was raining, snowing, sunning or blowing a hooligan, all of which you can get in the space of half an hour down there. But it takes time and I shall never forget the shock, and there is no other word for it, the shock of discovering that I was disabled by the heat on my first exercise in Oman.

We moved around the country in Land Rovers or Bedford lorries. Tracks or roads were not roads as we might understand them. The main ones used by the oil company vehicles were maintained by huge graders, mobile monsters which one would normally only see on a new building site flattening and shaping the landscape. Every now and then the oil company would send its graders along the road to iron out the corrugations which always seemed to develop after a week or two of use. Driving along a road shortly after it had been graded was a joy. Provided you could see where you were going, you could get up a fair speed and a wonderful trail of dust and sand would spew out behind you. If there was another vehicle in front, you either had to fall a long way behind or resign yourself to driving in a sand storm. If a grader had not passed recently, driving along the corrugated road was a bit like driving on a cattle grid – the faster the better – except that cattle grids usually extend only a few metres. Driving on a cattle grid for miles was a different experience. And if you met a grader coming the other way, it was best you got out of the way sharpish. Like Norwegian snow ploughs, they did not take prisoners.

Routes not used by the oil company were not maintained at all. You travelled as best you could by the easiest most direct route from A to B and took the track as you found it. Where it became impassable, you found a way around the obstruction. The driving wasn't all that bad in Oman even though vehicles were a relatively new phenomenon. Nevertheless, traffic accidents seemed to be frighteningly common. One always seemed to see the remains of a new disaster each time one travelled. It rather amazed us that even if only two vehicles were to be seen approaching each other from opposite directions, in good visibility on an open road, the chances of them crashing into each other were depressingly high. It was a sad fact that we seemed to lose as many of our soldiers in traffic accidents as we lost through enemy action.

We also granted leave to soldiers when we were in the North. Many soldiers lived in the interior and, as there were no oil company roads, it could take a man four or five days to get to his village. So we added this travelling time on to their leave entitlement. The men usually walked, rode a donkey, or hitched a lift with the supply Land Rovers or lorries that used the unmetalled tracks.

Everywhere one looked, one saw evidence of a turbulent past. Every village had a fort, and some of these were substantial. Every hill which dominated a *wadi* or a route had a hill top fortification or observation post. Some of these were crumbling away, but many were still usable and probably had been used relatively recently, although they may have been several hundreds of years old. Sometimes one could see a series of these forts dotted all the way along an important approach. As in past centuries in the Highlands of Scotland, where a fort or castle could be found at every strategic point governing the many waterways around the coast, it was impossible to progress unimpeded into the interior of Oman without the permission of the masters of that region.

By way of getting to know the country better, I took some men in one of our lorries and set off like a school bus run to take them to their villages. However, this was unlike any normal school bus trip, because it took me four days to get to the far end, and two to get back. It was a difficult journey along *wadi* bottoms and up and down tracks which were not recorded on any map. The ground would appear completely barren and unpromising, until one rounded a corner and there would be some palm trees, a well, and mud houses. Sometimes there would be terraced gardens with irrigation channels, and perhaps an old mud fort or a mosque.

The time had passed when, as happened to Arthur Brocklehurst a short ten years before, on turning up at a remote village in a Land Rover, the villagers would offer the vehicle grain and water for replenishment. Nevertheless, an Army truck turning up at a village such as this was not an everyday occurrence and our arrival was invariably greeted by small boys running out shouting and waving, followed by the men, and particularly the family of the man whom we were bringing on leave. He of course was especially welcome because not only was he evidently safe and well, but would possibly be carrying up to a year's wages with him. Eventually the truck would come to a halt surrounded by the whole village. Much handshaking and greeting would take place and I would be included in this. The instant I stepped out of the truck, I would be surrounded by twenty or thirty men and boys – no females – all wanting me to shake hands with them. So I would start my way shaking hands around the circle and keep on going until I'd finished. But no one would tell me I'd finished, and because they all seemed to look the same to my inexperienced eye, I'd carry on shaking until I'd shaken hands with the whole village about three times. They all thought this hilariously funny. It was so funny that after I had done it by mistake once or twice, I started doing it deliberately just to get a laugh. It never failed. There was no dignity or face to be lost; it just didn't matter.

I encountered a similar difficulty when playing football with the soldiers. There were usually two sides and, very occasionally, there was a referee. But other conventional distinctions such as different coloured strips or shirts-on/shirts-off were unknown. And you could forget any rules like only eleven per side, or even sides of approximately the same number. Can you imagine playing football when you can't tell one player on either side from any other? And at the height of your confusion, the chap who you thought was the referee would take the ball off you, in bare feet or flip flops, and score a goal; sometimes for you, sometimes for the other side ...!

I was the biggest duffer on the pitch – or rather, the *wadi* floor. The soldiers thought I was rubbish at football, which indeed I was, and found it was all just hilarious. I didn't mind; so long as they thought it was funny.

Sometimes, after being entertained to coffee and dates by the family of a soldier, we would spend the night at his village. My Arabic at this stage was still very stilted, but it was improving, and my attempts at conversation as we sat on the floor inside their houses were the cause of much giggling and laughter. Nonetheless, my efforts were appreciated. But I discovered there was no such thing as an embarrassing silence. If there was nothing to be said, it was perfectly acceptable to sit and share time and space with the people in agreeable silence.

From my soldiers I heard a few of the many tales that passed from one generation to the next in this oral culture. Many of these involved *djinns* or spirits. The small whirlwinds of dust that one sometimes saw generated by the heat and cavorting across the *wadi* floor were *djinns*. It would not do to get caught up in one of these. There was no knowing what might happen to you. Incoherent or mad people were possessed by *djinns*. Perhaps they had been caught by a whirlwind.

Shataan or Satan featured frequently. It was said that if you washed your face in your own urine each morning for seven mornings, one of two things would happen to you. Either Satan would send a woman to you whom you could have for your pleasure, or Satan himself would appear and have you for *his* pleasure.

There was supposedly a network of caves deep under the village of Izki, and a whole body of tales was associated with them. There was of course a cornucopia of gold and jewels to be found there by the man brave enough to go and get it out. But they were protected by evil *djinns*. Any man who had ever gone in had gone mad or blind or both, if indeed he was ever seen again. David Nicholls equipped himself with lights and ropes and, with the help of Lieutenant Said Hamed, set off on an expedition to explore the caves. He got in about thirty yards and found the way narrowed to a water channel about a foot across. It would have taken too long to dig out the rock falls and sediment, and the expedition was terminated. So the tales remained intact, but now have an extra dimension to them!

And then there was the explanation for the enigmatic supercilious smile on the face of every camel. Allah has a hundred names: Allah the Bountiful, the Compassionate, the Merciful, the Generous, the Gracious, the All-seeing ... but no man could ever know more than ninety-nine of the hundred names. Only the camel knew the hundredth: hence the smile!

In the evening, I would find a quiet spot on the side of a *wadi*, cook my meal, spread a camel blanket out on the ground, smoke a cigarette, and go to sleep under the stars, which were as clear and manifold as one could ever see from anywhere on Earth. This was a delightful and fascinating journey and by the end of it I had a good feel for the temper of the people that I was going to live with and whose soldiers they were going to let me command – and of their country. I liked what I saw.

On another occasion, we took a couple of soldiers on leave in a Land Rover. They lived on the other side of the mountains from our camp, on the coast near a place called Al Ashkara. It took two days to get there and in the course of the journey I was offered some sour camel's or goat's milk by some people who insisted on giving us their hospitality. There was no question of refusing it as this would have caused great offence, but it was all I could do to swallow it, keep it down, smile and say 'thank you, and God be with you.'

The usual welcome awaited us at Al Ashkara, and that night I slept on a camel blanket on the beach under the walls of the village with the rollers coming in from the Indian Ocean. At dawn the following morning, the mist was down and the sea was still. As the sun rose, burning off the mist, I was able to make out a couple of small local fishing boats and see life begin to stir in the village. There were signs of modernity – tyre tracks, tin cans, flip-flops – but not many. The way of life here had not changed much over the millennia. It didn't take a great leap of the imagination to suppose that this was what it must have been like by the Sea of Galilee. I felt I had taken an excursion into the Old Testament.

In Dhofar too it was possible to transport oneself to another age. Through the *jebel*, there was a series of tracks which, although they threaded their way across a rough mountain range, never seemed to lose or gain height. They followed the contours very cleverly, and had probably been unchanged for thousands of years. Our enemy used these ancient trade routes for their supply trains. As we lay at night among the frankincense trees, their fragrance triggered by a knock or a cut in the wood, lying in ambush on these tracks with our machine-guns and mines designed to blast ball-bearings into human and animal flesh, I felt I was an intruder in history.

These were the tracks that the traders of antiquity used as they carried their valuable product down to the ancient city of Sumhuran on the coast, there to be shipped to the Mediterranean and elsewhere in the Biblical lands. Is this where the three wise men got their frankincense? Did the ancient Egyptians, who used frankincense in their rites, burn the resin of the ancestors of these trees? Strange thoughts to be having while looking down the sights of a General Purpose 7.62 mm belt-fed Machine-Gun with a rate of fire of up to 900 rounds per minute.

Salalah, the main town in Dhofar, was another place which was straight out of antiquity. Although vehicles drove through it, the houses, the *suq* – or market – and the Sultan's palace were straight out of Ali Baba. One day I stood and watched it change forever as the market square was laid with tarmacadam in front of my eyes. No event in the previous three thousand years could have wrought such a visible transformation; and I stood and watched it happen in a short hour and a half.

It was on the journey home from the 'Sea of Galilee' when on impulse, I ordered the driver to take the Land Rover onto a long, flat beautiful piece of beach to break the monotony of jerking and struggling across rocks and boulders. The tide was out, and a long beach of glorious sand stretched out in front of us. All went well for a couple of hundred metres, and then disaster – we sank up to our hubcaps. We were bogged in. We were a day's drive from mechanical help. But in any case we were out of radio contact with anyone. I dare say we could have walked until we got to a place where radio reception was better, but how far that would be was anybody's guess. I reckoned I had about two hours to get us out before the vehicle was engulfed by the incoming tide. We had a piece of rope and a couple of spades, and the driver, the signaller and I dug and heaved like men possessed by the Devil. We put rocks under the wheels and built a stone path some thirty metres back to firm ground, but could we break the suction effect of the sand? When I was beginning to despair and, with the prospect of the Land Rover being swamped by the sea staring us in the face, it finally came free. I somehow couldn't get the idea out of my head that I was performing in a Laurel and Hardy movie. 'Another fine mess you've got us into, Stanley!'

We are all of us shaped by our experiences. Throughout all the time I knew my father, he carried a shovel in the boot of the car – just in case. No doubt his experiences in Burma and driving in Scotland between the wars taught him that this was only prudent. My experiences thus far, driving for twelve hours from Devon to Ayrshire overnight before there were motorways and open filling stations, have informed my subsequent habit of keeping a spare fuel can in the boot. After this episode, I felt that Father's odd obsession with his shovel maybe wasn't so daft after all.

I thoroughly enjoyed visiting these villages, which seemed so self-sufficient and which had adapted so well to unforgiving circumstances. Once inside the village precincts, one was in an environment so utterly different from the one through which one had travelled to get there. Date palms, acacia trees, banana leaves, tamarinds; all served to provide a most welcome overarching protection from the sun. There was shade, blessed shade. Beneath the shade there were houses built out of stones and mud which had not changed in shape or function since time immemorial. The roads were dirt tracks and although the insides of the houses that I saw were always very clean, the sides of the tracks were usually covered in rubbish. On occasions it seemed that the road was simply a track between two lines of garbage. I never really worked out how they otherwise disposed of refuse. It was a pleasure, however, to move around inside a village in the shadows and across the water courses, perhaps to share a coffee or a meal, or just a blether, sitting on a carpet on the floor of these dwellings.

Water was of course scarce and precious, and an important feature of the villages and elsewhere is the system of *falaj*. These are channels or leats which carry and distribute water. The word itself means 'distribution'. They wind and weave from underground wells, springs and mountain streams to villages, in and between villages, providing life-giving water for domestic use, and for irrigation in what to outside eyes looks like the most unpromising landscape. Sometimes the wells which supply them are up to 180 ft deep. They are constructed by hand and made from stones, mud and straw bricks, with cement made from fired limestone. Like a Roman road which lets nothing get in the way of its straight linear progress, these *falaj* follow a contour across mountain and plain regardless, with a gradient constant and uniform, driven by the imperative to let water flow gently but unambiguously through them from source to where the water is required.

Sometimes they are on the surface, but for much of their length they are underground. To cross deep *wadis*, aqueducts are built or sometimes the U-Tube siphon principle is used. The tunnels through which they pass are often cut through solid rock. They were dug by hand, first down and then sideways – rather like prisoners of war escaping from the Stalag – the sideways tunnels all linking up to form a long seamless channel which may run for many miles under the earth. If you fly across a featureless plain where these tunnels run, you can see long straight lines of holes and heaps of spoil about thirty metres apart where the *falaj* have been dug out underneath. They are often maintained by a tribe of small wiry men whose pay is a bunch of dates from each tree that is irrigated by the *falaj* that they are labouring on. There is a complex system of water management, and rights to water can be bought, sold and inherited. In larger communities a staff exists to manage and maintain the local *falaj*, and the rights to use them. Not infrequently the water that is carried is the subject of litigation.

The oldest of them were constructed by the Persians over two and a half thousand years ago. Most were built over a thousand years ago. They were the only substantial piece of man-made infrastructure in Oman for most of the last two and a half millennia and they are one of the most remarkable and least known wonders of the world, ancient or modern.

On the fringe of the village one would find fields and vegetable plots all irrigated from the *falaj*. If the village was on a slope – and much of Oman seems to be on a slope – these cultivated areas would be terraced, which added to their charm. Onions, peppers, lemons, limes, mangoes, pomegranates, garlic, plums, tomatoes, apricots, bananas, melons, and the ubiquitous dates all flourished there. Alfalfa grass for livestock would be grown too. Omani dates are delicious, reputedly the best in the world. Watching a date tree being harvested was a sight. The harvester climbed up the branchless trunk with a rope and a huge flat basket. It looked effortless but I would not want to try unless I had been trained as a mountain leader.

While small oxen provided the motive power in the fields, donkeys did pretty much everything else. All the shifting and carrying was done by these most patient of creatures. They were worked extremely hard, and it seemed to us that the accepted method of loading a donkey was to keep piling stuff on until its legs buckled, then remove a bit. But they were not otherwise greatly mistreated. Omanis understood their worth and tended to look after their donkeys.

The larger villages and towns have a market or *suq*. Animal markets contain camels, oxen, 'humpity-backit' cows, sheep with long droopy ears and big flapping tails. And goats: brown goats, black goats, big goats, small goats, great proud billy goats, white shaggy nanny goats; goats asleep, goats awake, and everywhere, goats with attitude. Then food of all kinds: spices, cooking ware, rice imported from India, earthenware made locally. Weapons: Martini Henry rifles a hundred years old decorated with engraved silver bands and probably more dangerous to the firer than the one fired at; British .303 Lee Enfields; the occasional *jezail*, a long barrelled exotic rifle with an impossibly curved butt, the likes of which can be seen in depictions of the 1842 British retreat from Kabul; and swords that look as if they really might have been used. All these were carried by male Omanis as a badge of respectability rather as we might wear a tie. These, the camel stick and the *khunjar*, the distinctive Omani curved dagger inside an ornate silver-covered sheath, were everyday accessories. Favourite souvenirs for Europeans were the coffee pots, especially the silver ones.

All silverware, and much other jewellery besides, was hammered out from silver Maria Theresa *thalers* or dollars. The cost of any item was the value of the *thalers* used, plus labour. This coin was the currency before riyal notes were introduced relatively recently in the 1960s, and the story of how it came to be the universal currency in much of the Middle East and Africa is a fascinating one. Its promulgation was a conscious act of policy by Maria Theresa, Empress of Austria, in the mid eighteenth century, designed to facilitate trade. Valued for the reliability of its silver content, its intricate design – thus making it difficult to forge – and the durability of silver, it was used by traders throughout the Mediterranean, the Levant, and North Africa. Following the trade routes, it spread along the Red Sea to the Arabian Sea and the Indian Ocean, and beyond to East Africa, the Indian subcontinent and China. It also crossed the Atlantic to the Americas. The coins still in circulation all bear the same date, 1780, the date of Maria Theresa's death, and they are still being minted to this day.

Perhaps another point in favour of the *thaler* was the size of Maria Theresa's bust. Her image on the coin is not that of a pretty woman: she was, after all, sixty three when she died. But she is portrayed as being handsomely endowed with a substantial bosom. In his book on the Blue Nile, Alan Moorehead describes how the great explorer Samuel Baker insisted on carrying only the 1780 edition because it had a 'profusion of bust'. It is indeed an impressive coin, and Maria Theresa looks like an impressive lady. In a culture where any image of any living creature, animal or human, was frowned upon, and where women took their place behind men, it seems that Maria Theresa nevertheless was *persona grata*. Perhaps it helped that she was a foreigner, and no doubt the fact that she was no longer alive was an advantage.

It also seems likely that the name of the present currency of Oman and several other Arabian states, the riyal, derives from the Spanish coin the *real* which preceeded the *thaler* in its ubiquity.

Health and education services for these remote villages were pretty scarce. There was a hospital in Muscat and a number of clinics in the bigger towns, and our own military medical officers also spent much of their time serving the local population. But that was all. The village *muttawah* or *mullah* would be the only source of education for most boys: girls as a rule would receive no formal education at all. Islam has no priests in the Christian sense. The *muttawahs* and *mullahs* were scholars of Islam and teachers.

I always took a medical orderly, known as a *campowda* – either a corruption of 'camphor powder' or a 'compounder of medicines' – with me to attend to any ailments that we might come across on our travels, and he was kept busy.

On one occasion, a child of about eighteen months was brought to us for whom he could do nothing. My *campowda* told me the child would die within a few days if it did not receive proper medical treatment. The parents of the child – and it was most unusual for me to meet the mother – were plainly in considerable distress, so that evening at a prearranged time when it had been agreed we would open up radio contact with our Headquarters, I had my signaller crank up our radio and send a Morse message requesting a helicopter to evacuate the child and mother to the hospital at Muscat. The next day, the helicopter duly turned up with a rather grumpy British medical orderly who examined the child. The orderly reluctantly agreed with the diagnosis of my Baluchi medic and he duly climbed into the helicopter with the child and his mother and off they flew to the hospital.

When I got back to base a couple of days later, it was pointed out to me, not unkindly, that scarce and expensive helicopters were not really meant to be used for such tasks. There simply were not enough resources to meet the needs of every sick child out in the remoter parts of the country, and next time, would I perhaps try and exercise a little more judgement? This argument was sadly irrefutable, and was one of my first encounters with the moral maze – the dynamics of the allocation of scarce resources to meet pressing, and apparently bottomless needs – but regardless of the rights or wrongs of this individual case, I saw the gratitude and respect that this small, naive, cost-inefficient act generated for the Sultan's Army, and felt sure that Qaboos sat just a fraction more firmly on his throne as a result of it. And one Omani infant was given the chance to grow to adulthood who otherwise would not have lived out the fortnight.

For a while I was the garrison commander at Izki or Zikki about an hour up the track from the main battalion base at Bid Bid. My experience in Northern Ireland had guided me towards looking at the faces of the women of any given community for an indicator of that community's general well being. In communities under pressure, it's the women who take the strain; who get the children to school, who find and cook the food. While the men are on the run or in jail or simply unemployed, it's the women who keep the show on the road. Are the women wearing make-up? Do they take care about how they dress? Or are their faces pinched, pale, drawn and concerned? I had seen all this in different housing estates in Northern Ireland.

In Oman, women did all the domestic tasks and worked in the fields, but I did not get the feeling that the men sat around doing nothing while the women did all the work. Men did plenty of work too. Women all wore long dresses and their heads were covered but I sometimes saw the faces. It was difficult to tell if they looked strained, but I think they were not unduly so. Certainly in my visits to the remote villages, there always seemed to be much ready laughter and many scampering children.

However, our Company *campowda* held a regular clinic for the people of Izki. The patients were not what you would normally see in the doctor's waiting room at home. It was an eye-opener to see the sort of ailments people suffered from. Flies were everywhere, and babies and children always seemed to have flies in their eyes. Their mothers would wave desultorily at them but the flies always won. Consequently there were some really unpleasant looking eye infections. Trachoma, malaria, tuberculosis, dysentery, whooping cough: all were there, not to mention the injuries people sustained in the normal course of life.

Respiratory ailments seemed to be common. People seemed to cough a lot. If you go to an Islamic country today and listen to the call to prayer from the mosque, you will more than likely hear the 'click' as the sound amplification system is turned on. This will be followed by the microphone being tested, or in many cases, the tape recording being switched on. Not so in Oman in the 1970s. Testimony to the live transmission by a live *muttawah* was the fit of coughing and hawking that often followed the hauntingly beautiful and compelling call.

A number of people, including children, were scarred with what appeared to be burn marks on their arms. This was a result of the theory of treating pain with pain. So a child who complained of a headache might have a red hot knife applied to an arm. I guess they didn't complain twice.

Many old men had cataracts in both eyes. And the old men weren't old at all by our standards. They just looked old. There were no dentists and there were always people with teeth trouble. We couldn't do much about this except issue painkillers. It was clear to even the most untutored eyes that life in the remote villages was hard. It may not have been nasty and brutish, but it could be dangerous, and for some it was very short indeed. Child mortality was high, and life expectancy was about fifty-five years. A wound or a broken bone which you or I might find painful – but once attended to, little more than an irksome inconvenience – for Omanis was a life threatening crisis which before it could even be treated had to be endured and survived for miles in the open back of a pick-up truck, or on the back of a donkey crossing

41

difficult country with no hard topped roads. There were no phones, let alone mobile phones, and victims of a road accident could wait many hours before being discovered.

If ever one got carried away with the romantic notion that beautiful, fascinating, mystical Oman was fortunate in her undeveloped state, that unsullied and unspoilt by outside influences she was a pristine example of old times or better times, one simply needed to join the *campowda*'s queue at Izki.

We British officers, both contracted and seconded, were officers in the Sultan's Armed Forces and we wore the Sultan's uniform. The daily working barracks uniform was an olive green shirt and olive green denim trousers very similar to UK military dress. In barracks, and on the rare occasion when we visited Muscat, we wore our beret, each regiment having a beret of its own colour. The Northern Frontier Regiment's was green.

British officers usually stood out from their Omani comrades. Normally taller and fairer-skinned, we were pretty readily identifiable. So, rather as in the early stages of the Boer War and the Great War, the officers were an obvious and natural target. Omanis would say that, even at a distance, they could tell who the Brit was by the way he walked. However, this did not apply to everyone. Some tanned more easily than others. And if a Brit wore a neatly clipped black beard rather than the usual shaggy luxuriant version, he could be indistinguishable from his soldiers – at least to British eyes.

For example, a newly arrived senior British officer visited the Northern Frontier Regiment on the *jebel* one day. He approached a lone soldier in a *sangar* and carefully and hesitatingly practised his Beaconsfield Arabic on him. '*Kayf haalek*' – 'How are you?' and so on. The soldier replied in the same language but rather more fluently, and after an exchange of courtesies, the Commander ventured a little more deeply into his limited repertoire. 'Is the food all right?' 'Do your boots fit?' 'Where is your village?' 'What is your tribe' and so on. Having enjoyed his chat and having eaten a little of his companion's food, the senior British officer continued on his way. It was only that evening when he was entertained in the Officers' Mess tent that he discovered that he had been talking to Arthur Brocklehurst, the Regimental Second-in-Command.

Notwithstanding the apparent futility of trying to disguise ourselves, on the *jebel* we tended to wear the same as our soldiers. Only the most short-sighted guerrilla would think we were Arabs when we were moving, but if we were bearded, suntanned and lying down, perhaps it might be a different matter. So on the *jebel*, we wore a *shemaagh*. There were no helmets and, of course, no body armour. The *shemaagh* was a loosely woven square cotton cloth which you wrapped around, or draped over, your head, depending on your inclination. It was wonderfully versatile. You could use your *shemaagh* as shade, or as a towel, a scarf, or as a nightdress wrapped around your midriff. It would protect your head from the wind, the dust and the flies. You could take it off and carry things in it, and you could use it as an arm sling or even a bandage or tourniquet. Immensely useful it was, and when you learned how to fold it and wrap it round your head properly, it was very comfortable and practical. Each regiment had its own colour, but on the *jebel*, everyone wore a field green one, which happened to be the Northern Frontier Regiment colour.

When I returned to the UK, I suggested that the *shemaagh* should be part of the field kit for Royal Marines, but I don't think they took me very seriously. A pity, because it is much more useful and stylish than a boring beret – except perhaps a Green Beret. In my fortress on the *jebel*, I sometimes wore my father's old felt shooting hat, but I never went anywhere on patrol without my *shemaagh*.

On duty, our soldiers wore shirt and trousers, or occasionally shorts, but off duty – in civvies – they would usually wear a white *dishdash* – a very loose overall a bit like an old fashioned nightshirt. This, together with a *shemaagh*, was the standard traditional dress.

One day at Izki I was invited to the village celebrations at the end of Ramadhan. During Ramadhan, Muslims are not permitted to let any food or water pass their lips during daylight hours. For the most devout, this prohibition extends to smoking, and even to swallowing spittle. These pious souls spend their daylight hours spitting. I was told abstinence even applied to sexual relations.

This practice had two manifest effects. Firstly, it was impossible to expect any energetic activity from anybody during the day. They couldn't eat or drink, and so very sensibly they conserved their energy. Secondly, the consequent dullness of the day was made up for by the parties at night. Alcohol was not present, at least not openly, but our soldiers would sit up much of the night eating, drinking and gossiping, thereby making themselves even more tired during the day. One might say that the whole social system went into a sort of night shift routine. But unlike night shift, where one gets some sleep during the day, many of our soldiers seemed to go the whole month without much sleep at all! We non-Muslims were not bound by these rules but we took care not to be seen openly diverging from them.

Exceptions were permitted to those for whom it might be unwise or dangerous not to take food regularly, such as travellers or pregnant women. Warriors at the front were included in this dispensation but they were expected to make up the fast later at a more convenient time.

The dispensation appeared in our standing orders and came in the form of a question to the Qadhi, the senior judge in the Sharia Court.

'Oh Qadhi, what is your opinion of a Muslim fighting an atheist enemy: is he allowed to break his fast during the month of Ramadhan if he were face to face with the enemy day and night? Food may be unavailable to him for one or two days. The Sacred Statement allows for those on journeys and for the sick to break their fast. Please give us your opinion.'

The Qadhi answers:

'The Muslim fighter is allowed to break his fast during Ramadhan. He even must if he realizes that fasting weakens his body. Fasting weakens the strength of a person, and fighting this enemy is a duty, and to fight him (God curse him) one needs one's full powers. Therefore let our Muslim fighter break his fast, and let him fight in the name of God, and if he dies, he will be a martyr. If he lives, he can make up his fast from the other days of the year, and he lives in peace, and we ask God to assist the Muslims in upholding the Holy Word.'

As can be imagined, the celebratory party at the end of Ramadhan was a celebration indeed. It would start the moment the new moon at the end of the Ramadhan lunar month was sighted, and continued on through the next day, the first daylight party for a month. I was invited to join the Izki village party at daylight. The party took the form of a large communal meal taken squatting around a monster platter of rice and goat stew, and dancing.

I was accompanied to the village by my Omani officers and our Company *muttawah*, who introduced me to the *Wali*, the Sultan's local governor. There was much handshaking and enquiring after each other's health, the health of the animals, the price of dates, and so on before we entered into the shade of his house after removing our footwear. The house was the usual mud brick and stone structure and sparsely decorated, but the traditional Islamic arches with their beautiful simple curves reversing to the hint of a point at the top were to be seen in the windows and doorways.

We squatted on a carpet with the other diners. As one squats, one takes great care to ensure that the soles of one's feet are not presented full frontal to the view of other people – a bit like making sure your flies are done up. Your feet are discreetly folded behind you – not always easy to begin with, but the body adapts. In time most

44

Europeans found squatting perfectly comfortable and natural. It is prudent to make sure that you have no holes in your socks.

The other diners – all male of course – were local youths and men of a variety of ages and stations. The youths were mostly teenagers and sons of the men present. Some of the middle aged men looked quite prosperous and were possibly shop owners or merchants. There were other more venerable gentlemen, all with beards of varying shades of grey. And there were others still who looked charmingly wild and woolly and whose accent I found unintelligible. All the men wore white *dishdashes* and *shemaaghs*, the latter mostly white too, but it seemed that the more rustic the man, the more colourful and more individualistic his *shemaagh* might be.

A serving boy brought water and we washed our hands. Water was also brought to drink. In due time, two people appeared carrying a huge engraved circular metal plate on which was heaped white rice and goat stew and fronds of green salad. This was set down in the centre of the carpet. After much thanking of Allah (*b'ism Illaahee ar Rahman ar Raheem*) I, the senior guest, was invited by the host, the *Wali*, to help himself. Typically, he would select a morsel from the centre of the meat and lay it in front of me, and invite me to help myself, always with one's right hand: *t'fuddhle* ('help yourself') *shukran* ('thank you') *afwan* ('don't mention it'). I, like everyone else, had heard of being offered sheep's eyes as a delicacy. I never saw this happen in Oman although Nick Holbrook was once offered a goat's eye while in the Musandam Peninsula. He declined it. At this, his host squitted it between his thumb and forefinger and threw it away saying, 'we don't like them either'.

Flat pieces of unleavened bread very similar to chapattis – *khubbs* – were passed round and one tore them into convenient sizes to scoop from the communal platter. Take a small handful of rice, incorporate a small piece of meat, squeeze into a convenient mouthful, and pop it in. Goat meat cooked long and slow Omani fashion is very delicious. The rice is flavoured sometimes with saffron and the ubiquitous cardamom seeds and is always garnished with lemon or *loomee* – limes.

One had to be careful not to overeat, so good was the food. Besides, there were others who were not at the table, or rather the carpet, who had not eaten. It was most important that sufficient remained for the women and children of the household to eat their fill afterwards. I wondered why, having cooked it, they simply didn't take their share and pass our share in to us. But no, it was important that we saw how much there was, and how bountiful Allah had been to our hosts. Seeing only half of what was there would not do.

45

Thus the meal and the conversation progressed. Eventually a sweet dessert of *halwa*, a kind of Turkish delight, was served, and then coffee. The coffee was cooked with cardamom seeds over a fire and served in very small cups. One never refused to take coffee. It was strong, tangy and very refreshing, and it would have been impolite to decline. One would be offered a second cup, then a third. After the third, you shook your cup indicating sufficiency. Then a few not too discreet belches of appreciation, slowly 'thank yous', more extensive hand shaking, and farewells.

My Arabic was still pretty rough but I understood enough to get the gist, and people were kind enough to ensure that I was included from time to time. These occasions were great fun. This is surely the way to eat. The sharing, the giving, the receiving, the interest in others, the exchange of food and conversation, and the thanking. Every meal is a celebration – a rejoicing that one has food and an appetite to enjoy it. If one is in good health and in the company of someone congenial with whom to share the celebration, so much the better. Surely there is no greater pleasure in life than sitting down thus and eating with friends?

Then there was dancing. The dancers were all male, of course; women as usual were not in evidence and, happily, I was not invited to dance. I don't remember how the music was produced. I seem to remember of lot of drumming. But it was a fascinating delight to watch the men and boys performing in the way their ancestors had done since time immemorial. I said there were no women, and there weren't, but females were not entirely absent. After a while I noticed that one of the older dancing gentlemen was holding a bundle resting on his shoulder as he cavorted in the dust with his fellows. I looked harder. It was a tiny girl child, apparently asleep, with her arms tightly wrapped around his large ochre yellow headdress.

Chapter Five

The Cast

The company commander of A Company was an Irishman from County Wexford called Johnny Braddell-Smith. He had had a short service commission in the British Army in the Lancashire Regiment where he was probably too unconventional to be appreciated by his masters, and so he gravitated to Oman as a contract officer. Being tough, understanding, tolerant and utterly unflappable, he was ideally suited to the country, the people, and the job in hand. At twenty-six, he was three years older than I. I took an instant liking to him and looked forward to working for him.

I was, on the face of it, a reasonably experienced officer for those times. After initial Royal Marines Officer Training in 1968 and 1969, I had been sent to the Far East where I had been given my first command, a troop of thirty Marines, shortly before my twentieth birthday. I exercised with my troop in Singapore and in the Malaysian jungle, and had a spell in the British Colony of Hong Kong where we had garrisoned the border with Red China for a while. This was followed in 1971 and 1972 by two very active tours in Northern Ireland, one in Armagh and another in Belfast. I had a brief flirtation with the Special Boat Service; brief, but long enough for me, and for them, to decide I should not pursue that avenue further. I had recruited officers for a short while, and had commanded a team training Royal Marines recruits at the Commando Training Centre.

In the four and a half years since I had joined aged eighteen, I had done and seen much, but had not stayed with any one organization for more than nine months. I felt that I had not always been as successful as I should have been, and had not had an opportunity to prove my worth. With the benefit of thirty more years, I can now see that for many young people, regardless of what experience they may have had, the simple passage of time is a key ingredient in their progress towards professional maturity and soundly based confidence. I was one of those.

I quickly sensed that Johnny would give me as much opportunity to flourish as I could handle, but at the same time he would never ask me to do something that I could not do. As it turned out, I could not have asked to work for a better man.

We complemented each other well. He was an experienced, outstanding leader, and I discovered that some of the things I had picked up on training and administration from the Royal Marines were just what was required. The company had another British contract officer called Tony Heslop. He too had had a short service commission in the British Army, spending most of his time with armoured cars. He was slightly older than I and had arrived before me, but because I was a Royal Marine and therefore an infantryman, I was made second-in-command and he third-in-command. The distinction barely mattered. There was plenty of work for both of us and we fumbled our way into our new jobs together.

Johnny had been in Oman for about three years. He took command of A Company at about the time that I arrived. He made a point of visiting the soldiers' barrack blocks in the evening on a regular basis and from time to time I would accompany him. We used to squat with the soldiers and eat with them. I listened hard trying to follow the conversation and pick up new words. Johnny had developed an impressive knowledge of Oman and his Omani soldiers in this way.

His administration of his company was excellent. He left the equipment, vehicles, stores, weapons and ammunition to Tony and me. He looked after the people. He kept a list of the name of every soldier, the courses he had done and the leave he was due. This was the sort of stuff you would normally expect your sergeant major to do, but when your sergeant major is a Bedu and has only just learned to read Arabic let alone English, then you have to find another way of doing it. A number of courses would be available at the Training Regiment: reading and writing, signals, mortars, promotion courses, occasionally a language course. He was meticulous in ensuring that each man got the courses appropriate to him and his ability. He made the most of every opportunity to advance the education of his soldiers and carefully planned their careers by taking into account their potential and their ambitions. Unsurprisingly, he quickly earned the trust and devotion of his men.

The Commanding Officer was a seconded officer like myself called Bryan Ray from The Queen's Regiment, and he too was a quiet, tough, understated type with great reservoirs of patience, gaiety, understanding and goodwill. His approach was to tell us what it was he required and why; to give us the resources, and perhaps discuss with us how we might set about our tasks. But then he would step back and let us get on with it, and we always knew that there was support and guidance if we needed it. He was the very best sort of officer for this kind of job.

There were few training facilities, but of real estate and ammunition there was no shortage – and what more could an enthusiastic young officer require? We were not constrained by the rules and regulations of a middle-aged peacetime army. We were a nascent fighting force at war and the average age of the officers was very young. Therefore training tended to be imaginative, bold and sometimes dangerous.

Simon Hill of the Parachute Regiment and David Nicholls, a fellow Royal Marine, had brought A Company back from a very active successful tour in Dhofar. Johnny and I were to take over from them. I had a few days with them as part of my handover and they imparted a number of very important lessons to me.

They pointed out that it is only in the films that the goody knows instantly and precisely where to return his fire when someone shoots at him. If only it were so easy. In reality, finding out from where you have been shot at – locating the enemy – is often one of the most difficult things to do on a battlefield. Typically you are on patrol with your men and the crack of enemy rifle or machine-gun fire is simultaneous with one or more of your men dropping to the ground wounded or dead. Everyone else dives on their bellies and scrambles for cover. Someone attends to the stricken man or men and everybody else shouts; 'anyone seen the enemy?' – and nobody has. So you start from there.

Anything can happen. If you are lucky, the enemy fires again from the same place a couple of times and someone sees a wisp of smoke. Or one of your own party not in the immediate engagement area can move to where he can see more clearly what is happening and tell you about it, assuming both your radios still work. Communications always seem to break down as soon as the shooting starts.

By firing at likely enemy firing points you might also be able to entice the enemy to fire at you and to give his position away. Once you have established his position you then have the problem of directing and controlling the fire of your own side on to him so that you can win the firefight and recover the initiative. Equally possible is that while you thought you had taken cover, another enemy position rips into you with a machine-gun from another location and you have to move again under fire, with or without your wounded or dead.

If the enemy is supported by indirect fire, you can expect mortar shells or rockets to start crashing in amongst you within a couple of minutes of the first contact. Fear, utter confusion and blind desperation

49

are waiting to overwhelm you, and only the best trained soldiers with the coolest NCOs and quickest thinking officers can turn such a situation round. During the day in Oman, initial contact usually took place at a range of two or three hundred metres or further. At night, or by day in the luxuriant vegetation that appeared after the monsoon, it could be a great deal closer.

C Company once had a firefight at the edge of the tree line during which Viv Rowe, a Royal Marines batchmate of mine who was then second-in-command of the company, heard Hamed Said, one of the company officers, calling for mortar fire onto his own grid reference. When Viv pointed this out, Hamed replied that it was no mistake: the enemy were only six feet away. This was a daylight contact which lasted all day and by the end of which Hamed's platoon had virtually run out of ammunition.

The enemy were often as surprised as we were. We stumbled across each other. But they were extremely good at seizing the initiative and had a wonderful eye for ground. Any mistake that you made in reading the ground or assessing their dispositions was instantly exploited and you could very quickly find that you and your patrol were in danger of being surrounded. On the other hand, if you were able to seize the initiative, their command and control was not very responsive and, once outflanked, they tended to melt away. They were also reluctant to take on strength.

If one side spotted the other without being seen, a trap could be laid – an ambush – and the side that walked into an ambush killing ground instantly found themselves in a chaotic, terrifying, bloody hell.

I later spent much time on the *jebel* trying to catch our enemy – known as the *adoo*, the Arabic word for 'enemy' – in an ambush and I never succeeded, although others did. But we did bump into each other from time to time and once the *adoo* more or less ambushed me. On each occasion, I found it fiendishly difficult to ascertain precisely where the other side was shooting from. We always won our firefights eventually because we made sure that we never operated out of range of indirect fire support, either mortars or artillery, or both. We were also usually able to call up a supporting air strike within about a quarter of an hour. Moreover, we always deployed in such number and dispositions that there was invariably a second or third group free to react and come to the rescue of the group in contact. But if that group in turn lost the initiative ...

Bitter experience had taught this army that locating the enemy during a firefight is a most important battle drill, and one of the marks of professional soldiery is how thoroughly and well this is practised.

So, taking on board the lessons from Simon Hill and David Nicholls, we trained hard in this art.

A group of about half a dozen well armed carefully chosen men would disappear up a suitable *wadi* and choose two or three fire positions. These two-man fire teams would then lie in wait for the main body, usually a platoon, which would advance up the *wadi* towards them. The leader of the fire teams and the platoon commander would be in radio contact. The first fire team would open fire on the advancing platoon, firing just over the platoon's heads of course. They would then take cover behind the rocks. The platoon would return fire at where they thought the fire had come from. At an appropriate moment, the second fire team, and perhaps the third, would open up.

This exercised people in many of the difficulties of locating the enemy and directing and controlling fire during a firefight. And sitting behind the rocks while a platoon's weight of fire, about twenty rifles and two machine-guns, went over your head and smashed into the rocks around you – or not, depending on how accurate they were – was also another new experience. I once did it with the entire company, but only once. This exercise required careful planning, reconnaissance and coordination, and eighty rifles and eight machine-guns were too unwieldy, not to say hairy, for peacetime safety. We switched people in the fire teams with those in the platoons as much as we dared so that each experienced as many different dimensions of the exercise as possible. We did this many times while training in the North. It was excellent training, and no one got hurt.

We were also fairly ambitious with our live firing mortar exercises. One of these did go wrong one night and I found myself being mortared by my own tubes while I was withdrawing from an exercise ambush. After the crashing around our ears subsided, I asked anxiously in Arabic 'is anyone hurt?' A pause, then Lieutenant Said Hamed's calm quiet voice came out of the dark 'only one; a slight wound'. One man had been hit by some shrapnel in his arm. I had been between him and the shell which wounded him. We carried on with the patrol and walked him home.

A board of inquiry was conducted by the regimental second-in-command, Arthur Brocklehurst. He found that I had not allowed for the difference in temperature between night and day. I had registered the fall of shot during the day. The exercise ambush had been sprung at night and the mortar shells did not travel quite so far in the cooler air. I expected a significant censure for my cock-up. I had, after all, wounded one man and endangered the rest, including myself. Arthur took a more pragmatic view than I could possibly have hoped for. He thought the training had been very realistic – it sure was – and believed that realistic training saved lives. He did not want to discourage me from doing it and he was quite certain I wouldn't make the same mistake again. The Commanding Officer, Bryan Ray, endorsed his findings and I was given a rather gentlemanly reproach and told to be more careful next time.

The war in Dhofar was overseen by a body called the Dhofar Development Committee. This was chaired by the Sultan's civilian representative the Wali of Dhofar, Sheik Braik bin Hamoud. All the stakeholders in Dhofar were represented on this committee which met weekly. I never met the Wali. He seems to have been a remarkable man and we felt and saw the benefit of his political leadership. It was he who had been shot and wounded by Sultan Said during the coup in 1970. Braik evidently had been one of the movers and shakers in getting the old man out and the young man in. He survived the coup and he survived the war which he had helped to win, but he was killed in a road accident some years later.

The aim of the Armed Forces in Dhofar was 'to secure Dhofar for civilian development'. This is what, in modern terms, would be called our 'mission statement'. Predating the formal articulation of British Army doctrine by about fifteen years, it nevertheless complied perfectly with that doctrine. It would have been easy to have been distracted by the desire to 'defeat the enemy' or 'free Dhofar from Communism' and so on, but no. It gave the end-state that the Armed Forces in Dhofar were to achieve and the overall purpose behind it. There is an element of brilliance in those six words. Unambiguous, crisp and entirely to the point, it was an exemplar of its type. Moreover, our Commanding Officer and our Brigade Commander made sure we all knew about this articulation of our required end-state, so nobody was in any doubt about the goal to which their efforts were being directed. We were happy with that and, under the leadership of this committee, we saw it all turning into fact. We felt this committee with the redoubtable Wali at its head knew what it was doing.

While on the *jebel* in Dhofar, we were visited frequently by our own Commanding Officer, Bryan Ray, and our own regimental officers like the Operations Officer, Tony Willis, and the Intelligence Officer, Mike Kingscote, who made sure they kept themselves well informed about the realities of life on the *jebel*. Our Brigade Commander, firstly Brigadier Jack Fletcher, who was relieved in turn by Brigadier John Akehurst, also visited us from time to time. The force in Dhofar was called the Dhofar Brigade. Numbering about 10,000 men it was about twice the size of any other normal brigade and contained Omanis, Baluchis, Indians, Pakistanis, Iranians, Jordanians, Egyptians, and British; the Brigade Commander, who sat on the Dhofar Development

Committee, had his own navy and his own air force under direct command. Some brigade.

Both Fletcher and Akehurst were first class soldiers and were the right men in the right place at the right time. Jack Fletcher died of cancer within two years of going home. This was a personal loss to all whom he visited on the *jebel* with his no nonsense but soldierly sympathetic approach. His wife Mary, whom I also met on a couple of occasions, was a delightful person who also succumbed to cancer a number of years later.

John Akehurst continued seamlessly where Fletcher had left off in prosecuting the war and took a real first-hand interest in what was happening on the *jebel*. Both men had that essential quality for all leaders of men under pressure. They gave people confidence. They gave them hope too; even if they themselves didn't always feel much hope.

This lies at the very heart of successful leadership. If people cannot feel, even though things are bad and may get worse, that if they follow this particular person, then there is a real prospect of ultimate success – then that person has failed as a leader. There are many different styles of leadership for many different circumstances, but ultimately the boss is the banker of hope, and he can never allow himself to appear bankrupt. If he doesn't display and impart hope, then he is hopeless – a no-hoper. Fletcher, Akehurst and Ray gave us hope. I have no doubt that Jack Fletcher would have gone further up the promotion ladder had he lived. John Akehurst did just that and became a four star general and the Deputy Supreme Allied Commander of NATO Forces in Europe before he retired. We weren't surprised.

The overall Commander of the Sultan's forces was Major General Tim Creasey, who was based in the North but kept in touch by visiting us on the *jebel*. He too was the right man in the right place at the right time. The soldiers called him the Bull Elephant, partly on account of his bulk, but also because he could be gloriously forthright. Unsurprisingly, Oman was the target of numerous representatives of commercial companies wishing to sell arms to this 'oil rich' country at war. I was present in General Creasey's house on one occasion shortly after British Aerospace had made a pitch at selling an anti-aircraft missile called Rapier to the Sultan. A discussion was underway on its possible roles. Given that the *adoo* had no aircraft, we rather had our reservations. Creasey was in no doubt. 'This country needs Rapier like I need a second arsehole'. Spot on!

For all his bluntness, he nevertheless had great political sensitivity and boundless military common sense. He was also skilfully persuasive. Creasey's predecessor, Brigadier John Graham, had won the confidence of the new young Sultan. But it could not be taken for granted in 1972 that the Sultan would continue to take and act on British advice. Together with his ambassadorial counterpart, Donald Hawley, Creasey played a most important part in winning and maintaining the confidence of Qaboos, sometimes in the face of competing sources of advice from other international players. He developed further the thinking of John Graham and successfully pushed forward the appropriate action. He felt that it was difficult to see how the *adoo* could win militarily – although they could just possibly. It was equally difficult to see how we could lose militarily – although we could just possibly. But the likely prospect, he felt, was a long drawn out war of attrition bleeding the country white with the end result being inevitable victory for the Communists, allowing them to achieve their aim of overthrowing the regime and controlling the Gulf. As Kissinger said, 'the guerrilla wins if he doesn't lose; the security forces lose if they don't win'. So Creasey determined on an active burst of military and civil activity which would force a decisive and early conclusion.

Rises in the oil price and its increased flow gave him new resources and he used them well. Our clothing and equipment began to improve perceptibly. He coaxed and goaded the British Government into being more open-handed with its support, and helped to persuade other Middle Eastern nations that, since their national interests were being served by Oman's war, some tangible contribution might be appropriate. He was thus instrumental in securing active Iranian and Jordanian participation. He also had a good memory. I bumped into him a number of times over subsequent years in some surprising places: at Staff College, in the caves in Gibraltar, in the garden at Buckingham Palace, and he always recognized me, enquired after my comrades and shared a conspiratorial joke with me. He is dead now, but Oman owed him much, as indeed did we all.

These officers, and most of my fellow denizens of the *jebel*, came from the British Army. As a Royal Marine, I belonged to the Royal Navy. This, my first exposure to the British Army, albeit in disguise, was an interesting exercise. The British Army sent about a hundred serving officers at any one time to Oman including some of its best people. They, like me, were seconded officers. A number of officers, having served in the British Army, had left and taken a contract in the Oman Army. They were the contract officers. Those who served on the *jebel* were usually excellent.

When I went to the Army Staff College at Camberley in the early eighties and saw the British Army full frontal so to speak, I discovered that as an institution it was then rather introspectively obsessed with what might happen in its sector of West Germany if the Soviets invaded. Anything that was not directly related to the British Army of the Rhine (BAOR) was of secondary importance. Just in case one was in any doubt about this, the downbeat nature of expressions such as ROW (rest-of-the-world) and OOA (out-of-area) allowed little room for misunderstanding. Needless to say, Oman fell into both these categories.

Some careers were made in Northern Ireland, but all the best jobs were in Germany. No ambitious officer could avoid this fact and, unless his card was marked with the right jobs in Germany, sooner or later he would find himself in a dead-end. There were some blithe spirits who didn't feel overly constrained by this reality, and who volunteered for the more exotic, interesting and operational jobs 'out-of-area', like Oman, but they were regarded by the mainstream set – perhaps not without a wistful twinge of envy – as vaguely irresponsible.

The Royal Marines, approach was somewhat different. The Royal Marines *were* the Rest-of-the-World; they *were* Out-of-Area. Oman was *the* place to be. Throughout much of the Cold War, the Royal Marines were looking for roles that they could use to help them in their battles for money from the Ministry of Defence. They weren't armoured troops and so were of limited use in the armoured scenarios in Germany. Amphibious warfare was out of fashion. They eventually carved out a valuable niche in North Norway and became the acknowledged experts in mountain and Arctic warfare. But in the 1960s and 1970s, they were in danger of being cast into the wilderness. This culminated with John Nott's attempt to disband the Royal Marines in 1981. They were saved at the last moment by the IRA and the Argentinians.

The Royal Marines saw Oman as an ideal opportunity to make themselves useful and to give their officers valuable operational experience which couldn't be got elsewhere. The possibilities for gaining experience were endless. There were very few artillery observers and no mortar fire controllers in Oman. So we did those jobs. There were no aircraft controllers, so we controlled the aircraft. Apart from the constructors of the barbed wire obstacle which became the Hornbeam Line in 1974, there were no engineers, so we built *sangars* with explosives, laid mines and constructed wire entanglements. In addition to the primary tasks of training and commanding infantry, the widest variety of operational and administrative jobs had to be done by someone. That someone was us.

We young officers competed for the eight or ten posts that the Royal Marines filled in Oman. NCOs were also sent to the Training Regiment in the North, but they always gravitated to Dhofar at some stage in their tour so that they could gain first hand knowledge of what they were training the soldiers for. This meant that over the ten years of the war perhaps seventy or so Royal Marines officers and a fair clutch of NCOs saw active service in Dhofar. In an officer corps that doesn't number much more than 450 at any one time, Oman became part of the Royal Marines culture.

The second-in-command of the rifle company in 42 Commando in which I had been a troop commander had been Peter Ward. He had fought in Oman. I had served at the Commando Training Centre with Jeremy Lee, Rick Williams, Donal Douglas and Hugh Affleck-Graves, all of whom had seen active service on the *jebel*. I was about to take over from the officer from whom I had bought my first car, David Nicholls. All these officers had distinguished themselves on the *jebel* before I went there. Peter Leicester, whose troop I had taken over in Singapore and David Sayers who had been the Assistant Adjutant, were in Oman now. Alan Howard and Ernie Cook whom I also knew from previous appointments were there too.

We all knew who had been there, who wanted to go there, and who had been selected to go. Stuart Rae, a well-liked and respected officer whom I also got to know in Singapore in 1970 had been killed on the *jebel* the year before I arrived. Steven Bidmead, the childhood friend who had persuaded me to join the Royal Marines rather than the Army, had recently been wounded there. Friends were there now and friends were planning to come with me. Ex-Royal Marines were on contract there. When two or three ex-Omani Royal Marines met in a bar, they would talk in Arabic to each other just to show off and get up the noses of everybody else who hadn't been there. It was *the* place to be: consequently the Royal Marines were disproportionately represented in Oman.

I was told that my Marines in X Company, 45 Commando Royal Marines, which I later commanded in the Falklands War, drew some comfort from the fact that I had been to war before. I know I did. I drew on the experience; it influenced my approach to training, and to planning and commanding in the battle for Two Sisters, and to all my subsequent operational appointments over the next twenty-five years.

So, those blithe spirits from the British Army who specifically volunteered for service in Oman, and who cared more about adventure and active soldiering than their careers, were, with my brother Royal Marines, my British companions on the *jebel*. Officers from the RAF Regiment, like Alistair Gilchrist and Tim Jones, whose normal role was the protection of airfields also somehow conspired to join us.

Some like Angus Ramsay had bright careers and high rank in front of them. Others left the Army soon after Oman and cut a furrow in other fields. But regiment, corps and arm became irrelevant on the *jebel*. All that mattered was: could you do your job or not? Almost all of them could do their jobs very well indeed. Officers from the Infantry, the Royal Signals, the Guards, the Royal Engineers, the Royal Artillery, the Cavalry, the logistics corps, the RAF Regiment and the Royal Marines, all put on the Sultan's uniform and walked the *jebel*. It was indeed my great good fortune to serve with them.

Oman was not a place for a person in a hurry. It could be infuriating trying to get things done. And sometimes things were done rather differently from what I had come to expect. As second-in-command, I took over the Company accounts, weapons, stores and ammunition from David Nicholls. The Company was at Izki at the time and living in its own small stand-alone company-sized barracks. Everything went well until I started counting the officers' mess crockery. I happened to notice a mess boy bringing crockery in through the back door from the sergeants' mess; crockery that I had already counted. I drew this to David's attention. He shrugged his shoulders. 'Do you want to start again?'

'No.'

'Fine. Let's go and have a drink.'

But the Omanis, far from being indolent, simply had priorities which reflected the prevailing circumstances. It was a hot, poor country. Hard labour and rushing about was energy consuming and rarely cost effective. How much easier it is for us western Protestant capitalists to exert ourselves a little, knowing that by so doing we will see a directly related benefit in terms of money, goods, status, or fulfilment.

In their country, the lesson of life was that if you worked hard enough to plant and harvest your date palm and keep a few goats, and if you were lucky, you could subsist at an acceptable level. Harder work did not guarantee any higher level of material satisfaction. There were no more material goods to be had. There were no jobs, no industries, no universities or schools as stepping-stones to wealth. More work only produced an incremental improvement – a few more goats or dates – not a quantum one, so the pressure to work just hard enough to achieve a sufficiency and no more was strong.

Being a religion ideally suited to people living in a harsh, unforgiving environment, Islam complemented this culture very well, but tended to add its own inertia. The very word Islam means 'surrender to God', and a Muslim is one who surrenders to God. The step from surrendering to God and accepting God's will, to accepting poverty, hardship and a short life is not a great one. Fatalistic is not quite the right adjective, but certainly Omanis had a resigned approach to life which was sometimes difficult to move. Convincing them that they could influence the course of events for the better if they tried harder, did things differently, or simply turned up, was not always easy. *'Insh'allah'* – if God wills – was the frequent retort in response to a proposal for action. This drove some British people to distraction and they did not usually stay in the country long.

The Omanis nevertheless were wonderful people to live with. They were superbly honest: I never had anything stolen from me while I was there and it wasn't as if there were no opportunities. They were generous to a fault and they had that elementary ingredient essential for a true sense of humour, personal humility – they didn't take themselves too seriously. In this we had a common understanding of inestimable value. Laughter and good humour were rarely far away. They were very tolerant. Devout Muslims don't drink alcohol and many of them were devout, but they saw no reason why we shouldn't drink if we wanted to, and indeed they tolerated their own people drinking as long as it was done discreetly and sensibly. Grapes are grown in certain areas of the Jebel Akhdar and unsurprisingly they are sometimes converted to alcohol. Nick Holbrook, while taking a patrol in that region, was once offered locally produced wine and brandy. He expressed his surprise that they should treat the strictures of Muhammad so lightly. He was told: 'we've been making wine for over 2,000 years. Muhammad has only been around for 1,400'.

Religion is like the weather. It is always around and always has been. It can do great good or great evil depending on how men take it. Recent events have served to highlight some less agreeable manifestations of Islam, but we in the West sometimes conveniently forget the innumerable acts of unspeakable vileness that have been perpetrated in the name of Christianity. So when we hear Muslims say that Islam is a religion of peace, we can hardly believe our ears. I hesitate to say that Islam is a religion of peace any more than I would say Christianity is a religion of peace. As with the Bible, in the Koran you can always find a quotation to suit almost every purpose or slant, and then find one which directly contradicts it. However, it seemed to me that Omanis were at peace with their religion and wished to be at peace with any man who was ready to be at peace with them. There was none of the fanatical fundamentalism that sometimes crops up in some other Islamic countries. Islam Omani style, while devoutly followed, was moderate, tolerant and an entirely appropriate guide and support to people living out their lives in this beautiful, barren corner of the Earth.

I found Omanis a pleasantly straightforward, uncomplicated people. There was a widely acknowledged and accepted social hierarchy, but they shared the Scottish approach to these matters, that however grand a person might be, he was after all only a man. Every man had his own personal dignity and individuality, so a *bedu* could look a sultan in the eye. 'A man's a man for a' that.' They were not naturally warlike but could be coaxed into enjoying soldiering. That said, there were some, fortified by Islam and great depths of character, who would and did fight to the death with barely a flinch.

There was plenty of talent there too. One of our platoon commanders, Said Hamed, whom I had inadvertently mortared along with myself, was a very steady and experienced warrior and I respected and relied heavily upon him. Yahya bin Nasser who joined us later was bright, committed and brave and thirty years later became a major general.

Ali Obaid, our Signals Officer was charming, enthusiastic and efficient. Said Nasser, who was second-in-command of C Company, also had a bright future. He took over command of C Company while I was in Oman and became the Commanding Officer of Northern Frontier Regiment within a couple of years.

Said Murr, the Company Sergeant Major of A Company, was of *bedu* stock. The Bedouin were nomadic people who lived in the desert and were regarded by respectable Omanis rather as settled bourgeois folk might regard Gypsies. In other words, they looked down their noses at them. By the lights of the British forces, Said was about as un-sergeant major-like as you could imagine – more like Sergeant Wilson from *Dad's Army* than anything else. Lining men up and taking names was not his forte but on the *jebel* commanding a platoon in a tight spot, he was unflappable and dependable.

Mohammed Said Raqaishi commanding Headquarters Company was a fascinating character from whom we all learned much. Having been used as a messenger by the enemy as a small boy during the Jebel Akhdar Wars of the 1950s, he had been a warrior all his life and there wasn't much that he didn't know about fighting on the *jebel*. Charming, amusing, fiery, loyal and tough, he was a born soldier and a man whose company it would be a pleasure to have at any time, but especially when things got rough. Raqaishi commanded the Northern Frontier Regiment within four years and then commanded the Brigade in Dhofar. Message boy and child soldier for the enemy, to brigade commander for the Sultan: a career that any soldier would be proud of.

And there were in our midst men of great talent and commitment like Hamed Said. Hamed was our Adjutant and had been brought up in Zanzibar where his family had been exiled. This was the same officer who, when he was Assistant Adjutant, was sent to C Company for some 'field experience'. When on the *jebel*, Hamed had sprung an ambush on the *adoo*. The *adoo* had counter-attacked his ambush and fatally wounded his machine gunner. During the course of this battle

Hamed had brought mortar fire down on the *adoo* who were only a few feet away from him. The measure of his calibre is the fact that he rose to be the Chief of Defence Staff of his country as a lieutenant general and then became Minister for Water Resources, a most important post in a country where the management of scarce water is vital. Hamed would have enriched and adorned any man's army.

There were also notable characters from the Indian subcontinent. Mercenary soldiers from Baluchistan in Pakistan, once part of the Sultan's empire, filled many of the posts that required technical skills. They had the necessary education to become signallers, mortarmen, medical orderlies, drivers mechanics and clerks.

Our Quartermaster, Yaqub Malik, was a splendid man, the very caricature of a Pakistani businessman, comfortably built, sleek and smiling; a real fixer and totally committed to ensuring that the right stores and ammunition were at the right place at the right time. He had arrived in Oman on secondment from the Pakistani Army ten years earlier. There was no harbour then and the boat in which he had arrived had dropped him off as close in to the beach as it could safely navigate. He had waded ashore to start his new life with all his worldly belongings on his head. He never let us down.

The Motor Transport Officer and the Paymaster were also Pakistanis and both highly efficient. We had two Medical Officers in my time. Medhi, an Assamese officer from the Indian Army, was an especial friend and in due course went on to command the entire military medical service in Oman. The capable Sikh, Manjit Singh, replaced him and brought his own colour and personality, as well as his own version of the *shemaagh*.

So, our job was to recruit, train and lead this polyglot army, many of whom were somewhat hesitant warriors, to fight against a formidable enemy. It required great tolerance, understanding, good humour, and above all an Atlantic-sized reservoir of patience – on the part of the Omanis as much as ourselves, for they must have found our driving, impatient ways pretty alien. For those of us who had any seeds of these qualities in us, Oman provided a warm, damp fertile soil for them to grow. Men who had no such seed had a barren time indeed.

Oman is also where I learned how to cope with O'Reilly's Law. Everybody has heard of Murphy's Law: anything that can go wrong will go wrong. Johnny Braddell-Smith taught me about O'Reilly. O'Reilly said that Murphy was an optimist. Then again, there was also O'Shaughnessy's Corollary to Murphy's Law which said that, on the rare occasions when Murphy's Law does not apply and something that could go wrong goes right, it will subsequently transpire that it would have been better if it had gone wrong in the first place.

So with the help of my British, Indian, Baluchi and Pakistani friends, and the Omanis who in their turn were very patient with me – and O'Reilly, Murphy and O'Shaughnessy – I quickly came to feel very much at home in this strange, beautiful country, and to respect and grow fond of the people who lived there.

Map 2 – Dhofar

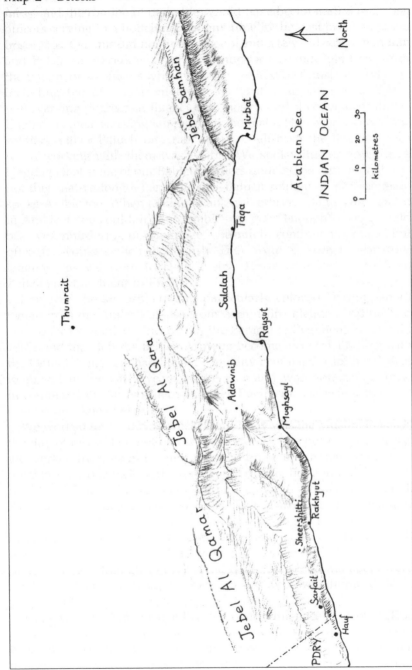

Chapter Six

The Play

It was normal for newly arrived officers in the Regiment to visit Dhofar for a month-long 'acquaint' before they went there for their nine month tour, so once I had found my feet within the Regiment after a few weeks I flew south to do a Cook's tour of the war.

As I arrived at Salalah airfield, I noticed a pair of Strikemaster light jet bombers landing in the vicinity of my aircraft as another pair took off. These small single-engined aircraft typically carried two 500 lb bombs, sixteen or twenty-four ground attack rockets and two 7.62 mm machine-guns. They were potent flexible weapons in our armoury, but they were not invulnerable. On enquiring what had generated this activity, I was told that another Strikemaster had been shot down by ground fire. These aircraft were bombing the wreckage to ensure that the *adoo* could get nothing of value from it. I was also told that they were making sure that the pilot, who had not parachuted out, was dead. This was not the only time that we resorted to this procedure, indeed on another occasion the Sultan's Air Force was asked to perform the same service by the Iranian Forces for one of their crashed helicopters. The *adoo* were ruthlessly brutal with their adversaries. We felt, therefore, that the chances of humane treatment for any of our people who fell into their hands were pretty poor, so we went to great lengths to ensure that none of our Servicemen was captured alive. I was to come across the implications of this later in my time in Oman.

I made a point of visiting places that I would not see when our tour came round so I first went to Sarfait, a fortified position high up on the escarpment close to the border with the PDRY (People's Democratic Republic of Yemen). On the map, it looked as if this place dominated the routes along which the *adoo* resupplied themselves. Surely all we needed to do was patrol actively in this area and we would have the *adoo*'s logistics by the throat? Then one noticed the differences in height.

Sarfait was at 3,000 feet. The *adoo* supply routes were mostly at sea level and certainly under 1,000 feet. Any operation from Sarfait to interdict *adoo* camel trains would require a degree of force protection and resupply for which we did not have the resources. Attempts had been made to patrol down to the sea but they had been ferociously resisted by the *adoo*. Now was not the time to develop operations from Sarfait, although that time would come. However, having taken Sarfait and put a battalion there, it would have been politically damaging to remove it. So it stayed.

Meanwhile it was a prime target for mortar attack. The *adoo* mortared it so often that the Army regiment based there, the Jebel Regiment, got quite blasé about it. Sarfait was so close to the border with the PDRY (People's Democratic Republic of Yemen) that it also received artillery fire from the town of Hauf on the other side of the border. The Jebel Regiment talked lightly about 'incomers'. The Sultan's soldiers there lived in hand-built stone bunkers called *sangars*. Sometimes these were partly underground, having been blasted into the limestone rock with explosives, but mostly they were simple stone huts. The roofs of course were a bit more substantial than the average hut roof and could withstand anything but the heaviest 'incomer'. But the danger of being caught out in the open was always very real. Forty or fifty incoming shells a day was not unusual, and yet some days there was nothing. The limestone surface was blasted to a white powder, and at the entrance to each of the *sangars* there was a little garden of tail fins and other bits of mortar shells gathered from where they had landed nearby.

The Jebel Regiment which was manning this position were resupplied entirely by helicopter. Fixed wing aircraft had been tried in the past and the evidence of failure was there in the shape of a crashed Caribou aircraft on a makeshift runway. The wing of this aircraft had been blown off and its engine set on fire by a rocket shortly after it had been unloaded. Astonishingly no one was seriously hurt. The high tailplane of the wrecked aeroplane had been a useful aiming reference point for *adoo* firing at the position from behind cover, until someone blasted it down with explosives.

Helicopters were more flexible and made more difficult targets, but it was always a tense moment as they took off and landed. They too were far from immune. Nigel Marshall, another Royal Marines friend and Mike Shipley, an Army acquaintance, were both killed together with Peter Davis, the pilot of the helicopter they were in, when it was shot down.

They and other aircraft were hit and brought down by small arms or Russian Sphaghin 12.7 mm machine gun fire. This was a powerful weapon which as well as being effective against aircraft, could and did destroy *sangars* and kill the men inside them.

We lived with the constant expectation that the *adoo* would sooner or later equip themselves with Russian hand-held Surface-to-Air-Missiles, so certain precautions were taken against them. Crossing the *jebel* was done at about 10,000 ft, and when approaching a position the helicopter would spiral down, benefiting from the protection that the friendly location offered. But there was a limit to what could sensibly be done without tying ourselves in knots. We rather took the view that it was just one of the many risks that one faced daily and simply hoped that one wouldn't be in the aircraft that the *adoo* chose to fire their first missile at. That very event did indeed happen close to the end of the war in autumn 1975 and a helicopter and a jet were shot down by hand-held missiles. But by then the war was as good as won.

Daft things could happen with helicopters. I was landing on a *jebel*-top position one day in a helicopter when a person ran out from a hole waving frantically at us to fly away. The pilot obeyed instantly. Seconds later we were shaken by a huge explosion that erupted from the position. They were blowing holes with explosives. We were undamaged. Oddly enough, some months later I myself was using explosives to blow holes in my own position. I took all the precautions I could by way of informing people and warning helicopters not to fly near us at the relevant time. Shortly after I had lit the fuse and everyone had taken cover I heard the familiar noise of a helicopter apparently approaching my position. I couldn't believe my ears. I climbed out of my protective hole and my eyes confirmed it. I had about forty-five seconds to shoo it away before it, or I, or both of us, were blown up. However, it turned and flew off in a different direction. It was one of the Shah of Iran's machines which he had sent to assist the Sultan in his battle against Communism. I don't know why it was there, or why it flew away. These things just happened.

While visiting the Jebel Regiment, I had a long talk with Mike Austen, a contract officer who had been in a long bloody, seven-hour battle a couple of months before – a firefight which had not gone well and in which his company commander, Paul Wright, had eventually been killed by a mortar shell. Many of their casualties had been caused by RPG 7s (rocket grenades) bursting in the air above them. There was no protection against airburst shells when occupying hastily constructed *sangars*. Overhead protection was only found inside the permanent bases. I listened with awe as he gently and simply recounted what had happened. Wright had been an inspirational commander and he was posthumously awarded the Omani Gallantry

Medal, the equivalent of the Victoria Cross, for this, his last battle. An Omani NCO was similarly decorated.

After my stay with Mike, I set off to walk to another part of this widely spread position to visit David Sayers, another seconded Royal Marine whom I had known in Singapore. He was commanding the most exposed position of all and rarely a day passed without it being attacked. David was in good spirits and as always he was full of amusing stories, but he looked thin and worn. He was in pain from a troubled back.

David's introduction to Oman and the war had been very different to mine. I had joined the Northern Frontier Regiment while it was training and recruiting in the North. My introduction had included time to acclimatise and a gentle easing into life with the Omanis in their fascinating country; and here I was visiting Dhofar for a month with no responsibilities other than to familiarise myself with the war and how it should be fought at my level. Not so with David. He had arrived from UK while his regiment was fighting on the *jebel*. He had spent one day in the Army headquarters in the North 'where I received an intelligence brief I didn't understand and was issued with kit I didn't know what to do with.' Thence he was flown straight to Dhofar and via Thumrait on to the regimental headquarters of the Jebel Regiment at Sarfait. He was immediately posted out to take command of the most exposed position of the Sarfait complex. Ten minutes after arriving he came under attack from sustained small arms fire, RPG 7 rocket grenades and mortars. The soldier in the forward *sangar* with him was wounded and David sustained what was to become a long term nagging back and neck injury. He had been in the country barely a week.

In spite of the injuries he sustained in this action, he continued to command his dangerous corner for some months. However, it became clear that the pain would not subside and he was eventually evacuated back to the UK, but not before he had been awarded the Omani equivalent of a Mention in Dispatches. In years to come we would both command X Company 45 Commando, he in Northern Ireland and I in the Falklands War, but this night we sat up late having a good gossip.

The following morning David offered me a chance to practise the observation and direction of artillery fire. This was an important skill for officers such as ourselves, requiring good map reading, the accurate judging of distances and slick radio work. The procedure involved getting the artillery to fire a shell at a chosen grid reference, and then giving the necessary corrections of range and bearing to ensure that subsequent shells hit the target. Much depended on seeing where the first shell landed. Only when that happened could adjustments be given. In the mountainous country of Dhofar this was not always easy as, more often than not, the first shell would disappear down a *wadi* or behind a *jebel*. Much time and ammunition was spent trying to get shells on the ground that one could actually see – without bringing them in so close as to blow oneself up. David, being a good host, shared his shells with me and I was grateful for the opportunity to practise a skill that I knew I would need for real soon enough. We fired our shells at likely enemy mortar base plate positions.

Shortly after the completion of the artillery shoot, the helicopter arrived to resupply David's position and to take me away. I boarded and it took off almost immediately. The helicopter had lifted to about 500 ft when I saw explosions around and among the *sangars* where I had spent the night and on the landing site from where we had just lifted off. David's position was being hammered again. The helicopter can't have been on the ground for much more than a minute. David said that it was my artillery shooting which induced this retaliatory barrage. Possibly, but he was mortared so often I don't know how he could tell!

That night, as I sat with David Daniels and other officers of the Jebel Regiment, we heard an explosion outside our *sangar*. One of the mines in our perimeter had exploded, set off by hyenas. What a racket they made. Only they could laugh in a minefield. The following day we went out and re-laid and reset the mines.

After a week with the Jebel Regiment on Sarfait, I visited the small coastal town of Mirbat some twenty miles north-east of Salalah. I flew there in a small transport aircraft called a Skyvan. We seemed to fly the entire journey over the sea, at sea level. Mirbat was in a delightful location with its cliffs and beaches tucked into its own little bay. Like many places in Oman, its situation was outwardly so idyllic that one couldn't help imagining it as a tourist resort in other more benign circumstances. But Mirbat was not yet ready to welcome tourists, except perhaps me. It had been the scene of a major and important battle precisely one year before.

The Sultan's policy of civil development, and the aggressive effective operations by his Army with its new equipment, had arrested the ascendancy of the Communist *adoo*. Support for the Government and confidence in the ability of the Army to provide security had gained real momentum. The *adoo*, perceiving the need to recover the initiative, decided that a major victory was required to turn the tide back in their direction. They chose the lightly defended garrison of this small seaside town to demonstrate the fragility of the Government position and their own omnipotence. The *adoo* assembled a force of about 300 men armed with anti-tank recoilless RPG 7 rocket grenade launchers, machine-guns and mortars. The idea was to approach the small town at night and silently establish a mortar firebase on Jebel Ali, a small hill not far from the town. Supported by these mortars the *adoo* would then assault the town before first light, overwhelm the garrison of about thirty soldiers, execute Government supporters, then disappear victorious into the mist and back up the *jebel*. As well as being a severe blow to the confidence of the Army, it would have gravely undermined all the good work which had been done in building up the confidence and co-operation of a suspicious, brutalized, sensitive population. There may also have been the intention to seize and hold rather than simply attack and destroy. In classic insurgency warfare there can be a transition from the guerrilla phase to a more conventional phase when the insurgents are strong enough. The holding of Mirbat, even for a limited period, thus demonstrating that the Sultan was no longer in control even of the towns on the Salalah Plains would have given the *adoo* a huge propaganda boost. It was relatively early in the *khareef* (season of mist) and the *adoo* may just have felt that this might constrain our airpower, and therefore make the capture and holding of Mirbat a serious possibility.

The first thing to go wrong was the silent capture of Jebel Ali. A small party of eight Omani soldiers had been posted by the defenders on Jebel Ali. Some were killed, but others escaped to alert the garrison. Furthermore, it had taken the *adoo* longer than planned to arrive at Mirbat and the attack, which was intended to enjoy the protection of darkness, started in daylight. Neither of these setbacks need have dislocated the attack severely. Three hundred well armed men supported by mortars and shielded by the monsoon mist against a semi-surprised garrison of about a tenth of their number – by rights there should have been only one possible outcome. However, the defence force, consisting of thirty or forty Omanis from a variety of local gendarmerie units and some Dhofari tribesmen, also included a Special Air Service Regiment (SAS) detachment of eight men. They also had a 25 pounder artillery piece in an emplacement next to the mud and stone fort they were defending. This gun and the fort defended by the gendarmerie were about 400 metres away from the house where the SAS were billeted.

As soon as the attack started, Mike Kealy, the British SAS officer commanding this detachment, called for air support and then joined his men in fighting off the *adoo* attacking his house. They had a .5 inch Browning machine-gun and a mortar as well as the usual GPMGs and rifles, so they were something of a prickly hedgehog even though there were only six of them in the house at the time. The other two members of the detachment, both from the Pacific island of Fiji, were with the 25 pounder gun 400 metres away.

Three Strikemasters took off from Salalah but were severely constrained by the low-lying monsoon mist. However, they found that at Mirbat they were able to come in from the sea at wave level below the cloud base and were presented with so many targets that they hardly knew where to begin. The Strikemasters were able to inflict much slaughter, especially on those *adoo* who were massed by the wire outside the fort. All the planes were hit by small arms fire and one was seriously damaged and had to limp back to Salalah. But, however skilful and gallant the pilots might be, airpower alone was not going to save the garrison against such overwhelming odds. The *adoo's* hand-held anti-tank weapons were bit by bit reducing to rubble the protection offered by the mud and stone buildings.

After the initial furious battle of about an hour, there was something of a lull, perhaps induced by the Strikemasters. Mike Kealy, taking advantage of this, took his medical orderly to attend to the wounded in the artillery gun pit by the fort 400 metres away from the SAS house. He also called for a helicopter to take the wounded out. Before he reached the artillery gun team, the battle started in earnest again and he and the medical orderly were very fortunate to get to the other side alive. The helicopter arrived but had to withdraw riddled with holes and without picking up any of the casualties. By now the *adoo* were so close that they were throwing grenades. One went into the gun pit but did not explode. Others landed in the fort and inflicted much carnage among the Omani soldiers inside. The 25 pounder was by now being fired over open sights, in other words at point blank range. Since this weapon was designed to provide indirect fire out to a range of seven and a half miles, this was a desperate measure, and one which had not been resorted to since the Second World War. Of the three men manning the 25 pounder gun, one Omani artilleryman and one SAS man were severely wounded. Kealy and the remaining man, who was also wounded, continued to fire the artillery piece. The medical orderly had by now also been fatally wounded. The rest of the garrison was pinned down inside the fort and the odds were high that Mike and his surviving comrades would very soon be overwhelmed.

However, Mars rolled his dice and threw a double six for the Sultan's forces that day. Normally there was only one squadron of SAS in Dhofar and they were spread in small groups around the war theatre. By extraordinary good fortune, Kealy's squadron was about to be replaced the very next day and the soldiers of the relieving squadron were in Salalah, about to fly out to their appointed posts dispersed all around the *jebel*. Indeed, they were actually on the firing range, fully kitted up and adjusting their weapons, as news of the battle arrived. As the drama at Mirbat was about to reach its only possible conclusion, they piled into helicopters and flew en masse to a point just to the southern edge of the town, from where they mounted a counter-attack.

The mortar position on Jebel Ali was destroyed by Strikemasters and Omani troops were helicoptered onto the hillock. The SAS reinforcements swept up through the town to the beleaguered SAS house and the gun pit by the fort and beyond. The *adoo* force was shattered.

The *adoo* took away with them as many dead and wounded as they could carry. The *adoo* were very rarely captured. They fought to the death rather than be captured, even though many of them 'surrendered' in their own good time when it suited them. On this occasion they left nearly forty of their number dead behind them. Perhaps as many again were wounded and a substantial proportion of them would die on the *jebel* from their wounds. Yet more still would die in the violent recriminations that took place in the aftermath of this action.

Shortly after the shooting was over a Skyvan cargo plane was sent into the Mirbat strip. The pilot, Barry West, assumed he would be shipping people out after the battle. He waited on the strip while his aircraft was loaded from the rear. Shortly before take off, he looked back from his pilot's seat into the cargo bay behind him. He was faced with a vision of carnage. His plane was full of corpses. He made two flights. There were no body bags and afterwards, before the aircraft could fly again, it needed a major refurbishment to clean the leaked body fluids out from the electrical wiring and controls under the cargo bay floor.

Nearly thirty years later, Peter Sincock, who had been chief of staff to Brigadier Jack Fletcher at this time, fell into conversation with an Arab gentleman wearing a smart suit in the Army and Navy Club in London. 'Where are you from?' he asked.

'I am an Arab.'

'Where in Arabia are you from?'

'I am from Oman.'

'Where in Oman are you from?'

'From Dhofar.' Seeing he was of a certain age, Peter asked him if he had been involved in the Dhofar War. To Peter's astonishment, he proved to have been a member of the *adoo* force that had attacked Mirbat. During the course of conversation, Peter remarked that the Army had reckoned the *adoo* casualties had amounted to perhaps sixty or eighty. His new acquaintance said that given the number of people who had died of wounds after being removed back to the *jebel* it was more like 200.

How long it would take the Sultan to rid his country entirely of its cancer was still an open question, but after this catastrophe it seemed highly unlikely that the *adoo* would ever 'liberate the occupied Arab Gulf'.

The *adoo* were very keen on anniversaries. They named their regiments after special dates – a conference, the start of the revolution, or some other such inspiring event. The Ninth of June Regiment, for instance, was eventually our opposition later that year. It was felt that the *adoo* might want to use the anniversary of the defeat at Mirbat the previous year, 19 July 1972, to turn it into a glorious victory, so I was to be in Mirbat to assist the garrison on 19 July 1973 – just in case.

Ernie Cook, another Royal Marines friend who now, serving with the Desert Regiment, commanded the garrison at Mirbat, welcomed me looking like a biblical prophet with his long hair and beard and gave me a fascinating, detailed battlefield tour. There was plenty of evidence of a furious fight still there in the form of bullet holes, shell craters and empty cases and I absorbed it all with great interest. I had already heard the old soldier's saying that there are three and only three types of military operations: Adjustable Military Fuck-Ups (AMFUs), Semi-Adjustable Military Fuck-Ups (SAMFUs), and Complete Military Fuck-Ups (CMFUs). The point is that nothing ever goes to plan and the unexpected is the only thing you can expect in battle. I now noted with interest that the principle of AMFUs, SAMFUs and CMFUs applies to the other side as well as one's own.

Nothing out of the ordinary happened at Mirbat on 19 July 1973. I sat on top of Jebel Ali all night gossiping with Ernie Cook. But it was exciting enough in its own way.

Waled Khamis, the Omani artilleryman who, together with the SAS Trooper Labalaba from Fiji, had been firing the 25-pounder over open sights, was awarded the Omani Gallantry Medal, an equivalent of the Victoria Cross. He had only stopped firing when he had used up all the available ready-use ammunition. He had then continued to fight with his rifle until he was shot through the spine. He survived. Trooper Labalaba, who died of his wounds, was recommended for a posthumous Victoria Cross. This was not awarded. He was instead awarded a Mention in Dispatches which was the only posthumous alternative at that time. Mike Kealy was decorated with the British Distinguished Service Order.

Those officers who served on four month tours with formed units like the SAS and certain artillery and engineer units were eligible for British awards and decorations, whereas individual British officers and

71

NCOs on loan to Sultan's Armed Forces, and British contract officers, usually operated outside the British system of honours and awards. As members of the Omani forces, we came under the Omani system. As a result, acts of gallantry by loan service soldiers remain rather obscure outside the circle of people who know that system. On the other hand, getting a separate Arabic campaign medal instead of just another clasp to add to one's General Service Medal was exciting and good for the ego.

Soldiers like medals. The British have in the past been very sparing with them. It was theoretically possible to fight your way through the entire First World War at the front in every theatre and end the War with only three medals: the Mons Star, the War Medal and the Victory Medal. Since 1962 active service had been marked by the award of a General Service Medal and a clasp on the medal ribbon for each theatre. Thus a man might have served in say, the Malay Peninsula, Borneo, Radfan and Northern Ireland and only have one medal. However many clasps he had on his medal, he only had one medal ribbon on his tunic. So a rookie who had done a mere twenty-eight days in Northern Ireland was indistinguishable from a man who might have served for years in half a dozen campaigns. I knew one officer who had fought his way around the world for years with the contracting British Empire and had six clasps on his medal ribbon – but only one medal. There wasn't any room for any more clasps. So we were quite pleased to have this opportunity to earn another medal. It might seem rather trivial, but that surely is why medals exist after all – to encourage soldiers to do daft things that no rational human being would otherwise contemplate!

I met Mike Kealy, the commander of the SAS detachment which had fought off the *adoo* on that day, as he passed though our mess at Bid Bid some time later. Having seen the battlefield, it was of special interest for me to hear something from him of the battle. He was a pleasant and unassuming person about the same age as me and was kind enough to talk a little about Mirbat to me. He died of exposure a few years later on an exercise on the Brecon Beacons in Wales.

My month in Dhofar passed without further incident and I returned to the North to continue preparations for our own battalion tour. Not everyone had such a gentle introduction to their time in Dhofar and I knew other officers who got involved in a full-scale battle during their tourist's 'acquaint' to Dhofar.

The immediate prize that the *adoo* were fighting for was the capital town of the Dhofar province, Salalah. The *jebel* adjacent to the town in the central area was relatively highly populated, with small villages like Mirbat along the coast and nomads in the *jebel* living by waterholes and moving their herds of goats and cattle from scrub to scrub looking for grazing. Bands of *adoo* used to live in the plains and the mountains in the hinterland, terrorizing and intimidating the population. They tortured, they burned, they threw people off cliffs and murdered them in other ways. They assassinated community leaders and abducted children from their parents for indoctrination in a school in Hauf just across the border in Yemen. They also mortared and fired rockets at the town.

In previous years, the *adoo* had been successfully contained by our predecessors for nine months of the year. However, during the period when the *khareef* (monsoon mist) covered the *jebel*, they had had free range of the place because, prior to the arrival of helicopters, the Army had not been able to sustain itself in the mist.

The *adoo* used to assemble camel and donkey trains near Hauf in the PDRY with food, ammunition and other supplies for their fighters in the mountains and the plains. They would slip under the escarpment in the shadow of Sarfait, then work their way eastwards parallel to the sea, through the mountains towards the juicy targets in the plains. By 1971 they were able to strike Salalah itself with indirect fire and in June 1972 they hit Salalah with Katyusha rockets. One of these struck the Officers' Mess at the RAF air base near the town and wounded a number of people. This incident effectively indicated that there was nowhere in Dhofar safe from *adoo* strikes. Would Salalah itself become untenable as a base? If that happened, the war would be as good as lost. But the pieces in the Government's strategy were beginning to fall into place.

The battle was now being won by the Government in the plains and the central and eastern *jebel*. A series of permanent, static, defended locations surrounding Salalah, and aggressive patrolling and ambushing, had severely constrained the *adoo*'s freedom of action. The Army's task now was to hold and protect the cleared areas and allow them to be developed. Once an area was safe for civil development, a well would be drilled, a school, a shop and a clinic built, and possibly a mosque. A track would be bulldozed for vehicular access and a means of getting the fattened cattle to market was provided. Projects like improving the bloodstock of the cattle could then be set up. A salient feature of these projects was the speed with which they were initiated. Work began immediately the area was cleared and major efforts were made to demonstrate to the population the real tangible benefits that were theirs when the *adoo* moved out and the Sultan's forces moved in. These projects were devised and overseen by the Civil Aid Department led by Martin Robb, who had recently transferred across from the Muscat Regiment. This helped to ensure that the military and civilian efforts worked hand in glove and that the emphasis flowed naturally and seamlessly from one to the other at the appropriate moment. And of course, there was the implicit threat that if the *adoo* were allowed to interfere with any of this, it would be taken away again. The *adoo*, who ultimately depended upon the support of the civilian population were made to understand that they were no longer welcome. Many either left, or came over to the Sultan.

In this way, the Sultan sought to offer the Dhofaris a prospect of prosperity and freedom within their own culture and religion, a far more attractive option than the alien, atheistic, totalitarian ideology being imposed upon them. The *adoo*'s ideological strength had been founded on the grievances that the Dhofaris had endured under Qaboos's father. Qaboos removed those grievances and this was not lost on the people of Dhofar. Thus a virtuous circle was created.

It was part of the Communist strategy to infiltrate the north of Oman too. On several occasions evidence was discovered of plans for selective assassinations. The Army barracks at Bid Bid had its perimeter mined. Another barracks at Izki was attacked with gunfire. On another occasion, a Land Rover had been stopped in a road block and found to be full of weapons, money and explosives. Had the Communists been successful in the South, there is little doubt that conflagration would have spread to the North. A coup against Sultan Qaboos or an assassination was undoubtedly on their agenda. Certainly a second front in the North was seen as a natural progression from the insurgency in the South and the authorities were always alert to this possibility. At various stages the Communists planted insurgents in key places. In early 1973 a number of serving soldiers had been uncovered as Communist agents in the Army. They had been executed by firing squad.

We conducted frequent patrols and snap road blocks as part of our routine duties in the North. On one occasion we were deployed to search for some named individuals who were seeking to foment rebellion in the villages along the Batinah coast. The rules of engagement were pretty elementary to anyone who had served in Northern Ireland and were reminiscent of the Wild West. 'The Government of His Majesty the Sultan will pay rewards to whoever brings the undermentioned to the nearest Government Post – Dead or Alive' said the posters in Arabic and English. There were the photographs of four men. For two of them there was a 10,000 rial reward; and for the other two, 5,000 rials. One of our companies, B Company commanded by Angus Ramsay, a Royal Highland Fusilier, actually found one of these 10,000 rial characters and took him alive. Angus distributed the money, which amounted to about £15,000, around his company. At about £150 per man this was a glorious windfall indeed.

A month after the Katyusha strike on Salalah, the *adoo* had attacked Mirbat. Hindsight being the only exact science, it is possible now to look back and see that the attack on Salalah was the high tide for the *adoo*. If they had succeeded at Mirbat, it might have gone higher still. But it never got so high again.

The next step for the Army in Dhofar was to isolate the *adoo* in the centre and east from their resupply and support from the PDRY in the west. This had been tried before. The military presence at Sarfait was part of an earlier attempt – a rather loose cork in the bottle – and the so-called Leopard Line in 1971 had been a series of positions north of Mughsayl to try to interdict these supply trains before they could get to the *adoo* who depended upon them. These efforts had been severely constrained by lack of resources. The Army now had the resources to construct an effective sustainable obstacle on the *jebel*.

During the Northern Frontier Regiment's previous tour in 1972, the regiment, operating out of Adawnib, had conducted extensive patrolling and ambushing operations in the area north of Mughsayl. Helicopters had been used to insert troops by surprise on to likely *adoo* transit routes. Simple but effective deception ploys were adopted. Typically, helicopters would land in a certain area, but take off again without disembarking troops. They would then land somewhere else, drop off the troops and then perhaps land again at a further site without dropping troops, and so on. In this way, the *adoo* had to assume that the Army was operating in their territory, but had no idea where they were, or in what strength. A number of furious, bloody but successful punch-ups with the *adoo* were thus generated, and the fight was taken to the *adoo* in territory that they had come to regard as their own. At least one camel train heading from west to east was attacked and destroyed.

One such search operation west of Adawnib involved A Company Northern Frontier Regiment. The company had been driven in lorries to the foot of the *jebel* on the western edge of the Salalah plain. A long approach march during a warm starlit night had taken the company up onto the *jebel* and well down the ridge that separates Wadi Adawnib to the north from Wadi Madom to the south. As dawn had broken, the company had fanned out and progressed west in a classic 'advance to contact' arrowhead formation. Junior leaders were well to the front. Major Simon Hill of the Parachute Regiment commanded the company. Two Royal Marines, Captains Bob Hudson and David Nicholls were part of the team.

As the sun rose the soldiers were feeling the effects of the long night approach march over the sharp stones of the *jebel*. They were hungry, tired and footsore. As the light strengthened, and the company reached the line between Killi and Ashawq, a burst of fire rang out and Corporal Mahmood in the lead section dropped dead. Soldiers flung themselves to the ground and looked desperately for firing positions that offered cover from view and protection from incoming bullets. The ground was as flat as a billiard table; there was little cover to be found. The prospects of a serious firefight looked decidedly one-sided if the *adoo* could use the cover offered by the sharp *wadi* edge from where the initial burst had originated. This edge was about 300 metres away to the west. Whoever held that edge held the initiative, as they had not only cover from view but, importantly, cover from fire.

A short pause followed the initial firing. David Nicholls was with the lead platoon in which Corporal Mahmood had been killed. He took stock and realized the tactical significance of control of the *wadi* edge. He jumped up and started to zig zag towards the *wadi* edge yelling in Arabic to the platoon commander and the remaining section commanders to move forward with him as quickly as possible to seize the *wadi* edge before reinforcements of *adoo* arrived. Had the *adoo* taken the *wadi* edge in large numbers the company would have been severely at risk in the open ground.

As David reached the edge of the *wadi* carrying his AK47 a young *adoo* climbed up towards the *wadi* edge some fifty metres to his north. David shot him with a burst of automatic fire and he fell backwards toppling off a large rock platform to disappear down into the *wadi*. David looked around expecting to find the rest of the lead platoon with him. There was nobody there. Firing had by now broken out some 500 metres to the north as more *adoo* came up out of the *wadi* and engaged the other lead platoon. A shout from just below David Nicholls revealed a bearded *adoo* some twenty feet below a rock overhang. His surprise at coming face to face with a similarly bearded British officer was evident. Wide bursts of fire at each other followed. David lobbed a grenade down into the *wadi* for good measure.

It was clear some *adoo* were just below the lip of the *wadi*. David, isolated and some 300 metres ahead of the company, made some urgent radio calls to encourage the platoon, which was focused on recovering Corporal Mahmood's corpse, to move up in support as quickly as possible. Simon Hill, the company commander, ordered Bob Hudson who was with the Company's 81 mm mortar sections to lob mortar shells down into the *wadi*. Simon also called for artillery on the Salalah plain to fire at maximum range to provide airburst in support to the north. A furious firefight was brewing up between A Company and the *adoo*. The company slowly but surely worked its way towards the wadi edge. At last, to his enormous relief, the platoon joined David Nicholls in his firing position. The battle continued for two hours with neither side gaining the upper hand.

At last the weight and volume of A Company's fire prevailed and the *adoo* withdrew. A search followed down into the steep-sided *wadi*. About twenty knapsacks and other kit were found at the bottom of the *wadi* in a large cave. Bob Hudson with the mortar section found a cave full of Russian AK47 ammunition and Chinese made 82 mm mortar bombs. It was evident that a camel train had brought these stores thus far and the *adoo* had been caught trying to carry supplies for their fighters engaged on operations further to the east. The body of the young *adoo* that David Nicholls had shot was found laid in a small cave just below the lip of the *wadi*. He was around eighteen years old. A Company left him with leaflets at his side encouraging other *adoo* to surrender. Corporal Mahmood's body was recovered and some six wounded soldiers were also evacuated by helicopter. The company moved to the south over Whale above Wadi Ashawq to spend the night before descending down to Mughsayl for a swim and recovery to Salalah.

Similar night operations of silent deployments out to the west of Mughsayl were rewarded by successful ambushes on small parties of three or four camels carrying small arms and mortar ammunition to the east.

These and other operations doubtless unsettled the *adoo* and had a perceptible effect on their ability to operate in the centre and east. They were now forced to break down the camel trains into more easily concealed man-sized loads for parties of load-carrying men, well before they reached this part of the *jebel*, if they wished to slip past the patrols of the Northern Frontier Regiment. But serious interdiction of their logistics movements from Hauf in the PDRY towards the Salalah plain could only be achieved by a more permanent presence.

From the knowledge and experience gained in these operations, Bryan Ray, the Commanding Officer, and his company commanders, notably Simon Hill and Tresham Gregg, identified a number of positions that would need to be held if the Army wanted to dominate completely this part of the *jebel*. Brigadier Jack Fletcher saw the potential benefit that such a line of positions would offer. The lie of the land was such that, while the *adoo* might try and bypass these positions by taking their camel trains further north, the effort for them to do so became exponentially greater the further north they went. Four or five positions on the *jebel* north of Mughsayl dominating the Wadi Jizalawt, the Wadi Ashawq and the Wadi Adawnib, stoutly manned and vigorously patrolled, could virtually close down the *adoo*'s logistics.

Men might still get through from time to time, but the days of substantial camel trains supplying the *adoo* attacking Salalah and the plain could be gone forever. The *adoo* might be able to buy, extort or steal food in the central area. However, every mortar round, every bullet, every weapon would need to be carried by a man running the gauntlet of this barrier. Moreover, the positions themselves might distract the focus of the *adoo*. The *adoo* might be tempted to attack them. So be it. Every ounce of energy spent attacking these positions was effort diverted from attacking that which we were trying to protect. Every mortar round, every Katyusha rocket fired at them, was a round not fired at Salalah. It might not always be pleasant for the men manning these positions, but if the positions were properly con-structed and supplied, and the men well led, they should be fine. So the concept of the Hornbeam Line was born.

The Northern Frontier Regiment completed its 1972 tour in Dhofar and returned to Northern Oman in January 1973 to rest, recruit and retrain in preparation for its next tour starting in November 1973. In this tour they would build on the work done in 1972, creating the obstacle and patrolling vigorously the new Hornbeam Line. The positions identified by Bryan Ray and his centurions were established and manned initially in 1973 by the Frontier Force, a Baluch regiment. Ray and the Northern Frontier Regiment returned to Dhofar and took over these positions in November 1973, and quickly set about con-structing the physical obstacle which would be a key feature in the plan to cut the *adoo*'s lines of communication between the PDRY and their target.

The Hornbeam Line consisted of a chain of eight platoon and company positions starting at the sea at Mughsayl and stretching up into the mountains towards the desert about thirty miles away. It was at right angles to the enemy line of communications and was intended to cauterize the relatively fertile, more populous, eastern area from the barren western *jebel*. It was used as a base for patrols and ambushes. From each position one could usually see the position on either side, but in the north they were as much as twenty kilometres apart. Very few people lived in this part of the *jebel* and those who did had either been recruited by the *adoo* or moved to the east. We did not therefore have to worry unduly about killing innocent civilians. The innocent had all gone. The only people we were likely to meet were *adoo* and this made our job more straightforward.

By day we could see most movement, but at night our line was pretty permeable. During my time there, we built a barbed wire and

78

Map 3 – The Hornbeam Line

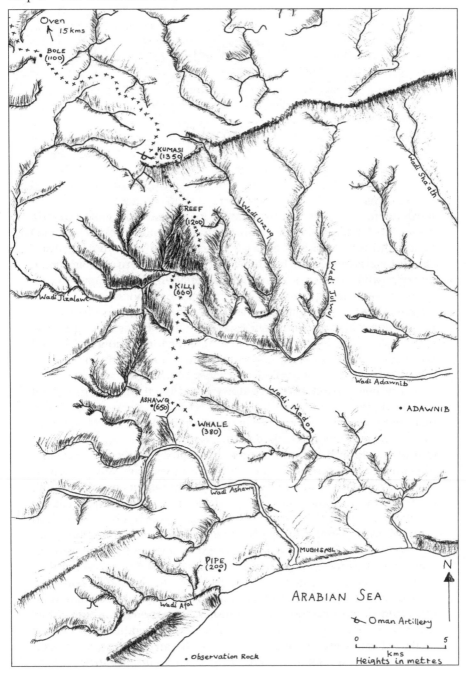

Oven
↑ 15 kms

BOLE
(1100)

KUMASI
(1350)

REEF
(1200)

Wadi Uruq

Wadi Sha'ath

Wadi Julvul

KILLI
(660)

Wadi Jizalaw

Wadi Adawnib

ASHAWQ
(650)

WHALE
(380)

Wadi Madom

• ADAWNIB

Wadi Ashawq

MUGHSAYL

PIPE
(200)

Wadi Afal

N

ARABIAN SEA

Oman Artillery

0   kms   5

Heights in metres

• Observation Rock

minefield obstacle the whole length of it. I was closely involved in the construction of this, and in the protection of the constructors. It was a major feat of military engineering, all done by hand by our own soldiers supervised by Royal Engineers. The Royal Engineer squadron in Oman at that time was commanded by John Blashford Snell, the expedition leader, with whom I worked later in Kenya. The subaltern who worked in my area was John Hoskinson. I enjoyed his company greatly and we were to serve together again several times in our later careers.

This wire and mine obstacle was a major investment in treasure and labour but it was worth it. It helped to focus things and it was a significant complication for the enemy who knew they had to overcome it if they wanted to continue fighting in the central and eastern areas. We did not allow ourselves to sit around waiting for things to happen. The line was not impervious and the *adoo* dreamt up some ingenious ways of getting over and under it with wooden beams and ropes. Its strength depended upon vigorous patrolling and ambushing and that was our job. In time, it played a major part, perhaps even a decisive part, in the defeat of the enemy.

Thirty years later, the mines are now being lifted. But it is a slow business. John Hoskinson and I had made meticulous records of every mine we laid and marked the minefields. We felt that we could have returned and lifted each one of them, including the dummy ones, and the anti-lift devices. These records are no longer to be found. The Iranian Forces did not make records, and of course, neither did the *adoo*. But even with the records, one would have been at risk. There was a fair chance that the *adoo* had lifted a few and replanted them where we might be expected to step if we were looking for our mines. There was also the problem of animals moving the mines. The small anti-personnel mine called a Dingbat had a piece of green hessian cloth glued to it. On several occasions, we found these had been disturbed and moved by foxes which seemed to like the glue that stuck the cloth on. Some were jumping mines with trip wires and I was always rather wary of them. So it will be a long time before the area is completely and safely cleared of mines. I was told recently by an Omani officer that the Jebalis have removed the wire to make stock enclosures for their animals. It was good to hear that someone is still finding it useful.

So, we had no civilians. We also saw very little of the Media. The modern soldier probably cannot imagine what it is like to have no camera or microphone poking over his shoulder, but that is how it was. Our war came at a time when, to the British public, our Forces seemed to have been involved in a number of colonial conflicts – Malaya, Borneo, Brunei, Kuwait and Aden. Northern Ireland was also grabbing people's attention. So, if anybody had heard of our doings, they probably thought it was just another post-colonial scrap. Besides, the Americans in Vietnam absorbed much of the world press attention. Our story was a piddling little affair compared to theirs. News teams did appear very occasionally but they depended entirely on us for their survival and although I don't believe we had anything to hide, they only saw what we were able to show them, which wasn't much. Besides, Oman did not encourage reporters and it was a difficult place to get to. So any press person who got as far as the *jebel* was usually a specialist in the area and fairly well informed already.

Helicopters were an important part of our lives. Resupply in quantities sufficient to keep large numbers of men operational on the *jebel* was only possible because of helicopters and the flexibility they offered. Fixed wing strips dotted the *jebel* but they had to be prepared and cleared, and they could be registered by *adoo* mortars as I had seen all too clearly from my visit to Sarfait. It would not do to use a strip too frequently and the work involved in clearing the stones was usually disproportionate to the value of the strip.

The workhorse helicopter was the Augusta Bell 205, an Italian built version of the ubiquitous US Huey seen in every American film since the 1960s. They were really solid, reliable aircraft and very powerful for their size. They carried a deceptively large payload. I don't know what the official figure was – probably about twelve passengers. All I know is that, again and again, we seemed to fill them up until they were bursting and the pilots never seemed to demur. We stuffed them full of everyone and everything: soldiers, food, ammunition, stores, Dhofari tribesmen, goats, anything – like students into a telephone box. They took underslung loads too: water, artillery pieces, donkey fodder and *burmails* full of water. A *burmail* was a forty-five gallon oil drum, or anything that looked vaguely similar to one, '*burmail*' being a corruption of Burmah Oil. They even took donkeys, after being suitably sedated, as underslung loads. They bulked out before the weight was too much for them. They flew everywhere in the most unpromising conditions by day and, where life was at stake, also at night without any of the modern night flying aids.

They never failed to respond to requests from us to evacuate wounded men from the battlefield or resupply us with ammunition during a battle. On many of these occasions helicopters were damaged by enemy fire. The pilots too were wounded from time to time and the risk of being shot down and killed, which also happened on several occasions, was ever-present. Never was an army more faithfully supported by its air force. The pilots of these machines were real heroes. Many were serving or ex-RAF but the Royal Navy and the Army Air

Corps were well represented. Some, like Dave Duncan, Steve Watson and Bill Bailey, had been Royal Marines.

To assist in the surge of logistics tasks associated with building the Hornbeam Line, a deal was done with the RAF whereby a flight of four Wessex helicopters was detached to the Sultan's Air Force complete with five pilots and about thirty support crew. Flying coils of barbed wire, metal fence posts and boxes of land mines around the place doesn't sound much of a demanding task. But when one considers the ruggedness of the terrain, and the extra labour involved if the kit were not dropped in precisely the right place, the job demanded the highest degree of flying skills. Again and again I saw this team put a machine down, with perhaps one wheel touching down and the rotors a few feet away from a cliff, to ensure that we did not have to hump tons of stores up or down the mountain. I have never seen flying like it before or since.

The detachment was commanded by a Polish pilot called Alek Tarwid. Nothing was too much trouble or too risky for him or his team where we were concerned. A solution would be found. Alek, who was somewhat older than most pilots, had flown Spitfires during the Second World War. Once, he got me up beside him in the cab of his Wessex and gave me a demonstration of what it was like to fly a Spitfire. The Messerschmitts wouldn't have stood a chance! 'A Spitfire is like a woman' he used to say in his marked Polish accent. He never amplified. I think it was meant to be a compliment to Spitfires. We were always left to speculate what kind of women Alek liked, assuming he favoured women who were like Spitfires.

Our predecessors had fought without helicopters and I bow to them. The advent of these machines transformed sustainability on the *jebel*. We simply could not have done without them.

I spent much of my ten months in Dhofar commanding and operating from a number of different A Company positions high up on the Hornbeam Line. My first position was called Reef. I commanded two small platoons – about forty Omanis and a few Baluchis – at Reef. For a while, an SAS team with a group of Dhofari tribesmen shared the position with us. At a height of about four thousand feet, near the edge of the escarpment which was the beginning of the *jebel* proper, the views down over the escarpment across to the plain and out to sea were spectacular. The next position to my south west, Killi, was the first of B Company's locations. It was only five kilometres away as the crow flies, but to get to it, one had to climb down three and a half thousand feet to the bottom of the Wadi Adawnib or Jizalawt and then three thousand feet up again on the other side. This meant half a day's strenuous effort to get there, and another half day's even more strenuous effort to get back again, so we didn't do it very often. But we could shout across the chasm and be heard if there was no wind and the conditions were right.

I made the effort to cross this chasm on Christmas Day 1973. Angus Ramsay commanded the neighbouring company, B Company. He had two British officers to support him: Charlie Daniel (another Royal Marines batchmate) and Nick Knollys of the Scots Guards. Nick stayed on his own position on Ashawq, but I joined Charlie and Angus for Christmas in the company headquarters at Killi. We were joined by another batchmate, Viv Rowe. So three Royal Marines batchmates spent their Christmas on the *jebel* together in 1973. We didn't feel very Christmassy because the war had to continue. But it was quiet enough on the day itself, apart from our own mortars. The *adoo* got their revenge on Boxing Day and mortared us back.

Life on top of our mountains was spartan. We lived in dry stone bunkers called *sangars* to protect us from mortar and shellfire. If the position was especially exposed we used explosives to blast down a few feet into the limestone, thereby reducing the profile of the structures and improving protection. The *sangars* were lit by a kerosene fuelled hurricane lamp and could be made to be quite cosy, which in winter, when the *Shimaal* – The North Wind – was blowing, was an important factor at four thousand feet. Occasionally our water froze. I was the only European: no one else spoke English so my soldier's Arabic became pretty fluent.

Our soldiers were hardy and uncomplaining. The food they ate was sufficient but monotonous. They needed no entertainment, being content to gossip, smoke, and drink tea and coffee when time allowed. Very few of them could read before they joined the Army and, although the Army provided reading and writing courses, most were still illiterate. The tea, – *chai* – particularly Baluchi *chai*, was liberally dosed with condensed milk and cardamom seeds. It didn't taste much like tea as we understand it, but it was rather good.

By the time I arrived, the weapons had been upgraded, but there were still soldiers who had not been issued with new desert boots. Pakistani gym shoes had long been all that was available. These lasted for about the first five kilometres of a patrol before they started to fall apart. Admittedly many soldiers spent their lives barefoot at home and so this didn't bother them too much. But the *jebel* was rough even for Omani feet. Webbing and equipment were British Second World War vintage and were adequate. Omanis were adept at adjusting and adapting what they had to make the best for their purposes. A blanket and a piece of string for a rucksack was luxury for many.

Manpower was also run on a shoestring. Sending people on leave and on courses had to be continued even throughout operational periods, so we were never up to nominal strength. Platoons therefore tended to have about twenty men and were often a good deal smaller than that.

I found myself with an orderly. His living quarters were in my *sangar* with me, but he took his turn on sentry with everyone else. Eventually, I decided I had no use for an orderly, except perhaps to cook for me, but Hamdan Suleman couldn't cook and wasn't interested in learning. So, given this and the shortage of manpower, he rejoined his platoon as a normal soldier. But he was a bright cheerful soul from slave stock and wanted to learn English. So I taught him some elementary English. I also taught him to salute and say 'Hello Matey' when he saw British officers. In this way he was always guaranteed a smile or a laugh from my fellow countrymen. This taking advantage of the ignorance of each other's language was not a one way thing. In another regiment there was a British officer called Nick and who was known to his soldiers by his first name. The Arabic word for 'fornication' is *neek*. The amusement that the Arab soldiers got from wishing him 'good day' frequently and throughout the day is not difficult to imagine.

After Hamdan moved out, I lived on my own, but while we were not on patrol, I spent a fair amount of each day in the *sangars* of my soldiers, moving from *bayt* to *bayt* – house to house – listening to the crack, drinking tea and coffee, eating, and smoking cigarettes, just as all soldiers always do anywhere in the world.

I usually stayed on top of my own particular mountain for about three weeks at a time, operating out of our *sangar* dugouts by day and night. We changed positions during the course of our tour in Dhofar and in time, I lived at Reef, Kumasi and Bole. Johnny Braddell-Smith was the Company Commander, but through sickness and leave, I ended up commanding the Company for nearly three months of our ten month tour. Tony Heslop shared Bole with me briefly but for much of the time he was at Oven some twenty kilometres to the north where the *jebel* began to flatten out. A patrol along the Hornbeam Line to Oven was something of an expedition and Tony remained remarkably sane in spite of his long periods of isolation.

My first location, Reef, was perched high up on the side of the Wadis Jizalawt and Adawnib. The dry bed of the *wadi*, rocky, narrow and cavernous, was about 3,500 feet below to the west. This *wadi* between Killi and Reef was a feature of major tactical significance and had to be patrolled properly if the *adoo* were not to use it as a thoroughfare. A Company occasionally joined in these patrols but the lion's share was done by B Company. They did not have quite so far to climb. Operating in the Adawnib was hard work and, when we came to build the physical obstacle of the Hornbeam line, it was harder work still. It also presented a great challenge for helicopters flying down into this relatively confined space and I was glad never to have had to carry a casualty out of there.

Occasionally I would patrol as far as Johnny's position about five kilometres to the north. More often, I went out to the east and, from Bole, to the west. About every three weeks, I might take a helicopter down to the regimental base by the sea at Mughsayl for a night. There I would swim in the sea, perhaps scramble among the rocks for crayfish, and catch up on the news with my British and Omani friends.

Mughsayl was another of those places like Mirbat that one could imagine as a tourist resort. There was a beautiful, long, pristine beach there, and the scenery with the *jebel* as a backdrop was magnificent. Indeed, it occurred to more than one of us that, with our Arabic language skills and our local knowledge, it might be an idea to start a tourist business in Oman. One might even get in at the ground floor and build a hotel at Mughsayl. We discussed which spot the first hotel would be built on. Meanwhile, putting our dreams to one side, we enjoyed the rare pleasure of bathing and watching long-legged wading birds walk the sands at sunset. One had to be careful of sharks though, and from time to time we would go on shark-grenading expeditions to see if we could catch one. Two men each with two grenades would stand ankle deep in the water and do a co-ordinated hurl at the shark seen at knee depth. The hope was that we would get a grenade at each of four corners round the shark. We never managed it, but the mess boys were more successful and we ate the results of their hunts occasionally.

Every six weeks, one would hitch a lift from a helicopter into Salalah and take a room either in the Army barracks at Umm al Gwarif or in the RAF mess next to the airfield there.

The Sultan of Oman's Air Force – SOAF, which was really the RAF in disguise, was peopled by outstanding warriors whose company I sought and to whom I owe my life. They flew their aircraft – helicopters and jets – with the greatest gallantry and skill in the most formidable conditions in the face of the enemy, always mindful that we on the ground depended on them. We knew their individual voices on the radio and trusted them implicitly and, when the opportunity to thank them arose on these six weekly visits to civilization, we did so with heartfelt sincerity, a wild gaiety, and a purposeful alcoholic vigour. It usually took a couple of days to get rid of the hangover. They were supported by ex-RN and RAF ground crew on contract who also were dedicated to ensuring that aircraft spent as little time on the ground as possible.

Some of the pilots went on to high rank. Tony Nicholson, who flew helicopters, became Equerry to HRH Prince Philip and ended up an air vice marshal. Jock Stirrup, a Strikemaster pilot, reached the very top and became the Chief of the Defence Staff – the head of the British Armed Forces – and an air chief marshal. Others served a few more years and started new lives outside the Service. Like us, almost all of them found their experience in Oman a seminal one which in many ways shaped the rest of their lives.

One morning after one of these bacchanalian sprees, Bob Mason, a Strikemaster pilot and a good friend, took me up on a sortie in his plane. I still remember his pre-flight briefing. 'If I say, "eject" he said, 'then eject. If you hear me saying it a second time, it won't be me, it will be the echo'.

We took off and very quickly I found we were flying over the Hornbeam Line. It was uplifting, and yet at the same time somewhat depressing, to fly so quickly and so effortlessly over the small piece of real estate where I had shed so much of my sweat by day and night over the previous months.

We went west deep into *adoo* country looking for camel trains and soon found one. I was in the left-hand seat and operated the machine gun. Bob fired the rockets and dropped the bombs. Once I had started firing, I found it difficult to stop. Bob had to tell me to take my hand off the trigger. When we pulled up the 'G' force took me by surprise and I started to black out. On levelling out, I regained consciousness and promptly brought up the curried sausages I had eaten in the bar at 4.00 am. I felt a lot better after that.

Bob was wisely disinclined to hang around and examine our handiwork. We had either done them damage or we hadn't, and if the latter, we weren't going to risk a second pass. Many a pilot has come a cropper by having first woken up his enemy, and then given him a second chance to hit back. So we then went on a speculative strafing run at Raykhut and the Sheershitti Caves, a notorious *adoo* stronghold. We plainly made ourselves unwelcome there because they shot back at us and I could see orange tennis balls passing behind the cockpit. We were unhit and returned home.

For one whose natural habitat was firmly on the ground this was a most interesting exercise. I was fascinated at how little one could really see from the air unless one knew precisely where to look and what to look for, especially if one was travelling at speed. I now understood why the pilots always preferred to have a soldier on the ground to talk them into their target. On the other hand, as we flew out over the sea, we could see creatures like manta rays and turtles just below the surface of the clear blue Indian Ocean.

This was a thrilling, exhilarating trip, but not one I wished to repeat. Better down here wishing I was up there, than up there wishing I was down here. People who fly in war earn their extra pay.

I always found it a moving experience flying over the *jebel* and none more so than when I hitched a lift in the front seat of an AB 206, a small communications and liaison machine. The pilot, Dave Duncan, flew at low level over the most spectacular country. One moment the *jebel* was scudding past about 200 feet underneath us, then, as we flew over a cliff, the ground would disappear a thousand feet below. As we headed towards another towering cliff, it seemed that we would be sure to collide with it, but no. A little flick of Dave's wrist and we were over the lip and the ground was scudding past underneath us again. No film, no IMAX cinema, could replicate the sensation of flying like this.

Neither were our Air Force comrades averse to seeing what life was like on the other side of the street. Several pilots, both fixed wing and rotary wing, went to the trouble, discomfort and risk to join us on the *jebel* for short periods. Usually they stayed for a night or two. And often they came out with us on patrol or on an ambush, thus giving them a deeper understanding of what they were doing when they were flying in support of us, and of course, cementing our relationships even further.

As well as amusing ourselves with the Sultan's Air Force, we would sometimes play with the Navy. Although hardly the Royal Navy in disguise, the Sultan of Oman's Navy was run by serving and ex-Royal Naval people in much the same way as was the Army. My closest contact with them was through an ex-RN man called Gordon Gillies. He commanded a wooden motorised Arab dhow, which, for its size, must have been one of the most heavily armed ships in the world. It had four .30 inch machine-guns, a recoilless 106 mm Iranian anti-tank weapon in the bow with a range of nearly four miles, and two .5 inch Browning machine-guns.

The coastal strip at the bottom of the Qamar Mountains offered the best and easiest route for the *adoo*'s resupply, and Gordon in his formidable battleship used to patrol it and try to deny its use to them. By day, if he could not get in sufficiently close to strike himself, he was able to direct Strikemasters in to hit targets that he could observe. On dark nights, he was able to get in close without being seen. Any *adoo* within sight of the coast had to take into account the possibility of Gordon spotting them through his first generation night viewing device and blasting off at them with his formidable battery. Campfires were obvious targets. In late 1972, these operations had destroyed or seriously damaged three *adoo* camel trains. On one occasion a number of high-ranking adoo leaders were killed by the combined fire from the dhow and Strikemaster aircraft.

Brigadier Jack Fletcher was in no doubt that Gordon and his pocket battleship, crewed with sixteen men and able to strike the *adoo* by day and by night in places where land forces could not go, was among the most cost-effective forces under his command.

At this stage of the war, there were only two dhows – one in the North, and Gordon's operating in Dhofar waters. Latterly, when the Navy acquired more craft, they would work in pairs. One would fire off some rounds into the *jebel* at a putative target from a range of, say, two or three thousand metres. Meanwhile a second craft would work its way well inshore in the hope that the first vessel's antics might tempt the *adoo* to return fire and thereby give away their positions. The inshore boat would be in a good position to identify more accurately the firing point, give it a good short-range walloping, and then skedaddle out of range.

There were also unscrupulous captains who took advantage of pilgrims seeking a passage by sea to Mecca from the Indian sub-continent. Having taken a rapacious fare off them they would some-times dump them on the Omani coast assuring them that Mecca was just over the next sand dune. The lucky ones were stopped at sea by the Sultan's Navy, or seen by them on the beach and rescued before they succumbed to thirst and starvation.

Mike Kingscote and I joined Gordon on his battleship for one of these interdiction shore bombardment operations. Having come straight from the *jebel*, we had a rather light-hearted approach to this less physically strenuous but no less serious form of warfare. I had a wonderful time sitting in an armchair drinking whisky, looking through the binoculars and the night sight and blasting off on the main armament. Ah – that's surely the way to go to war! We plainly were not far from the target because we attracted some return fire, but the *adoo* must have had some difficulty estimating our range at sea at night because the fire fell short.

But there were more serious moments on other occasions when the *adoo* got an approximation of Gordon's range with their mortars or 76 mm rockets. Zig-zagging in a slow moving dhow to outwit the mortarmen or rocketeers was an interesting game which fortunately Gordon always managed to win.

The dhow would conduct patrols of four or five days' duration with only one or two days off in between patrols. Much of the patrol was spent in action or at least under threat of fire from the shore. Gordon was the only officer in the dhow and he seemed to be on watch all the time. His bravery and endurance were recognized with the award of the Omani Distinguished Service Medal for Gallantry.

A small number of the British officers had similar tri-Service experiences, which must make us some of the few people of our generation, not to mention any other generation, who have been to war and been shot at on land, at sea, and in the air.

It was easy to sympathise with officers who joined us, or visited us, while we were in the mountains. We usually hadn't washed for a week or two, we were bearded, and we all looked a bit gaunt. We had also probably picked up a few jungly habits like sleeping on piles of rocks and squatting on the ground in preference to sitting on a chair.

One day Christopher Barnes arrived on the *jebel*. A Royal Signals officer, he had spent most of his service hitherto in Germany with the British Army of the Rhine. He had rather sportingly volunteered to serve in Oman in the infantry role and joined the Northern Frontier Regiment. He had flown from UK a short time before and had been sent to assist me as I was hard pressed and on my own. Not only was I commanding the company because Johnny was on leave, but I was unwell and couldn't keep my food down; and all this at a time when the *adoo* were being particularly active trying to get through our line. I had been out on an ambush most of the night and every night for the previous six days.

He landed on my position at first light. The helicopter took off and left him standing there, surrounded by silence: no sign of any welcome. He found a sentry and made his wishes known in pristine, virginal Beaconsfield Arabic. *'Wayn al qaa'id assareeya'* 'Where is the company commander?' A directional shrug towards my *sangar*. Barnes walked towards the low dry stone edifice more reminiscent of Neolithic Skara Brae than a pukka BAOR infantry company headquarters, and approached the small waist-high hole that passed for a door. He knelt down, moved the sack curtain to one side, poked his head in, peered into the darkness and announced himself. No response. He announced himself again. Something moved in there. A living creature stirred and a filthy, gaunt, bearded apparition swathed in blankets, emerged from the dark nether regions and was sick over his feet. Such was his introduction to *jebel* life.

Chris soon became an experienced and respected *jebel* soldier. However, part of his preparations for Oman had been to buy a very expensive and smart pair of desert boots in London. Was he not going to the desert after all? Well, not quite. The rocks in the Dhofar jebel were no respecter of boots, and his soles soon had great chunks torn out of them. He quickly resorted to the cheap flexible versions that the rest of us wore – bought in Barretts and made in Poland. When back in London on leave some months later, he returned to the shop that had sold him his desert boots and made plain that he was less than satisfied. 'Ah, Sir, our desert boots aren't actually intended for the desert; they are really at their best when padding around St James's.'

I had a similar experience with my boots. I had brought to Oman what I thought were the very best of British military boots with a 'Commando' sole. I even wore them on the flight out to save on weight and space in my luggage. The *jebel* very quickly tore great chunks out of the rubber and they were soon regretfully discarded.

For food on the *jebel*, we ate what the soldiers ate, supplemented with what we could lay our hands on in the way of fresh and tinned food. The staple was tinned pilchards in tomato sauce, rice, onions, pistachio nuts and *khubbs* – unleavened bread. These flat round pancakes are better known in India and the UK as chapattis. Comprising simply flour and water, they were cooked in situ over an open fire on the cut-out lid of an old oil drum. We wondered whether Messrs Crosse and Blackwell had pulled a fast one with the contract for their tinned pilchards in tomato sauce. It was ubiquitous. At one stage there was so much of it on my position that there was nowhere to store it; so we built a *sangar* out of the tins and stored the rest of the food inside it. There were risks attached to this. While the protection afforded by Messrs Crosse and Blackwell's product was probably as good as that provided by its equivalent bulk in sandbags, the stink that the *sangar* gave off if hit by a mortar rendered it uninhabitable after a day or so. On other positions, *sangars* would be built out of pilchards in tomato sauce to decoy *adoo* away from the genuine article. Just as well that the stink was invisible; otherwise the *adoo* would have been able to identify the dummy *sangars* from the reek emanating from them!

The soldiers quite liked pilchards in tomato sauce, but not *that* much. We found this diet monotonous so we got quite good at making it interesting with spices and other additives, and it was in Oman that I developed my interest in cooking, building on what I had learned from my mother, who was a quite excellent cook. The diet could be brightened up with fresh meat occasionally and we also supplemented it with tinned or fresh food bought in Salalah.

I once got, at a special discount, a consignment of tinned food that had been in some kind of flood. The tins and their contents were in perfectly good order, but the labels had all been washed off. So for several weeks, my meal times were enlivened by a culinary guessing game: shake the tin; listen to the flop; what would it be today? – Anything from fruit salad to mock turtle soup! After a while I got quite expert at divining the contents of my anonymous tins.

I also kept a couple of small goats called Flip and Flop. I wrote their names on their sides in indelible ink, Arabic on one side, English on the other, and they became well known personalities with the soldiers. Rather like cats, they had free run of the place, and you would find them absolutely everywhere. I didn't mind too much finding two goats asleep by my face when I woke up, but they had a habit of eating everything and anything. One day they started eating the wad of cash I kept next to the sleeping space in my *sangar* for paying the company. I had to make up the loss, although fortunately they had started at the end with the lower denominations. I decided that they were safer and cheaper dead. So we killed them and ate them before their time. This was a pity in a way, as their propensity to try and bugger each other provided the soldiers with hours of harmless amusement. But they were delicious.

In a further effort to vary our diet I acquired a pair of hens. Surely the eggs they would supply would help to enliven our diet? Dhofari hens are about the size of Bantams and their eggs are correspondingly diminutive, but nothing ventured nothing gained. Any attempt that I made at penning them was somehow frustrated by the soldiers, and they conspired to make almost as much mess in the wrong places as the goats. They didn't lay any eggs. Or at least if they did, the eggs didn't stay around long enough for me to collect them.

After a while, Said Hamed jokingly asked me if I knew what my new nickname was. No I didn't. *'Ra'ees Degaaga'* he said.

'Eh? Captain Hen? OK – so I keep hens.'

'No', he explained; the soldiers were speculating on whether I was doing to the hens what the goats were trying to do to each other.

'Good grief – what an idea – is that what happens in this country?'

'Very occasionally, but only *in extremis.*' Well, you learn something new every day. I suppose a man's got to take his pleasure where he can find it. We ate the hens.

I never went hungry in Dhofar and the food was wholesome enough if you took care to eat a balanced diet. Some people did catch malaria but prophylactic pills usually kept it at bay. Patrolling up and down mountains made us extremely fit. I saw myself in a mirror one day in the RAF mess in Salalah. I could count every rib on my chest and my legs looked like a ballet dancer's. One certainly did lose weight, perhaps through being pretty constantly on one's guard. Water needed purification and diarrhoea was always a risk but, it seemed to me that, apart from the risk of violent and terminal interruption by the *adoo*, the life we led was healthy enough.

So I was somewhat surprised when I went to the excellent British Field Surgical Team in Salalah one day with the intention of donating

91

blood. As an O Negative universal donor, I thought they'd be pleased to see me. Besides, you never knew when you might need it back yourself; it seemed to be a sensible investment to put some aside beforehand. The British doctor took one look at me and said,' 'Where are you based?' I told him I was on the *jebel*. He said, 'You just go away, my boy, and keep your blood. You look as if you need it all. We've got enough here to keep you alive for twenty-four hours and, if you need any more, we'll fly it in from UK for you'. I began to wonder if I shouldn't just ask for a wee transfusion there and then.

Cigarettes were an important part of life. Arthur Brocklehurst, our Regimental second-in-command, smoked nothing but Gauloises and he made sure they were always available in the supply chain, so somehow many of us ended up smoking Gauloises too. There were some non-smokers, but many if not most men found cigarettes essential. The Omanis and Baluchis seemed to find no objection in Islam to smoking, although I believe that strictly speaking it is forbidden. Indeed, there was evidence that tolerance of smoking did not spread much beyond the Army. A soldier from C Company went home on leave and tried to impress his civilian friends by nonchalantly lighting up in public. He was promptly locked up by the local *wali*.

The soldiers sometimes chewed a leaf called *qat* which has a narcotic effect. I heard that some of them smoked hash too but I don't recall seeing it. For me, cigarettes were a prop to my nerves and an aid to concentration; in even the most uncomfortable or dangerous situations, it was a consolation to find a cigarette that one hadn't sat on and broken, light it up and take a deep drag. And passing them round, or sharing one's cigarette with a fellow soldier regardless of rank or race, or even which side you've been fighting on, is, and has always been, an easy act of friendship, even solidarity, between men sharing a common predicament. However, at night, a lighted cigarette can be seen for hundreds of yards, and even the smell may give away your presence or your direction. So smoking at night on patrol or ambush was out of the question, which is unfortunate because that was when I usually felt most in need of a puff.

During the Second World War, in March 1945, British parachute forces landed behind German lines as part of the operations to cross the River Rhine. After twenty-four hours fighting off the surrounding Germans, while they hadn't run out of ammunition, they had run out of cigarettes. So one of the platoon commanders was rather surprised when he saw some of his soldiers smoking on the second day. He asked his sergeant major if they had received a parachute drop resupply. No, they hadn't. The mystery was solved by the Chaplain who got the truth out of the men. One of their comrades had been killed during the initial landings – before he could have smoked the tin of cigarettes that he would have been carrying. The surviving soldiers surmised that they had buried his cigarettes along with him. So they had gone back and dug him up, relieved the corpse of its precious fags, and then buried him again. As well as making me laugh, this story struck a real chord with me when the platoon commander himself related it to me in 2005.

Of course, smoking should not be encouraged, but I have come across officers who have sought to deny their men cigarettes while they are in the field. What folly! For some they are as important as food, and this is no time to impose your sanctimonious twaddle on men who deserve all the help you can give them. Keep them supplied with ammunition, water, food and smokes, and if you can keep them alive long enough for them to die of lung cancer, you'll be doing pretty well.

Sanitation on the *jebel* was elementary. One simply walked to a relatively unexposed area designated as the 'boule area' outside the perimeter of the position and dropped one's trousers. There might be a gentle aroma attached to this spot but in the hot sun crap dried very quickly and hygiene was maintained.

Not everybody did it this way however. Chris Barnes took over a position called Pipe from Ian Gordon, an officer in the Muscat Regiment. After showing him all the *sangars*, the sentry positions, the mines and the obstacles, Ian took him over a lip on the west side of the escarpment and along a ten metre ledge which was about two metres immediately below one of the sentry posts. There, Ian proudly showed him the officers' loo, in a shallow cave, comprising an upturned wooden ammunition box with a suitably carved seat – a veritable throne overlooking the Jebel Afal. Immediately to hand there were several rolls of brightly coloured loo paper. It did occur to Chris that his grand view of the Jebel Afal could be reciprocated by any *adoo* on the Jebel Afal looking in his direction. There was no cover against sniper fire and a dash to safe ground back along the ledge would include an undignified scramble up the escarpment, possibly with one's trousers around one's ankles. However, he used the throne happily enough for a week or two before disaster struck. Forgetting Ian's final admonition to keep the loo roll secured under a rock, he had left it loose. To his horror, one morning, he found strips of brightly coloured loo paper strewn on the hillside below him, sticking to the camel thorn and the frankincense trees, and clearly marking his location for any *adoo* who might yet have been uncertain where to direct his spare firepower.

Normally, there was no such thing as loo paper. One simply equipped oneself with a selection of suitably shaped pebbles before one went. All very ecological, I'm sure. You could use whichever hand you wanted but you had to be conscious that the widespread assumption throughout the Middle East is that you use your left hand for this function, and so you always used your right hand for eating and for greeting. Given that one usually ate from a communal platter, any breach of the latter custom would be sure to offend.

This emphasis on the cleanliness of the right hand of course adds great force to the Sharia punishment for theft: the amputation of the right hand. So far as I was aware, the Omanis did not go in for chopping off limbs, but in those countries where it is practised the result for the amputee is cataclysmic in that he either has to resort to unclean non-Islamic practice, or starve.

Farting too was regarded as extremely rude – far ruder than in the West. The word for fart was *mutafujaraat*, the same word as 'explosion'. There was a story about a young man called Mussa Osman who once was heard to fart. Such was the disgrace that came upon him that he was obliged to leave his village and seek his fortune in another country. Mussa prospered and became a rich and respected man in the land of his exile, but before he died an old man, he longed to return to his home village for a final look. So he returned, unknown and unrecognized by his own folk. In the course of his visit, he spoke to a young boy and enquired of him if he had ever heard of a man called Mussa Osman. 'Oh yes' he said, 'He was the man who farted in the time of my grandfather'.

It was possible to sleep on a camp bed in the *sangar*, but Johnny insisted on sleeping on a pile of gravel-filled sandbags. To begin with, I thought this was a little too austere for my taste, but I tried it. One spent so much time lying around the rough rocks at night in ambush, that I too got used to it. Everything took some getting used to, but the body does adjust remarkably well. One slept rather as a mother sleeps. Her ear attuned to certain specific sounds, like her child crying, she will sleep through other far noisier interruptions. I would always hear a voice on the radio that lay next to my head however deeply I was sleeping. On the other hand I was eventually able to slumber through the nightly barrages of mortars that we fired off into the *jebel* at likely *adoo* routes and water holes.

We also got used to wearing the same clothes for protracted periods. It was possible to send clothes down to Mughsayl on the helicopter resupply to have them washed by the *dhobi-wallah* who operated in the Headquarters there. But the date and time of return was uncertain and it was as well not to depend upon this. On patrol, one could expect to sweat a great deal, so I got into the habit of having a patrol set of clothes and a *bayt* set of clothes, *bayt* being the Arabic word for 'house' or 'home'. However, after a couple of weeks, especially during the *khareef*, the distinction between the *bayt* clothes and the patrol clothes could get somewhat blurred, and in the end one simply got used to wearing less than pristine clothes. It certainly didn't do to be too particular. The rumour that we would wear our socks for three days, then turn them inside out and wear them for another three days, then swap feet for another three days, then inside out again for another three days was not entirely true, but not entirely false either. On the other hand, the additional rumour that on completion of this cycle, we then boiled them and ate them, had no foundation in fact whatsoever; although we did nothing to dispel it!

Danger, fatigue, discomfort, dirty clothes, beards, indifferent food, isolation, loneliness; these and other privations were constituent parts of our lives, and all were accepted with soldierly equanimity. However, in our mountain top hermit-like cave dwelling life, I discovered the importance of being able to brush one's teeth. This easy, simple act of bodily hygiene had a disproportionate effect on my physical self regard. With a fresh, clean tasting mouth, I could never quite be a complete troglodyte. A good toothbrush and an inexhaustible supply of toothpaste: these would be my preferred luxuries on my desert island.

One day His Majesty the Sultan visited us at Bole, high up on the *jebel* on the Hornbeam Line. We were given little notice. Surprise offers its own security. So he saw us in our natural state, but he didn't seem to mind. Fortunately he brought his own picnic with him otherwise he would have had to eat Crosse & Blackwell's pilchards in tomato sauce and less-than-perfectly-fresh onion. The British ambassador, Donald Hawley, was in his entourage accompanied by two rather young children. It was a strange sight to see European children on the *jebel*. I had barely set eyes on a European woman for about a year, let alone children. While it was pleasant to see them we felt a tad uneasy for their safety. The first mortar round or Katyusha missile was always the most dangerous one because usually you didn't hear it coming until a couple of seconds before it struck. Although, with the air cover which was in place to protect the Sultan, it was probably unlikely that the *adoo* would risk a shoot, and I suppose our fears were groundless.

Also in the Sultan's entourage were half a dozen *khudaam*, body-guards with very black faces descended from slaves who enjoyed a special privileged position in the Sultan's household. Big burly negroid men dressed in coloured dishdashes and turbans and carrying rifles and camel sticks, they were like something out of the Arabian Nights.

The Sultan took time with the soldiers and was very gracious. He talked to everyone and took an interest in everything. He shared his picnic, food was eaten, and coffee was drunk.

At some stage some smarty pants suggested that perhaps His Majesty would like to fire a machine-gun? He indicated his assent. The Royal Party proceeded out to a sentry position. The soldier on sentry duty looked as if he'd seen a hundred aliens arrive in a flying saucer as the great and good ousted him from his *sangar* and took up positions to watch the regal burst of machine-gun fire. Sultan Qaboos lay down behind the General Purpose Machine Gun and waited for someone to tell him what to do. Silence. He looked quizzically from one side to the other, trying to catch the eye of his courtiers. The courtiers, avoiding his eye, looked at each other as if to say, 'not me Chief, I'm airframes.' He caught my eye. Hitherto content to be an innocent bystander – none of this was my idea – I decided I knew what he wanted. 'GUN GROUP: WITH A BELT OF FIFTY ROUNDS, LOAD. THREE HUNDRED. REFERENCE DEFILE BY LARGE ROCK; 12 O'CLOCK. TWO O'CLOCK FROM ROCK, PILE OF WHITE STONES – BURSTS OF THREE OR FOUR ROUNDS – FIRE!' His Majesty Sultan Qaboos bin Said bin Taimur Al Busaidi, on hearing this time-honoured standard fire control order such as a corporal would give to his two-man gun team, suddenly became Private Al Busaidi of The Cameronians (Scottish Rifles) again. He pricked up his ears, picked up his machine gun, loaded it, went through the drills perfectly, and put a couple of bursts of machine gun fire smack on target. Much congratulating and courtly clapping. He had forgotten nothing. He probably even recognized the Scottish accent.

The visit was a great success. The soldiers talked about it for days. They had taken coffee with their Sultan.

Sultan Qaboos was not the only royalty to take a personal interest in his warriors on the *jebel*. King Hussein of Jordan sent a squadron of his engineers to help his fellow monarch in need and, in due course, he too came to visit them. On the King's arrival in Dhofar, Ian Ventham of the Oman Artillery was ordered to provide a twenty-one gun salute. However, there were no blank rounds in the ammunition inventory of this army at war. Ian solved the problem by using live, high explosive ammunition and fired twenty-one rounds from his three guns at pre-recorded targets on the *jebel*. So each bang was followed by the crunch of the explosion on the *jebel*: twice the number of bangs for his buck. One senses that King Hussein's eyes would have twinkled at this. What the *adoo* made of it is not recorded.

Chapter Seven

The Action: East of the Line

Ambushing was our bread and butter. We were there to stop the *adoo* getting through the Hornbeam Line. We could observe much of the Line by day and, although some bold men might try a daylight breach, and might even succeed, they would not get through in the numbers or carrying the quantities that would affect the course of the war. So while we did patrol during the day, daylight was in the main used for rest, or reconnaissance for night operations. Darkness was a commodity to be used by both sides, and the night ambush was our staple.

When conducted properly, an ambush is a complex, delicate operation and demands well trained and well drilled troops. A less-than-fully-baked ambush improperly planned or rehearsed is liable to go wrong. And there is much which can go wrong, especially when trying to ambush an enemy as alert and as wily as ours.

If time allows, planning for an ambush can start days before the operation itself. Since we frequently went out on ambush on several consecutive nights, we tended to start the planning, preparation and orders process in late morning when all the participants had had some kip after their exertions of the night before. An ambush site would be chosen. Ideally this would be indicated by intelligence which we had received, either from headquarters or from our own local tribesmen. More often, it was the local commander's assessment of likely spots or routes where the *adoo* might be channelled in their efforts to cross the Hornbeam Line.

Time spent on reconnaissance is seldom wasted, and we usually made sure we had a daylight look at the ground that we were going to tiptoe around at night. The daylight recce would take place some days before the planned ambush, and would take the form of a routine daylight patrol. It would not do to be seen to be taking too close an interest in any one piece of ground, and certainly not within twenty-four hours of the intended ambush. We had to assume that the *adoo* were watching us and making careful note of our movements. The ambush commander would certainly go on the recce and ideally might take a couple of his subordinates. However, pressure of commitments rarely allowed this.

With the recce complete, the planning could begin in earnest. Which direction was the *adoo* likely to come from, and in what numbers? Was the ambush site observable by the *adoo* from a distance, thus necessitating a complete night move, or could we do part of the approach unobserved in daylight? Would it be a simple linear ambush on a track, or would it have to be a more complex area ambush? What cover could the *adoo* use in his approach to the site, and therefore at what time in the night would they be likely to try and get through. As a rule they would want to be as far away through the Line as possible before sunrise, thus suggesting a break through as early in the night as possible. But they of course went both ways – east and west – through the Line and we had to take account of that possibility too. Would the *khareef* be down? What would be the state of the moon and when would it rise and set? A bright moonlit night in the light coloured limestone mountainscape of Dhofar could be almost as bright as daylight. And if the moon set while the ambush was in position, near daylight could turn very quickly into black darkness. All these factors and others, including the availability of our own men, shaped the size, timings, and locations of our ambushes.

The commander would then make his plan and allocate his troops to the essential tasks. He would choose a killing ground in the centre: the best ground to give him the main chance of killing as many enemy as possible in as short a time as possible. He would nominate a killer group, usually with his greatest firepower. The commander would always be in the killer group. He would nominate cut-off groups who would be furthest out from the killing area to give either early warning of *adoo* approach, or to cut off an escape, depending upon from which direction the *adoo* came. He might also site a rear area group to provide protection against a surprise approach from the back. Some means of communication would have to be arranged between these groups. If the early warning/cut-off groups were close to the track, they might not be able to speak on the radio without giving themselves away. A series of presses on the radio transmission button might be used, or they might have to resort to a long piece of string and an agreed code of tugs.

Mortar and artillery fire support must also be planned. But again this should be done well before the ambush in order not to give the *adoo* notice of an impending operation. Ideally the targets would be registered and pre-recorded in order to ensure first round accuracy. One might want to record the killing ground if it was not too close to the killer group. One might also record likely enemy escape routes, or routes by which the enemy might follow you up as you withdrew. And in any event, to avoid the sort of mistake I made while training in the North when I mortared myself, account would need to be taken of the different temperatures between night and day. You might also consider the use of the mortar or artillery 'starshell' to help you see the target when the ambush is sprung.

What other aids might be useful? Trip flares? How will they be initiated? If you leave them to be triggered automatically by the intended victim, there is a risk that you find yourself killing a pack of hyenas or wolves. So who will pull the trip wire and on what order? Claymore mines are a useful addition to the armoury. The Claymore is a shaped slab of explosives designed to blast a load of ball bearings in a specific direction. The effect can be devastating at close quarters. But they have to be sited and aimed properly, and very clear instructions given on when they should be fired. There are risks with these mines. I recall an exercise in the Malaysian jungle where the enemy somehow got into the killing ground of an ambush without being spotted. They found the Claymore mines and turned them round to face the killer group. It was only an exercise and the mines were dummies, but the point was obvious enough.

How will the ambush be sprung? A shout? A whistle blast? It was generally felt that the best way was for the ambush commander to spring it himself with a burst of machine gun fire or by firing a Claymore mine. But there must be a means of springing the trap if the enemy come from an unexpected direction or the commander cannot see them for whatever reason. And when the shooting is over, how will the 'cease fire' be signalled? A whistle blast or a shouted order could be heard by any surviving *adoo* who, knowing the ambush was over, might make good his escape, or might choose to wait until the ambushers reveal themselves and shoot back. So a series of false 'end of ambush' signals might be devised before the real one was given. But everyone would need to know which was which. Once the shooting was really over, it was best to leave the area without going into the killing ground. There was a strict limit to what could safely be discovered from the results of an ambush in the dark. If there were survivors, they would be lying down and you and your people would be silhouetted moving on your feet. You would, in effect, be ripe for an ambush by them. Any investigation or follow up would be done in daylight.

Great care also needed to be taken to ensure that everyone knew the signal to withdraw, and that they all got the message. A rendezvous point in the rear would be set and everyone must be clocked through it. So passwords would have to be published and understood.

The commander must also cater for the many what-ifs associated with this operation. What if the *adoo* appear before you are settled in position? What if the weather or the light level changes unexpectedly while you are in position? What if the *adoo* come from an unexpected direction? What if they come in greater numbers than you had anticipated? What if they bypass your early warning groups? What if they counter-attack you? What if they appear while you are withdrawing? It will be seen that the opportunities for confusion and cock-up are considerable. Groups of men moving around in the dark not knowing precisely what they are doing, where they are going and what the others are doing, while there may be *adoo* about, is a recipe for disaster.

So, the ambush commander makes his plan and prepares and delivers his orders to all who are participating. He may then arrange to rehearse the critical phases of the ambush in daylight; for instance, the move from line of march through the rendezvous point into the separate groups. Similarly, the withdrawal might be practised. Time then for a hot meal, a crap and other final preparations. Take something that one can eat quietly during the night.

Eventually the men would assemble ready for the night's work. The commander might ask each man to jump up and down to ensure that no one rattled. Final kit checks would be made, a last cigarette would be smoked, then off we go.

It was not long before we knew the ground very well indeed. Soon our procedures became streamlined and many of the steps outlined above became routine. But there is always a danger of complacency. A man returned from leave or a new soldier from the Training Regiment had to be schooled into the routine. Fatigue too had to be managed. Long nights, night after night trying to stay alert at the end of a machine-gun, take their toll, and one had to be careful that one was not lying out on the *jebel* with a bunch of sleeping men. The sound of snoring was potentially lethal in more ways than one. And it was not always the *adoo* who surprised me. On one occasion, I had been puzzled by the shuffling and muttering that came from some of the positions. On closer investigation, I found that some of our soldiers were saying their prayers. They at least had the grace to say them quietly, but the operational nature of the situation hadn't stopped them getting out their mats, kneeling on them facing Mecca and going through the whole prayer routine. I waited till they finished then asked them not to do it again until we were back at base. They were happy enough with this once I had explained it to them.

Our first crisis on the *jebel* was when a patrol I had sent out to lay an ambush on a track was itself surprised by the *adoo*. Four or five *adoo* had approached the ambush from an unexpected direction in the darkness and had been able to fight their way out of the trap. A bright, pleasant corporal called Saif Jameel had been shot through the leg, and the patrol needed help to protect themselves and to get their wounded man back to base. All this information came through in garbled bits on our radio. Radio communications were notoriously poor at night. I was fortunate in that Tony Willis, an ex-RAF officer and now serving as our Operations Officer, happened to be spending the night with me at Kumasi, so I left him to mind the shop and try to keep communications open on our dodgy radios.

I got half a dozen men together to go to try and find the stranded patrol. It was bright clear moonlight when I left and I made good time to the site. On reflection, I should have been far more cautious, but I still had much to learn. We were few in number and there were *adoo* about. Another couple of casualties on this patrol could have presaged disaster. Moreover, whenever there was more than one patrol out, the risk of bumping into each other and having a blue-on-blue shoot-out was commensurately greater. However, I was lucky, I knew the ground well and found them easily enough. Normally one would expect to have to earmark two or even four men to assist or to carry a non-walking wounded man. However, the difference in physique between me and my soldiers meant that Corporal Saif Jameel, who was light even by Omani standards, was not much heavier than a full rucksack. I bandaged up Saif and put him over my shoulder to carry him home. It was only about two kilometres away. But the moon had now gone down. What had been so bright that it was almost like daylight had been transformed into the blackest of black nights. In spite of the fact that I had a compass and I knew the ground, I was disorientated. I hadn't a clue which way the base was. It wouldn't have taken a major mistake to have ended up completely lost and, in the blackness, a wrong turn carrying a wounded man could have been disastrous.

I tried to get through on the radio, but I couldn't make myself clear. What I wanted was for someone to fire a flare into the air so I could tell which way to travel. There was an artillery battery nearby and they were very keen to give me artillery fire support. 'No thank you – I don't want an artillery barrage, I just want a flare'.

'Are you sure, we've got three guns here, and we could put down three shells each in a minute'

'No no. Just walk out of your *sangar* and fire a hand-held flare up into the air.' I could feel the baffled disappointment in his voice, but eventually a flare went up; in completely the opposite direction from which I was expecting it. However, I walked towards it, and another one which went up half an hour later, and we made it home.

The following morning I returned to the site of the ambush and found a blood trail which we followed for a hundred metres or so until it disappeared. So the ambush had inflicted at least one casualty. We looked hard in the local area in the hope of finding a wounded man laid up, either with or without his comrades. We didn't find him. Either his comrades had managed to carry him away or it was an arm wound. You don't walk very far after you have been shot in the leg or the body with a FN 7.6 mm round.

Corporal Saif Jameel duly returned to the Company from hospital. He was pleased to be back and had not enjoyed the life of a patient or recuperating with the base wallahs in Salalah. He called them queers and old women. He told me that it was announced one day that the Sultan would come to visit the hospital. An apple was placed on the table beside each man's bed in advance of the visit. The Sultan came, was suitably gracious, and progressed on his way. An orderly then came round to collect the apples. Saif had eaten his. He was given a right royal bollocking.

My own choice of personal weapon was influenced by the possibility of ambush – both ambushing the *adoo*, and the threat of being ambushed by them. The standard issue rifle was the 7.62 mm Belgian Fabrique Nationale rifle. This was the weapon that the British SLR was based on and had very similar characteristics. It was a dependable self-loading rifle, at its best at ranges of several hundred metres. It could fire on automatic, in other words, like a machine-gun, but it wasn't particularly good for that. By day on the *jebel* it was a good weapon. However, at night where a fleeting opportunity in the dark might be all you saw, immediate high volume rapid fire was desirable. One had to consider too that you might be that fleeting target in the dark. Deliberate well-aimed single shots weren't going to help you much. The ability to spray bullets as you tried to escape from someone else's killing zone was your only chance. So I equipped myself with the AK47 Kalashnikov, the standard Soviet infantry weapon and the weapon that the *adoo* and every other third world soldier – and a few first world ones – could be seen toting around the globe.

I got hold of this rifle from the stock that had been taken from the Dhofaris who had surrendered to the Sultan's forces. In other words, it was an ex-*adoo* weapon. It had a large magazine containing thirty rounds and one could fire it all off in a few seconds. Its working parts

102

were very simple and had been machined with such loose tolerances that sand and dirt rarely jammed it. The calibre was also 7.62 mm but the ammunition was not interchangeable with the FN. The AK47 had a shorter, smaller cartridge and therefore lacked the long range hitting power of the FN, but it served its purpose well. The long magazine sticking out of the bottom meant that one could be a little exposed when trying to fire from behind low cover, and I found the distinctive clunk of the safety catch when released a bit disconcerting. I used to listen for it as the indicator of imminent ambush on the *jebel* at night, and wondered if the *adoo* were listening for mine. But on balance it was an excellent weapon.

We also had the General Purpose Machine Gun – the GPMG – also made by Fabrique Nationale, which was a belt-fed 7.62 mm weapon. The ammunition was interchangeable with the FN rifle. It was an excellent, well proven, powerful weapon but Omanis found it rather heavy and unwieldy coming in at 24 lbs. And then we had to carry the ammunition. But the weight of fire and its reliability outweighed this disadvantage.

On the position called Bole, we had two British made 81 mm mortars. These too were excellent weapons and had a range of about five and a half kilometres. While occasionally we would be out of range of our artillery, we never operated out of range of our mortars if we could help it. Even though artillery or aircraft might be able to support us, both had their disadvantages. The Strikemaster didn't operate at night and, even though the pilots would risk their necks and break every rule in the book to help us in poor visibility, there was always a limit to what they could do. Our old Second World War artillery pieces, served though they were by devoted and expert Omani soldiers, were not very accurate at long range. And communications with them were not always of the best, especially at night. Furthermore, aircraft and guns took time to organise. Mortars under one's own direct command on the other hand, were quick and responsive twenty-four hours a day regardless of the weather. They were accurate and their fire could be adjusted extremely close in to one's own position, if that was what was required. We were responsible for selecting and training our own mortarmen, so we got the quality of service that we deserved, for good or for ill.

I also had a couple of donkeys under my command. They arrived on my position as an underslung load – after first being sedated. A donkey will carry about a hundred and fifty pounds, which amounts to about ten mortar shells or four jerry cans of water. They were very patient and sure footed animals. In order to ensure that they never made a noise when they weren't supposed to, they had had their vocal chords cut. The chap who came with them – the donkey wallah – was a wiry old man, in fact probably no more than forty, with a glorious ear-to-ear smile and not a tooth in his head. These donkeys and their toothless, redoubtable handler were important members of A Company. They gave us our own integral heavy lift transport which allowed us to deploy our fire power to places that we might not otherwise reach.

If a patrol was going to go beyond the range of their mortar firebase, we would deploy the mortars with the patrol and set up another firebase, thereby ensuring that we always were able to call on them for help. The donkeys would carry the mortars, and each man on the patrol would carry a mortar shell. On arrival at the designated spot, the mortarmen would stop, dig their pit and set up their protected firebase to cover the patrol area. Each soldier would drop off his mortar round as he passed the mortar pit on his way out on to the patrol. It was perfectly possible to use helicopters to fly in the heavy stuff, and even to fly in the troops, and this was done too. However, helicopters make a noise, and one does not always want to fly them into unknown landing sites in enemy territory. Helicopter hours were also precious. The low-tech donkey solution allowed a fighting patrol to insert itself deep into *adoo* territory quietly during the night without any fuss and be dug in and established ready to take on all comers at first light, and with its own mortar support. In this way we were able to dislocate *adoo* expectations at ranges beyond normal patrolling distance from the Hornbeam Line.

At Kumasi, we sported another anachronism in this anachronistic country, the .5 inch Browning machine-gun, sometimes known in American war films as the Fifty Cal. This beast was anachronistic in that it was designed shortly after the First World War and, the man who conceived it, John Moses Browning of Utah, had been born in 1855. But it remained, and remains still, a superb weapon, and in no way obsolete. It was accurate up to about 2,000 metres and could pump its half inch slug out to nearly 7,000 metres. We were pleased to have this in our armoury, and I know the defenders of Mirbat certainly were. And having subsequently been at the receiving end of one of these beasts, I can vouch for its efficacy. It is curious to note that this weapon is still in service with the British forces, and the Royal Marines have just installed it on their brand new all-terrain armoured vehicle, the Viking. So it has been in service for over eighty years, and has the prospect of many more years in front of it yet; and this about a century and a half after the birth of its American designer.

None of the artillery pieces that supported us were new either. The 25 pounder was a British Second World War weapon and the larger

5.5 inch howitzer which could push a shell out to nearly 14,000 metres, was of similar vintage. Even the Omani soldiers, who were not spoilt with new equipment and weapons, called this piece the *Shaiba* – the Old Man. But they were adequate weapons, and they and the soldiers and officers who worked them served us extremely well.

None of the helicopter pilots spoke Arabic. None of the Omani soldiers at company level could speak English. Being the only people who could speak both to the pilots and to the soldiers, we were therefore pivotal to any successful evacuation operation. If you yourself were wounded during the day, and couldn't speak on the radio, there was a good chance that word would get through to the Air Force via our Regimental Headquarters where both languages were spoken. That being so, the pilots would certainly take off and look for you, and in daylight, they had a fair chance of finding you, unless you were down one of the deep *wadis* like the Jizalawt. At night, even supposing that news of one's injury managed to get through on our degraded communications, they hadn't a hope of finding you unless you were on an especially benign piece of ground, and your soldiers had put out flares or torches.

Although we soldiers used a primitive first generation night vision device which amplified ambient light, there were no such things as night vision flying aids then. Passive Night Goggles, the staple for all tactical night flying now, did not exist. As far as I could see, the pilots flew by moonlight if there was a moon, or by the seat of their pants if there wasn't. So we were always conscious of night being an especially dangerous time. This being so, we did what we could to train our soldiers to cope with such an eventuality and to use the small radio beacon that officers carried, but the language barrier and the lousy communications were always serious obstacles.

However, our difficulties were as nothing compared to those of our predecessors who had had no helicopters at all. Sometimes it had been possible to get wounded men to an improvised air strip out of range of enemy fire, but these strips were few and far between, and pilots of the small fixed wing propeller driven Beaver aircraft were understandably cautious about flying into a strip which had not been recently checked out by a qualified person. It was more likely that the casualties would have to be carried to the nearest point to which a vehicle might be driven. The carrying party would need to be escorted through *adoo* country and it may be that the plan for the original operation would have to be amended or even aborted, depending upon how many escorts were required, and at what stage in the operation the men had been wounded. So, long painful hours on a stretcher or a donkey were the prospect for a wounded man who could not be got quickly out in an aircraft or vehicle. And even once in the vehicle, the journey was never going to be too comfortable. Morphine might be used to take the edge off his agony, but only if the wound allowed it. Morphine administered to a man with a torso or head wound would just as likely ensure an early demise. You were lucky if you survived such an ordeal.

Communications were pretty good during the day. Officers and NCOs each carried a small hand-held very high frequency (VHF) 'National' walkie-talkie radio set which was good for short range line-of-sight communications. This was fine for its limited purpose but the *adoo* used something similar and one had to assume that they were listening to us. They also jammed the net from time to time. The set was not very robust and when one fell on it, or rolled over it as one tended to do in a crisis, it was easily broken.

We also used a high frequency (HF) back-pack radio for longer distances. HF radio waves skip and bounce between the Earth's surface and the ionosphere which surrounds the Earth. The ionosphere rises during the day and then the radio worked well. But at night, when the ionosphere moves nearer to the Earth's surface, the signal is severely degraded. This can be overcome by using a different antenna, but such an antenna would be so large that it would not normally be man packable.

We lacked a more powerful VHF radio. This made voice communications virtually impossible after dark, which was a grave impediment to our operations. Occasionally we harboured dark thoughts about those who had left such a gap in our inventory. Did the procurement officer take a kickback from the supplier to persuade him not to ask too many questions about the utility of the radios? Controls and checks and balances in those early days were few and far between and it would have been easy to cover up a dirty deal. Some time after I left Oman, a British officer was sacked for a dodgy deal that he arranged with equipment procurement, so it was not unknown.

Then again, it was just as likely to have been a cock-up. Had they been tested in theatre at night? Highly unlikely. Had there been a rigorous analysis of the operational requirement? Probably not. Had the buyer accepted the word of the supplier that they would meet the task? Almost certainly. Most likely of all is that there simply hadn't been enough money at the time to buy the extra radios that would have given us the complete capability. Whatever the reason, we were left with radios which wouldn't work in the dark.

However, while voice transmission at night was difficult or impossible, one could usually get through using Morse Code. I learned to transmit Morse Code while I was on the *jebel*, which is much easier than learning to understand it. But it had its uses. I once called for

106

pre-arranged artillery fire on a target by tapping out Morse letters on a key strapped to my leg as I walked. This is a most unusual procedure, but was the sort of ploy that we had to resort to from time to time.

There was no such thing as Global Positioning Satellite (GPS) navigation in those days and good map reading was an essential art for all soldiers. We had maps, but there were no contours; only an indistinct shadowing, and any reference to tracks, waterholes or other features had to be treated at best as approximate, at worst downright wrong. The best thing to do was to get to know the ground as quickly and as thoroughly as possible then mark up and correct your own map.

Artillery or mortar fire was a useful aid to navigation. In every area, the artillery had registered targets like real water holes, tracks and defiles chosen for the likelihood of approach. If these were marked accurately on your map, you could ask the guns to fire say, Alpha Three Nine. A shell would land on the spot and, assuming you could see where it had landed, you could work out where you were in relation to that point. But if there were no registered targets nearby, you could at a push choose a grid reference off your map and ask the guns to drop one on that. The risk of course was that you might be on that grid yourself ...

I had served in the Malaysian jungle so I was used to being permanently unsure of my position. The difference there was that, although you could rarely see much further than a few metres, the contours on the maps were dependable. You navigated by measuring distances and watching the contours. In Oman, you could almost always see a long way, but the precipitous moonscape in which we marched was no easier to read for that, and a mistake could mean a climb down, up, or both, of a couple of thousand feet, or finding a very long way round.

Between June and September each year, the south-west monsoon came in from the Indian Ocean and shrouded all ground below 2,000 feet in a damp, muggy, thick, drizzling mist. This mist was called the *khareef*. This was a particularly difficult time of year. The mist was reminiscent of the Scottish East Coast haar, except that it was thicker and wetter. If one was living and operating at this level, it was almost like living in the dark because visibility was usually restricted to close range; usually, but not always, because sometimes the mist swirled and lifted. One moment you could be trudging along trying to find the end of your nose and, the next moment, a vista of perhaps several hundred metres could open up in front of you.

This could be rather disconcerting. You couldn't depend on the *khareef* to screen your movements and neither could the *adoo*.

The possibility of suddenly finding yourself at close range with your adversaries when neither you nor they in the least expected it, in broad misty daylight, was always present. This served to keep one especially on edge. The *khareef* did eerie things to sound too. The volume was muffled, but a sound in the mist never seemed to come from quite the direction that you thought it did. Moreover, it did nothing to improve my already dodgy map reading.

The overall effect of the *khareef* on operations was also significant because helicopter movements were severely curtailed. This of course not only meant one's operational movement was restricted, but resupply and casualty evacuation were difficult too. The problem of resupply was largely overcome by building up a stockpile of food and water. For several weeks before the *khareef*, extra helicopter effort was devoted to bringing enough up to those positions that would be affected so that they could remain operational for the three months of the *khareef*.

The resupply to the *jebel* generally, and during the *khareef* in particular, presented a major logistics task both for the hard pressed helicopter force and the operations officers and logisticians. In the Northern Frontier Regiment, this burden was borne by Yaqub, our Quartermaster, and Tony Willis, the Operations Officer. Nick Knollys, after six months on Ashawq, took over the latter task for the *khareef* build-up. Typically we would have four helicopter hours allocated to us each day. Nick would receive the orders from each position and pass them to the Quartermaster who would assemble the stores. Nick would assess the bulk and weight of each load and write a helicopter flying programme for the next day's resupply. One had to be mindful of the *adoo*'s desire to disrupt our programme so we had to avoid routine and repetition when flying into the positions. The most vulnerable moment was the point of touch down and so we underslung as many loads as possible for quick turnaround. If there were troop movements of course, they had to land. Having written the plan the night before, it could not be left to work on its own. Like all military plans, it had to be adjusted and even rewritten to take account of unforeseen changes. The helicopter hours might be reduced or increased. A helicopter might develop a defect. Late urgent requirements would have to be met. The *adoo* might choose to interfere with a mortar stonk. The helicopter might turn out to be Iranian and this would require more careful supervision. We might even get two helicopters!

Since none of the pilots spoke Arabic there was a need to communicate with the receiving position to ensure they were ready to handle the load, and that the *adoo* were not in the process of attacking

108

them. It was also good to know that there were no blasting operations underway. The helicopters rarely had two pilots so Nick found that the best way to control all this was for himself to take the left-hand seat in the front of the helicopter. In this way he was able to communicate with all concerned and control the complex business of resupplying seven or eight positions with all they needed to prosecute the war. He also learned a great deal about flying and on occasion took the controls himself, although, had I known that at the time, I would have ensured I was never in the back while Knollys was in the front!

The scope and success of all military operations are completely dependent on what can be achieved logistically. The success of the Hornbeam Line was only made possible by the efforts of the logisticians like Nick, Tony and Yaqub and the helicopter pilots, both British and Iranian. I do not recall that we on the *jebel* ever lacked anything that we needed to do our jobs.

The creation of a stockpile of water on the *jebel* presented few problems, although water that had been inside a plastic barrel for three months didn't always taste just as delicious as it might have done earlier on. I know of at least one occasion when the would-be drinker of water found that, what had been a tadpole when the container was filled, had developed into something a lot bigger, and had died. When he opened his water bottle with a view to slaking a heavy thirst some weeks later, he had a rather disgusting surprise, and no water.

Dry food, like onions and bags of rice, did not improve in the continuously dank atmosphere of the *khareef* and there was an inevitable high level of wastage. One's skin too became white, soft and easily broken, and any wound had to be carefully protected against infection. All in all, it was not a pleasure living on the *jebel* during the *khareef*, and relief was often sought by climbing up above it, or walking down to base for a break.

But the *khareef* didn't stop helicopters altogether and, if they knew it was absolutely necessary, the pilots would take off in thick mist in the hope that it might be possible to find a workable gap at the far end. And there were days when flying was largely unhindered. It was this ability to fly during the *khareef* which allowed the Sultan's forces to continue fighting the war on the *jebel* throughout the year. In previous years, the *jebel* had had to be abandoned to the *adoo* because, logistically, it had been impossible to sustain operations. This of course had done nothing to help the successful prosecution of the war. Indeed, for this reason, the introduction of helicopters to the *jebel* was undoubtedly one of the most important turning points of the war.

When finally the *khareef* lifted in September, the *jebel*, which in July had been brown, yellow and barren, suddenly presented itself in a rich verdant green with leaves on trees and grass fit for grazing. The trees were usually very thorny and movement among them was often very difficult. The *shemaagh*, which otherwise was excellent headgear, became notorious for its tendency to get caught up in the thorns. Marked on our maps were 'densely wooded slopes'. For nine months of the year, it was difficult to imagine such a phenomenon in our arid patrol areas. But for a few weeks after the *khareef*, our maps were absolutely accurate, at least in this regard, if not in any other. Since they tended to move by day, this foliage favoured the *adoo* as it offered them cover which they would not otherwise have had. They were as adept at fighting in this near jungle environment as they were on the waterless harsh *jebel*.

Being mortared or shelled is an experience, which, once endured, remains branded on the memory for life. Much depends on the sort of cover available. It is unpleasant enough if you are under cover, but if you are in the open, it is one of the most frightening things that can happen to you. The noise is quite the loudest I have ever heard, and it penetrates through every pore in your skin to every brain cell in your head. As screaming death crashes down all around you, you think every moment is going to be your last. The assault is not so much on the body as on the mind and, once it has finished, you can't believe you have survived. Both in the Falklands and in Oman, I was always left after each artillery barrage on our position with a feeling of surprise at how many people had not been killed. How could we have survived that? The purpose of artillery is sometimes to damage and destroy, but more usually it is to neutralize while one carries out some concurrent manoeuvre. Neutralizing it certainly is. But the danger of sudden unheralded destruction was always present.

We had a good working routine for mortars. We usually posted a sentry 100 metres or so west of our position – sufficiently far away for him not to be distracted by the noises of the daily routine of the camp. His chief task was to listen for the 'pop' of a mortar firing. If he heard the pop, he would shout 'incomer' as loud as he could, and we would all dive for cover into weapon pits or *sangars*. Once inside, one would have been very unlucky to have been hurt and, indeed, remarkably few soldiers became mortar casualties. Even Nick Knollys who commanded Ashawq, which was the most exposed position on the Hornbeam Line, for six months and who was on the receiving end of several hundred incomers, including some twenty Katyusha rockets, sustained only a few minor casualties. The principal vegetation in the small valleys leading down from Ashawq was the frankincense tree. The smell was quite pervasive, the more so when the trees were damaged by mortar shells thus allowing the sap to bleed.

Ashawq's prominence and attractiveness as a target was not lessened by the Omani flag that Nick Knollys insisted on flying at the top of a long pole throughout his time there. Normally one would try and avoid providing enemy gunners with such a gratuitous aiming mark, but Nick felt that the place was so obvious in any case, that the flag would not make any difference. This act of defiance implied in flying the Sultan's emblem in territory in which the *adoo* had hitherto had had a free run was a boost to our soldiers' morale and, one hoped, of some irritation to the *adoo*.

It wasn't only the soldiers who drew encouragement from this flag. One day, Bob Mason was leading a flight of six aircraft on their way back to base from a strike in the western *jebel*. Last light was approaching, the weather was beautiful and the fluffy clouds were reddened by the setting sun. By way of a salute to the soldiers serving on the Hornbeam Line, Bob decided to do a flypast of every position from north to south. He received permission, and arranged for the artillery and mortars to hold their fire. Down they came to about fifty feet into arrow formation and started flying down the line. The colours on the *jebel* were astonishing – purples and blacks to the east, reds and oranges to the west, all against the backdrop of a sky of ever deepening blue. At each position they passed, they could see soldiers running about and waving cheerfully – until they got to Ashawq. As they approached this battered whitened fortress, they could see the flagpole with the Omani flag and, beside it a *sangar*, bathed in the setting sun. On top of the *sangar* stood a lone soldier standing stiffly to attention saluting them, the Sultan of Oman's Air Force. Having kindly come along to salute us and lift our spirits, they themselves went away with lumps in their throats.

To work out where the *adoo* was firing from, we used a procedure of crater examination. The residual tail fin would tell you the type of mortar that had been used so you would know the maximum range. On one occasion while we were being mortared on Boxing Day, the dry stone bunker in which Viv Rowe was taking cover was hit. The tailfin of the mortar bounced in through an aperture and fell into Viv's hands. He was unhurt. He examined the tail fin and saw that it was from a Chinese mortar with a range of 2,100 metres. He was able to inform our own mortars thus helping them to adjust their returning fire. The pattern of the blast marks would give you a good indication of the direction from which it was fired. Using the map, your knowledge of the ground and of the *adoo*'s tactics, you could then make an educated estimate of the location of the firing position, and perhaps of the location of the observer who had directed the shoot, and then fire back either with our own mortars, or with artillery.

111

However, the *adoo* also had Katyusha rockets. 'Katyusha' is the Russian diminutive term for Katherine – 'Wee Katie'. These were the rocket artillery missiles known as Stalin's Organs and used by the Russians during the Second World War. During that war they were fired in multiples from a rack on the back of a truck. In this war, single missiles were fired from a contraption of poles and sticks having been transported on a camel or donkey. They were 122 mm in calibre and had a range of between 11 and 20 kilometres depending upon what version was being used. They carried a 40 lb shaped warhead. A shaped warhead meant that it could go through almost anything that we were likely to be able to put up against it. If this was Little Katie, one wonders what Big Katie was like.

Because of their range, usually the only counter to the Katyusha was an air strike. However, it took time to rustle up an air strike and, in the time it took for a Strikemaster to appear, there was every chance that the *adoo* would have finished firing or moved the firing point. Moreover, the *adoo* would wait until evening before they fired their Katyushas. Since they were firing from the west eastwards on to our positions, this meant that the sun was in our eyes, and the horizon would be hazy and indistinct, making it almost impossible for us to identify the firing point. Although the Katyushas were essentially line of sight weapons they could be fired from a reverse slope which we could not see. Unlike a mortar, there was no warning 'pop'. However, if one was extremely lucky, one might be able to spot an initial trail of smoke. So we took to arranging for aircraft to be in the air just before sunset, out of sight and sound but close enough to be called in at a moment's notice. This Katyusha trap worked on at least one occasion.

Johnny Braddell-Smith's position at Kumasi was A Company headquarters and it was about five kilometres to my north. I watched him being hit by three or four of these brutes one evening as great plumes of smoke erupted around his *sangars*. No one was hurt. When I next visited him, I examined the holes. It was quite plain that a direct hit from one of these things would blow a *sangar*, and all that was in it, away. Indeed, this is precisely what happened on one occasion at Ashawq. However, Nick Knollys had sent the four or five men whose home it was away on leave a short time before. In due course they returned to the *jebel* at the end of their leave only to find a rubble-filled hole where their *sangar* had been. Allah is indeed merciful.

My own little fortress at Reef didn't seem to be a convenient target for these monsters and I never came under fire from them myself. I was not unhappy about this. However, when I took command of A Company while Johnny went on leave, I moved to company headquarters at Kumasi. It turned out to be a very active period which suited me well enough. The prospect of being Katyusha'd was a wonderful incentive to ensure that I was out on patrol as much of the time as possible.

I sometimes wondered why the *adoo* didn't use these powerful weapons to better effect. They were adept at using them and they were remarkably accurate with them. However, I suppose they had their difficulties too. They may not have had very many of them, and to move them by foot, donkey or camel to a good firing point in the *jebel* must have presented a significant logistics challenge. Furthermore, they no doubt were conscious of the possibility of being trapped by Strikemasters, especially since, on a couple of occasions, the pilots went and strafed likely firing points in the evenings just for good fellowship. This would not be lost on the *adoo*, and they didn't want to be Strikemastered any more than we wanted to be Katyusha'd, so I suppose we more or less unknowingly called it quits.

However, the *adoo* had some sophisticated artillerymen as Ian Gordon found out. Ian was with the Muscat Regiment and was attached to us with his troops on the Hornbeam Line. He operated out of Pipe at the southern extremity of the Line. He discovered that the *adoo* had mastered 'shadow register' techniques. The *adoo* could always be expected to mark 9 June, the date of the start of the Revolution in Dhofar. For several days prior to 9 June 1974 the *adoo* fired a 75 mm recoilless artillery piece, not at Ian Gordon's position, but apparently at our artillery position some 800 metres away. In any event, the shells were clearly off target. Ian dutifully examined the craters and concluded from a study of the ground and the maximum range of the *adoo* weapon, that they were firing from the only safe cover available, and that our artillery position was out of range from this safe firing point. He therefore looked forward to 9 June with some equanimity and anticipated that he would watch another failed attempt to hit our guns. He even went so far as to put his chair on top of his *sangar* and eat his breakfast while enjoying the *adoos'* discomfiture on their big day. The first shell was duly fired. Ian started counting the seconds of the time of flight, expecting it to explode futilely on the barren mountainside. He had barely reached the expected number of seconds when 'a hell of a bang a few yards away knocked me off my chair and sent my mess tin flying – not from the blast but from me jumping out of my skin with fright. I dived into the relative safety of my *sangar* as the *adoo* fired a dozen or more very accurate rounds smack into the position in a relatively short space of time.' Ian had taken the precaution of briefing the Strikemasters beforehand and he immediately scrambled the jets, although the *adoo* had probably scarpered by the time the bombs went down.

Shadow registering is the procedure whereby a feature a known distance, bearing and height from the intended target is chosen to correct the fall of shot and then the exact adjustment is applied to range and bearing to give a good chance of the first shot landing, unexpectedly, accurately on target. Ian on Pipe had been the intended target all along. As Ian said afterwards; 'Never underestimate your enemy nor think him a fool.'

I was on the receiving end of artillery fire again in the Falklands War and once again I brought mortar fire down on my own position, although this time, for the same reason as Hamed Said, I did it deliberately. The sensation remains indelibly engraved on my mind. While we may not have lost many people to indirect fire in Oman, the courage required to sit for several months on top of a hill, as Nick and his soldiers did on one of the easiest and most obvious targets in all Dhofar; hoping to hear the 'pop' in time to take cover before the 'crash', or in the case of Wee Katie, hoping she won't come anywhere near your *sangar* – the courage required to sit still and stay sane is not to be underestimated.

A Company manned and patrolled from the four northern positions on the Hornbeam Line; Reef, Kumasi, Bole and Oven. Sometimes we combined as a company and, leaving only a skeleton garrison at the bases, we mounted a concerted operation to disconcert the enemy's expectations and work a bit further out east from the Line. In early March 1974, Intelligence suggested that there was a party of *adoo* some five or eight kilometres out to our east lying up and waiting as a reception party for a camel train about to attempt a break through the wire. We decided to try and move them on so as to disrupt this resupply operation.

After leaving enough men to hold and defend each position, we divided the remainder of the company between us. Each half comprised two small platoons of about fifteen men each – about thirty men plus our mortar section. The SAS four-man team based on Reef came with me. The idea was that we would move at night, stop and go firm by first light in defensive positions, and lie in wait to see what happened. If the enemy had seen you, they would often attack. They rarely discovered all your positions, so one portion of the company was usually in a good position to give them a good pasting, especially since we always moved within range of our own mortars, and sometimes artillery. Aircraft were also available for these orchestrated punch-ups.

We tried to conduct our major movements in enemy-held country at night and then be established in a strong position at dawn. In this way the *adoo* would either have to move to attack us, or move to slink away.

1. HM Sultan Qaboos bin Said

2. Johnny Braddell-Smith

(Nicholas Knollys)

3. Fanja Village near Bid Bid *(Nicholas Knollys)*

4. Nick Knollys, Charlie Daniel, Angus Ramsay and Salim Said *(Nicholas Knollys)*

5. A Dhofari Firqat group

(*Nicholas Knollys*)

6. The workhorse of the war – AB 205 helicopter with underslung load

(*Nicholas Knollys*)

7. Baluchi soldiers with 81mm mortar   (Nicholas Knollys)

8. 75mm artillery with frankincense tree   (Nicholas Knollys

9. Dhofari Jebalis

(Bryan Ray)

10. Returning from patrol   (*Nicholas Knollys*)

11. Ashawq in the *khareef*

(Nicholas Knollys)

12. Wessex saving us a walk

(John Hoskinson)

13. 'Stand to' before dusk on the Hornbeam line

(Nicholas Knollys)

14. The author at Reef

(Author)

15. The author's home at Reef for six months *(Author)*

16. Cooking *khubbs* on the lid of an oil drum *(Nicholas Knollys)*

17. Gordon Gillies's battleship

(Nicholas Knollys)

18. Hamdi al Gamal with friends

(Nicholas Knollys)

19. Remains of mortar and Katyusha attacks on Ashawq (note the famous flag)

(Nicholas Knollys)

20. The author amusing himself with a .50 Browning *(Bryan Ray)*

21. Skyvan landing on a *jebel* strip   (*Nicholas Knollys*)

22. SOAF Caribou hit while landing at Sarfait   (*Nicholas Knollys*)

23 Strikemaster over Salalah

(Nicholas Knollys)

In either case, they would have to do it in daylight and therefore risk exposing themselves. We would move in daylight, but only when a substantial portion of the force was able to cover the moving force, or react quickly as a reserve. It was always essential to have an uncommitted force to act as a reserve. Strangely this was the area where the *adoo* was weakest. Perhaps they did not have enough radios. Once they were committed to a certain course of action, they were often unable to react to a surprise move of ours. So we tried to surprise them as much as possible.

On this occasion, I was operating near the head of the Wadi Sha'ath ten kilometres to the east of the Hornbeam Line. At dawn, there was no sign of anybody anywhere. By way of having a second cast, at Johnny's request, I moved my two small platoons a little further to the east, one on the ground, one moving. As I was crossing a low ridge, I came under machine-gun fire from my front. I hit the ground and found myself next to one of the SAS troopers, Trooper Kent. He had a huge rucksack and was carrying a General Purpose Machine Gun. As he got into position, I started calling on my hand-held radio for mortar and gun support. I loaded his weapon for him, lying next to him on his left side. As usual, I couldn't see exactly where the fire was coming from, but had a pretty good guess and directed him on to it. He fired a burst. Fire was returned. I redirected him to where I thought this had come from and he fired a couple of bursts in that direction, with me putting another belt of ammunition on his machine gun as he did so. He fired another couple of bursts then his head suddenly slumped forward onto his weapon and blood spurted out from his face, lying next to mine. He had been hit, but it seemed to me that if it had been a head wound, it might not have been fatal, because although there was a lot of blood, the head was not as damaged as it should have been if it had taken the full force of a bullet. But he definitely wasn't conscious, so I heaved at him, trying to pull and roll him backwards into cover. His huge rucksack did not help.

We were now under fire from at least two positions. I had, almost immediately on coming under fire, rolled on my radio and broken the antenna right off. I wasn't doing very well with Kent on my own, and was joined by four other brave men: Corporal Wildman and Trooper McLaren of the SAS detachment, one of my own NCOs, Corporal Hamed Khamis, and an Omani soldier from his section, Private Zayeed Khalifa. We grabbed Kent and tried to pull him back, but Corporal Hamed was soon hit and went down. Then Corporal Wildman was shot in the thigh so we scrambled back into what we thought was cover. Hamed's man, Zayeed Khalifa, was soon hit in the arm from a hitherto unseen position and so we had to scramble again with our wounded to find more cover.

So out of the six men involved in this little skirmish, I was one of two who had not been hit. Corporal Hamed, brave and faithful man, who had automatically come to my assistance without being asked, had crashed down very hard next to me and I had seen his face as he went. I thought he was dead. Kent was probably dead, but I was puzzled by the relatively mild nature of the wound to his face and couldn't be sure. The Northern Frontier Regiment had never left a body for the enemy, and the disgrace of being the first to do so was not something I much wanted for myself. Besides, they could be alive and, I felt, we should go to almost any lengths to avoid leaving them to the *adoo*'s tender mercies.

It was now clear that the *adoo* were present in greater numbers than we had anticipated, and they had caught us on the hop, moving in daylight on ground which was not to our advantage. In effect, they had ambushed us. They now made a concerted effort to surround us. However, Viv Rowe had arrived on the high ground to our rear, saw what was happening and moved to prevent it. At the same time, he requested that Regimental Headquarters deploy part of his company, C Company, into the area to secure our line of withdrawal back to the Hornbeam Line, and this was duly done.

Furthermore, I had by this time been able to get through on another radio and call up aircraft. Three pairs of Strikemasters supported us that day, and the first pair led by Bob Mason returned for a second and third sortie. They used all their ordnance types; bombs, rockets and machine guns. On one occasion, I gave directions to one pilot who dropped a 500 lb ground burst bomb about 400 metres to the west of where I wanted it. In a hasty frightened moment, in my next orders to him, I mixed up east with west, and the following attack was on top of us. Fortunately he had no bombs or rockets left and he only machine gunned us. I had never been machine gunned from the air before, and it was rather disconcerting knowing that, however low one lay, one could not take cover from the fire. Sand and stones spurted up all around us but no one was hit; God alone knows why not. A moment or two later, the empty brass cartridges came clattering down amongst us. One landed on my back. On another occasion, an air burst bomb landed sufficiently close for Viv to call an emergency temporary stop to the air action. But the overall effect of the aircraft was to bring the tide of the battle back in our favour. We eventually started to win the firefight.

The situation was still somewhat confused, but with the help of the other platoon commanded by Said Murr, our *bedu* Company Sergeant

116

Major, we set about consolidating our position, making it as safe as we could and fighting off attempts by the *adoo* to encircle us. I had also by now managed to arrange supporting mortar fire on another radio. To begin with, I controlled all the supporting fire myself including the aircraft. I found this a very confusing task. I was trying to guide Johnny in to the best spot to reinforce me. I was also trying to direct and win the firefight with my own platoon and the neighbouring platoon under Said Murr. At the same time I was trying to direct mortars and aircraft. All this involved operating on several radio nets at once – some in Arabic and some in English. My grasp of what was going on was frankly tenuous and a sense of 'system overload' was not very far away. The *adoo* meanwhile were of course shooting at us with both single shots and machine-gun fire. I remembered Mike Austen's account of the battle where his company commander, Paul Wright, was killed by mortar fire. When would the first exploding mortar shell burst in amongst us? Great was my relief, therefore, when Viv Rowe, having thwarted the *adoo*'s attempt to surround us, took control of the mortars and aircraft from me. He thereafter coordinated all the fire support most effectively with great skill and calmness.

Corporal Wildman now told me that Kent had been carrying a new type of radio in his rucksack, and he had been told by his masters that he shouldn't let it fall into enemy hands. I was pretty sure both men were dead by now, but the imperative to try and recover the bodies was still there. However, the Strikemasters seemed to have stunned the enemy as well as us, and the encircling movements were stopped at about the same time as Johnny arrived with the rest of the company.

In a rather agitated manner, I started to explain to him what had happened, but he wasn't listening. Johnny was not a great breakfast man. From him I learned about the smoker's three course breakfast: a cigarette, a cup of coffee and a cough. He had had his coffee before the shooting had started and before he had left his previous position. His breakfast had been disturbed by the onset of this battle. He was now fumbling around inside his equipment looking for his fags. He had moved with his troops at great speed across the *jebel* for two kilometres and wasn't now going to be rushed. He eventually produced a crumpled packet of Rothmans and passed one to me. I took it and lit up with him and drew in very deeply. So we lay there, not speaking, while the enemy fire went over our heads, and smoked a cigarette. I knew then that things were going to be all right. Incidentally, if anyone tells you that a bullet whines or buzzes as it passes you, you may safely assume that they've never been shot at. It's a crack, not unlike the sound of a loud whiplash. And it always sounds very very close to your head, even though it may be a few feet away.

Johnny soon recovered his breath, we finished our Rothmans, and he had the third course of his breakfast.

Johnny then started to deploy his men and at last we got to a point where we could set about recovering the bodies and their kit. Johnny got together a party of four men, briefed them, waited until another air attack went in, and ran out to grab Kent. The four men who went with him ran round the body and ran back again, leaving the body behind and Johnny out there on his own. Notwithstanding the lethal circumstances, both Johnny and I immediately saw the macabre comic humour in this slapstick performance. You may wonder how we could ever think that this was funny. Someone once said that humour is the human's way of taking a sabbatical from reality. That was just what we needed then and somehow we both found it in these crazy, dangerous circumstances. Johnny looking at me, shook his head and smiled, then too ran back, and, ever patient, briefed them again and arranged another air strike through Viv. This time they succeeded in bringing Corporal Hamed in.

Prodded by the example of my company commander, I did the same thing with another group of four men and we brought in Trooper Kent, but while I was doing this, Johnny was also under fire, nipping about the open ground on his own picking up bits of kit, including the famous radio. The enemy eventually seemed to think that the fun had gone out of the game; their fire subsided and we were masters of the ground. But they were still willing to take on the helicopter which came to evacuate our dead and wounded. It was hit by several bullets as it cleared out of the area from a terrific burst of firing, even though a pair of Strikemasters was again providing top cover. Pilots and vital systems somehow escaped damage and it disappeared flying on an even keel and made it safely to Salalah. The whole battle had taken six hours, yet it had seemed to me to flash past in an hour or so.

Both our men were dead. Kent had not been shot in the head at all. The face wound was from the rear sight of the GPMG as he had slumped on top of it. He had been shot in the heart through the right side of his body. Doubtless he had been hit by an AK47 Kalashnikov with its short 7.62 mm round. An FN 7.62 mm would have gone right through him so I felt fortunate that it had not penetrated through to me lying on his left. The *adoo* had approached the bodies and cut off Kent's epaulettes, presumably under the impression that they had killed an officer. They usually went for three things: officers; radio antennas because they knew there would be officers near them; and machine guns. I was dirty, sun burnt, bearded and wearing a *shemaagh* on my head like my soldiers. The British Army, even the SAS, seemed to insist upon their men being clean, bright and wearing normal uniform. Not

118

only was Trooper Kent firing a machine-gun and carrying a radio, he was clean-shaven and fair of face. He was therefore the natural target.

Throughout the entire battle, I did not once set eyes on the human form of the *adoo*, although others did.

I don't really know how many enemy we were up against. Probably not very many to begin with, but certainly a good deal more than the half a dozen that we had come out to do battle with. I now know that the supply party had been through and the reception party had been reinforced by a number of men from that. Later, Johnny told me that half a dozen *adoo* had been about to walk into his killing ground when they had heard the shooting from my contact. At that moment, they had quickly disappeared in my direction. Johnny had started moving his half of the company towards mine as soon as he had heard the shooting, but he was a good two kilometres away. There is always a risk of overestimating the numbers of the enemy, but I guess maybe fifteen or twenty *adoo* eventually joined forces against us. It certainly seemed to me that every *adoo* within ten kilometres had heard the noise and had come over from the east to join in the fun.

At first sight this action was a Complete Military Fuck Up. It certainly felt like it at the time. For two men dead and two wounded, it seemed we had achieved nothing but to scare the pants off ourselves. I also felt we had been extremely lucky that I had not killed more of our own people through my misdirection of the air strike. We only escaped the ghastly consequences of my mistake because the pilot had run out of bombs and rockets, and I was not very proud of this, my second attempt at killing myself and my own people.

However, Johnny was more sanguine. He assured me that every soldier of any experience on the *jebel* had been involved in an 'own goal' or a 'blue-on-blue'. Not even the most experienced or well trained troops were immune from them, including the SAS. I have since discovered the truth of what he said. They certainly happened fairly regularly in Oman. Indeed the only mutiny that I was aware of took place as a result of a 'blue on blue'. It was most unfortunate that the commanders against whom the men had mutinied were not themselves responsible for the mistake.

Nor was this to be my last experience of own goals. In the Falklands War, my company and I were machine gunned by the Commando Logistics Regiment who thought they were shooting at low flying Argentinian aircraft. They may well have been shooting at aircraft, but they failed to appreciate that the aircraft were flying so low that we on the hill behind them were also in the line of fire. Later in that war, I also listened on my company radio to the aftermath of the incident

119

where one of our own patrols bumped the mortar section which was moving out to provide the patrol with mortar cover. Four of our own people were killed on that occasion.

Own goals are all too common and no soldier of any experience would deny it. War is the province of the knackered and the confused. It is therefore the province of the cock-up. Frightened, tired men under pressure are always going to make mistakes. Desperation is never very far away in battle and these things seem to happen very easily. Many years later, I heard this observation being made to a gathering which included a number of Second World War veterans. One of them stood up and said that he had landed on D Day, fought his way to the Elbe, and had been bombed by every air force *except* the Luftwaffe. *Plus ça change* ...

But on this occasion, subsequent intelligence slowly revealed that we had killed five of the enemy and wounded at least as many more: ten casualties out of a force of perhaps fifteen or twenty men. This cheered us up, and was a useful lesson that, however badly the battle may seem to be going for you, it is well to remember that it may actually be going worse for the other side. 'War is a clash of wills' said the great Prussian military theorist Clausewitz, and he wasn't wrong. You are not beat until you think you're beat. It is also very important to remember what the overall goal of any operation might be. We had made it more difficult for the *adoo* to resupply themselves through the Hornbeam Line, and that, after all, was what we were there for in the first place.

After we had returned to base, Johnny and I went round our soldiers and talked to them and debriefed them and put together our reports. How many *adoo* had they seen? Had they shot any? And so on. They were sorry about the dead and wounded but satisfied that all that could have been done was done. They were all soldiers after all.

Said Murr received the Sultan's Commendation, an equivalent to a Mention in Dispatches, for anchoring our position so reliably with his platoon. I was decorated with the Omani Distinguished Service Medal for Gallantry for my part in this action; a rough equivalent to the British Military Cross. Johnny, who had already been awarded the Sultan's Commendation in 1971, was decorated with the Bravery Medal. We assessed this medal as sitting alongside the British Distinguished Service Order.

I don't feel I was especially brave on this occasion. How does one measure bravery? I suppose one starts by looking at the difference between what you are naturally inclined to do, and what your sense of duty tells you you should do. Courage is what it costs you to cover the deficiency. I don't feel there was much of a gap to bridge in this case. In the heat of battle, the things I did, the things we all did, came naturally.

We were trained to do them. I gladly own that I was very proud to have won a medal, and that I wear it with great pride and pleasure. I know it gave my parents great pleasure too, particularly since they didn't know about it until after I had left the country and was safe. But the only man who knows the cost of the little coloured ribbon he wears on his chest is the man himself. This action didn't cost me much. However, that is only part of the story.

One month before, in February 1974, I had been on yet another night patrol out to the east of the Hornbeam Line above the Wadi Urzuq with my two platoons.

Troops on patrol in any type of country, when they stop for more than simply a short break, usually create some protection for themselves from surprise attack. The form this takes will depend on the ground. In temperate countries, they scratch out a depression in the ground or dig a trench. In Oman they built dry stone nest-like *sangars* with the abundance of stones that were always lying around. There were certain parts of the *jebel* which had been the scene of many operations and were now freckled with old *sangars*.

On this patrol there was a number of old *sangars* about. It was standard procedure never to go into these old *sangars*, because the *adoo* had a habit of placing mines and booby traps in them. Every soldier was taught never to use old *sangars*, however tempting it might be; always build a new one. But it had been a long march, and the temptation was too great for one of my men this night. I felt, rather than heard, the explosion some metres behind me. I knew instantly what had happened.

I arrived at the low-walled roofless *sangar* and I could hear a sound like a cow pishing as his lifeblood squirted away. He was groaning loudly and shouting for his mother in Arabic. In the dim moonlight, I could see the light reflected from his blood. We had to get him out, but how? One mine had gone off in this *sangar*. I did not know of any instances where the *adoo* had put two mines in a *sangar*. But then there were lots of things I didn't know. What I did know was that if I were trying to kill British officers, that is precisely what I would do. I had been in Northern Ireland and, even in the early 1970s, the IRA had been in the habit of conducting one incident in order to catch us out with a second. Were the wily *adoo* into setting up secondary incidents too?

No one seemed to be able to tell me by which route the soldier had entered. All sorts of horrible thoughts went through my head, but the man needed help desperately. Eventually I instinctively clutched my genitals – thereby probably ensuring that if I stepped on something I would lose my hands as well as my balls – and tiptoed into the *sangar*, knelt down, picked him up and walked out with him, undamaged.

His wounds were consistent with him having stepped on a Russian PMN anti-personnel mine – designed to maim but not to kill. Dead men are easy to deal with. You leave them until you are ready to bury them, or ship them out and get on with the battle meanwhile. Wounded men need other men to attend to them. Groaning, screaming wounded men can unnerve their comrades. This man had lost one leg from just below the knee. The other leg was wrecked, with his bloody bare foot flapping about like a half put-on sock. His genitals had gone and he had a sucking chest wound. The naked bone jutting out from his knee made a sickening grating sound on the rocks in the dark as Lal Bux the Baluchi, our excellent *campowda*, and I patched him up as best we could. It took us some time in the dark to find all his wounds.

I suppose one's sense of smell is accentuated in the dark in the same way as one's sense of hearing, and I remember smelling burnt explosives and blood. I wondered what sort of life lay in front of a man in Oman with such crippling injuries. It did occur to me to overdose him with morphine and give him a quick quiet death, but I didn't have the stomach for this; especially since I had done everything I could to try and save him.

It was not going to be a straightforward business getting him out. The moon had by now disappeared and a mist had settled down on our part of the *jebel*. I managed to get a message through to Headquarters with our grid reference, and a helicopter took off from Salalah. Soon I could hear his engine noise and the beat of his rotor blades. I established contact with him and gave him a reverse bearing of his noise so he could head towards us. He was also able to home in on our radio beacon. Then radio contact was lost. He went past us in the mist and went down about a thousand feet below and beyond us. I knew we were on top of a fairly precipitous cliff. I wasn't at all keen on heading in that direction. At last I heard him turn round and head back towards us – but below the cliff face. Balancing the risk of a helicopter crash against the possibility of there being *adoo* near enough to be able to do something to hurt us, I threw caution to the winds and pulled the tab on a couple of very bright long burning flares. I heard him come closer and rising. At last I saw the helicopter rotor blades in the light of our flares emerging out of the mist, nosing its way up the edge of the cliff at our feet like a man peering over a wall. He landed, lifted our man out and flew back to Salalah. The soldier died before he got to the hospital.

The helicopter, piloted by Dave Duncan, an ex-Royal Marine then on contract to the Sultan's Air Force disappeared and silence and darkness returned to the *jebel*. God knows, I needed a cigarette; but even though I had just illuminated half the *jebel* with my flares and ruined everyone's night vision for a fortnight, I refrained.

We rallied the patrol and carried on with the operation. Our troubles were not over, however. Tony Heslop found another soldier flicking stones off another old *sangar*. As he flicked each stone, he jumped away before it hit the ground believing he was thereby safe from booby traps. And yet another soldier went to sleep during one of the stops on the way home. His absence was not noticed, or reported, by his fellows until some two hours had passed, and so Tony and I had to mount a major effort to retrace our steps, find him and recover him. We each took a party to the two separate places that we thought he might be. Tony found him. He had only just woken up. He didn't seem unduly concerned when we turned up. His faith in our ability to save him was touching, although we thought it a little misplaced.

When I got back to base, I was exhausted and somewhat shocked. It was standing operating procedure not to use old *sangars*. Had we done enough to explain this to our people? The dead soldier had very newly joined the company from the Training Regiment. Had he been briefed, or had he slipped through the net? I talked it over with Tony Heslop and the Omani NCOs who had witnessed it all, and that helped. Tony had been a rock of support during the night; unflappable, dependable, tireless and willing. Talking about these things is never a bad idea, and the Omani soldiers, in their quiet undemonstrative way, were appreciative that I had tried to save him, and that made me feel a bit better.

Thirty years later Peter Isaacs told me a story that put a final piece in the jigsaw. Peter was serving with Frontier Force, the regiment which relieved us on the Hornbeam Line in October 1974. In May 1975, Peter went out east from the Line above the Wadi Urzuq with two ex-*adoo* who had recently come across to the Sultan's side. They said they knew where there were some mines and were anxious to claim the bounty given to those who brought them in. They took Peter to the *sangar* where our soldier had met his end. His foot and leg bones were still there, as were the covers of the field dressings Lal Bux and I had used to bandage him up. The two ex-*adoo* then went to a *sangar* nearby and lifted out two Russian PMN mines. So, the *adoo* did indeed put double mines in *sangars*. My fears of a secondary incident had not been misplaced.

These *adoo* also had a sense of humour. One of these men, unseen by Peter, removed the detonator from one of the mines and then, standing in front of Peter, pushed the pressure plate down with his hands. The mine triggered and the spring-loaded plunger, with no detonator to obstruct its progress, sprang out and hit Peter in the chest.

So I do wear my medal with pride, not so much for the hot-blooded widely observed battle of the Wadi Sha'ath, but for a very lonely moment on a dark, misty night, when I had to reach a long way down into my soul before I found enough to make me do my duty. It was a bad night and, when I think of my little piece of coloured cloth and tin, I think of the sound of a cow pishing, and a stricken, dying soldier calling for his mother.

At first light the following morning I found my clothes, my hands, my arms and my face were covered in the dried blood of this soldier. And I didn't even know his name.

Mines were rarely far from our minds. The *adoo* laid them and sometimes were very clever with them. On one occasion they evidently found a couple of mines that the Northern Frontier Regiment had laid during their 1972 tour on the *jebel* west of Ashawq. Assuming that one day we would either come and lay an ambush round them, or inspect them, or even come and lift them, they laid a pattern of their own mines to catch anyone who approached. This duly happened in October 1976, after the official end of the war. The Frontier Force mounted an operation against a group of *adoo* reported as still operating in the area. A Baluch soldier stepped on an *adoo* mine and lost his foot. But it didn't end there. Peter Isaacs eventually led a casualty evacuation operation to extract him. After the wounded soldier had been flown out, Peter inspected the mine crater and satisfied himself that the mine had indeed been a Russian one and not one of ours. Following his footsteps back to the large rock where the rest of the patrol was waiting he himself stepped on a mine just short of the rock. Peter lost a leg and an eye. After he in turn was evacuated, a specialist engineer team was flown in to clear the area thoroughly of mines. They found a further nine mines all placed round the rock to catch anybody who might take cover while ambushing or approaching the original Northern Frontier Regiment mines. One mine had indeed been stepped on but had failed to detonate.

We tried to avoid tracks that were used too often, and we tried to walk on hard ground, but both were impractical, especially at night. So they became just another risk we lived with.

We laid mines too. Apart from the conventional marked and recorded patterns associated with the wire of the Hornbeam Line, on one occasion we found a water hole and stitched it up with mines. Again we marked and recorded them. The conventional approaches, the approaches that might be used if one was trying to avoid mines, and the immediate environs of the waterhole itself: all were covered. The official doctrine of always observing one's mines and covering them with fire was impossible to follow here. But the waterhole was within hearing distance of one of the *jebel* positions, so we registered it with mortar or artillery fire too, the idea being that if one heard a mine going off, one would then stonk it with indirect fire, thereby turning mere hell into a ghastly screaming torment. We were not successful with our mines at the waterhole. Animals were probably the only casualties.

On one occasion we doctored a couple of hand grenades by removing the four second fuses and replacing them with gunpowder from our rifle ammunition. Then we left them lying around with other discarded kit where the *adoo* might find them, in the hope that they might suppose that a slovenly soldier had dropped them. It was surmised that any *adoo* who tried to throw them would be killed instantly – a pretty hare-brained idea on reflection. It was equally possible that our own soldiers, or their successors, might also pick them up, so when next in that direction we recovered and destroyed them.

Just as hare-brained, but less lethal, was the tinned cheese ploy. Which tracks were the *adoo* using? The rocks were usually so hard that we couldn't track them. So we came up with the wizard wheeze of leaving small tins of Army cheese around in the hope that the hungry *adoo* would pick them up. Who after all could resist a bite of Army processed cheese? Cheese gone? Aha! *adoo* must have been here.

Unsurprisingly, water was always a major consideration governing everything we – and the *adoo* – did. Our water was supplied to us by helicopter in *burmails*. It was estimated that by the time it had been transported up to us on the *jebel*, it had probably cost more than the equivalent volume of champagne. We would not even have preferred champagne under these circumstances, although perhaps a little chilled smackerel would not have gone amiss from time to time, or even a beer, or a drop of the Scottish amber liquid. But the only thing that satisfies your thirst when you are truly thirsty is water. Pure, undiluted water; chilled from a *chargul* or a goatskin, it was the very essence of Heaven.

We waste so much water in our every day lives in the West. I have never been able to have a bath, or see a wantonly running tap without a twinge of something approaching guilt ever since.

We also took pains to find places which the *adoo* might use to get water in their journeys through our area. Some of these were marked on the map, but the maps were so imprecise that they were only rough indicators. The Jebali tribesmen called *firqat* who worked with us told us about some water holes and we occasionally found others. The word 'waterhole' may give you the wrong impression. These were damp spots at the bottom of *wadis*, perhaps in a cave, from which if you were patient and lucky, you might be able to extract a few dribbles over an hour or so. They were of use to small animals, but the *adoo* too used them from time to time. However, mostly they resupplied before they got to our area. Nevertheless we made it as difficult as possible for them to use such water as there was near the Hornbeam Line.

We tried to work out the most likely tracks for the *adoo* to use on their long treks from the PDRY through our mountains to the central plains and, without restricting our own movements unduly, tried to catch them out with land mines. Occasionally we were successful.

One night a man went up on a mine laid by B Company on the slopes of the Wadi Jizalawt below my position. We didn't make any move to bury the body of this man, chiefly because we were afraid of our own mines. They had of course been recorded, but there was no knowing which other mines might still be there and perhaps had been moved by the explosion. It seemed imprudent to rescue an enemy corpse from a dangerous minefield at risk to oneself. Besides, the sight of his corpse might be a disincentive for others. So he became something of a tourist attraction for patrols operating in that area. Photographs were taken. Soon the foxes had a go at him. He had once been an individual with his own name. Now he was the disarranged detritus of a sudden and desperate action in the night. He was rubbish.

In luxury and safety after my return to UK, I reflected that I had in the past been surprised when I had seen pictures in books about the First World War where soldiers were to be seen filing past corpses of their enemies with apparent indifference. Now I understood.

During the battle, compassion for one's enemy can be fatal. After the battle, it is a central mark of one's humanity. The dividing line between the two has to be crossed at the appropriate – and often the most dangerous – moment, and this does not always come naturally, even when one is dealing with the living, let alone the dead.

In the Falklands, when we found some dead Argentinian soldiers whom we had killed while capturing the Two Sisters, we started digging a grave. We were in a hurry, and artillery fire was landing on our hill in a random and intermittent fashion, and we were disinclined to hang around too long in the open. The grave we dug was too small. My Marines wanted to break the legs of the corpses to make them fit the inadequate grave. I stopped them and, notwithstanding the sporadic artillery fire, we made the grave fit the corpses rather than the other way round.

The British sometimes have been very good at recognizing the individuality of the soldier, including the soldiers of their enemies. Even in graveyards such as Tyne Cot at Passchendaele near Ypres in Belgium, where thousands of soldiers of the First World War lie buried, there is a sense that each and every man has his own special place. Each person has his own gravestone – identical to thousands of others, maybe – but uniquely devoted to him so that other men, and God, might know him by his name. And if his name is unknown, then he is 'known unto God'. But he is always known unto somebody. This is not an automatic response and it sometimes has to be taught. In Oman, I discovered how easy it can be to lose sight of the individuality of other men and, it is with a certain unease that I reflect that I too had something to learn in this field. But at least in the Falklands, I was able to pass the lesson on.

After our company operation in the Wadi Sha'ath, it was decided to conduct a battalion operation in the same area to make the point that we dominated that area and that the *adoo*, if they felt that they could use it again with impunity, were mistaken. Silent night insertion on foot using donkeys to carry mortars, ammunition and water was achieved. Helicopters were ready to resupply us during the day. By dawn, about two hundred and fifty men were in positions spread across a wide area of *jebel* ready to take on anyone that dared poke his nose out. Nobody did, but it was a useful exercise and further complicated the job of the *adoo*, who could never be sure when and where we might appear. And if we did appear, he could be sure that if he attacked, he himself would probably be attacked by another group that he could not see.

As we returned to our hilltop bases after this operation, we heard that Nick Knollys on Ashawq was being hit by Katyushas yet again. The Strikemaster/Katyusha trap was sprung and artillery and jets were quickly called in to respond. They were being directed by Angus Ramsay from Killi which was not under fire. The setting sun and the usual indistinct lines on the horizon made it very difficult to gauge the range from which the weapons were being fired. However, Viv Rowe, who happened to be withdrawing into Kumasi with Bryan Ray our Commanding Officer, being about a thousand feet higher and off to an angle, had a grandstand view and could see the smoke from the firing point ten kilometres away. They quickly guided the jets on to the target, and three kills were achieved and later confirmed by Radio Aden.

Radio Aden was usually a fairly reliable source of information on *adoo* casualties, presumably because it was information that the PDRY authorities couldn't hide from the families of the dead *adoo*. On the other hand, the claims they made about the death and destruction they were inflicting on us were gloriously nonsensical. On one occasion they announced that they had blown up and killed 250 soldiers garrisoning Ashawq, together with their British commander. The thirty or so live soldiers who garrisoned Ashawq, and their very alive British commander, found this highly entertaining.

127

I learned many things from these actions east of the Hornbeam Line. I learned why men fight. Queen, Sultan and Country, a sense of duty, glory, money, religion, ideology, family, a sense of adventure; these and many other motivators may play their parts in getting a man through the gates of the training establishment and to the battlefield. But for most men, none of these will sustain him in moments of extremis and impel him to fight to the threshold and beyond. The real reason is very simple. A man fights for the respect of his friends. He doesn't want to be seen to be the weak link. He doesn't want to let his friends down. This applies to all soldiers mercenary or regular, whatever their motive for becoming soldiers may have been. This need for self-respect in the individual is the glue which holds together all men in adversity. Throughout the Wadi Sha'ath action, I was very conscious that others depended on me and were looking to me to lead and guide them. I did not want to be shown up. Johnny had taken his group of four men to bring in the first body. There was still a body out there. How could I let him do it again? I had to go for the second one. The same applied to the soldier in the mined *sangar*. If I had not done something to get him out, how could I have looked my men in the face ever again? How could I have lived with myself?

I have since spoken at length to many warriors with much more experience than me, and none have demurred from this view. Most fighting soldiers will risk even death to avoid losing the good opinion of their fellows.

I learned too what Churchill meant when he said something to the effect that the most exhilarating feeling a man can have is to be shot at and missed. The surge of elation and gratitude was almost over-whelming. This exhilaration is often directly proportional to the level of anxiety felt before the battle, and can be very great indeed.

I also found that everything that David Nicholls and Simon Hill had told me about the difficulties of locating the enemy and directing and controlling fire had turned out to be true. I learned how constrained a patrol becomes as soon as it starts to take casualties. In a conventional set piece battle, the casualties are left for others behind the immediate front line to deal with, or to be treated and evacuated after the battle. In the heat of the moment, they do not, or should not, directly affect the action, except in the sense that your numbers are reduced in line with the casualties you receive. It could even be that the other side takes your wounded as prisoners and, although there have been some notable exceptions, one might expect one's wounded to be reasonably treated by a civilised conventional enemy. We had no reason to suppose that the *adoo* would mistreat unduly any soldiers of ours that they captured, but given their brutal treatment of those who stood

128

up against them, we could never be sure. Indeed towards the end of the war, they did kill in cold blood some men they had captured. Furthermore, if they thought that they could make any propaganda mileage out of captured soldiers, wounded or otherwise, no doubt they would do so. So far as we were concerned, leaving people behind in *adoo* territory was not an option. Omani soldiers were also keen not to leave a body to the infidel *adoo*. It was most important to get the corpse out and give it an Islamic funeral, ideally before sunset on the day of death.

So, on patrols such as ours, regardless of your fine, square-chinned, forward-leaning intentions of taking the fight to the *adoo* and dominating the ground, as soon as you take your first casualty, the game changes. The first priority becomes the protection and evacuation of your casualties. Any other approach would quickly deplete the morale of your men, and probably invite mutiny. One dead man takes four fit men to carry him any distance over rough ground. A walking wounded man will need help to carry his kit – yet another man who is not immediately ready to fight. Non-walking wounded buy up even more men: four or six to carry each one. Thus your fighting power and mobility become exponentially reduced for each casualty you have to protect and move. In this way, a well-founded, strong, aggressive fighting patrol can very quickly become a crippled, vulnerable bunch of men fighting for their lives.

I had learned this truth the hard way. Our friends in B Company operating across the Jizalawt out to the west were soon to have it thrust in their faces too.

Chapter Eight

The Action: West of the Line

B Company, commanded by Angus Ramsay, also conducted many operations out of their positions to dominate the *jebel* and make life difficult for the *adoo*. The nature of the ground meant that they tended to go west while we in A Company went east. The enemy to the west had had a more or less free run of the *jebel* up to the Hornbeam Line and were nearer to their supply bases in the PDRY. B Company also had to consider how they could limit the freedom of the *adoo* to hit Ashawq with indirect fire. Ashawq could be seen jutting above the surrounding plateau for miles in all directions. From the west, the setting sun lit up the crag, battered white by constant bombardment, so that it stuck out like a stubborn bollard, complete with its 'up yours' Omani flag, dominating the *adoo*'s route to Salalah.

The usual enemy routine was to lie up and observe until the daily resupply helicopters had returned to Salalah, and then in the evening, fire about twenty mortar bombs without interference or observation from the air. Our return fire, be it from mortars, guns or aircraft, was always hindered by our need to squint west into the setting sun and the time it took to get aircraft over the target. By the time we were able to react effectively there was often very little daylight left.

In some ways the *adoo* were, however, creatures of habit who liked to use exactly the same mortar base plate position each time. This helped them to get the most lethal first round on target – but it made them predictable and vulnerable. Without water nearby, they could not stay in strength on the *jebel*, and B Company, like A Company, began to patrol at night with increasing vigour against them. In the moonlight, enemy mortar base plate positions were found and mined, sometimes with success, and the *adoo* began a steady retreat to the west. In time they ceased to shell Killi, and concentrated their fire on Ashawq.

130

The enemy supply route along the ridgeline was narrow and predictable, so B Company patrols reached ever further west to mine the approach tracks. The *adoo*'s response was to stop using the Russian 82 mm mortar with a range of three and a half kilometres in favour of the Chinese 75 mm recoilless anti-tank gun, which fired a low-trajectory shell nearly seven and a half kilometres – and finally they deployed their most frightening weapon, their Katyushas.

B Company continued to play cat-and-mouse games on moonlit night patrols, seeking and mining the *adoo* routes and firing positions. This also deterred *adoo* attempts to cross the Hornbeam Line, but it became an increasingly dodgy business, with B Company patrols operating so far to the west that they reached the extreme range of the all-important protecting Oman Artillery batteries at Mughsayl or Kumasi.

Technically, the Kumasi 25 pounders could not reach the western end of the Ashawq ridgeline – even at maximum charge, which was rarely used because it wore out our old guns. But Kumasi was a thousand feet above the Ashawq plateau, and a 25 pounder 'firing downhill' could gain at least an extra mile of range in the hands of skilled and experienced gunners. The guns at Mughsayl were closer, but firing uphill from sea level, they were limited to targets on the southern side of the crest of the Ashawq ridge. B Company sometimes backpacked its mortars west from Killi to provide extra fire support, but this was logistically slow and cumbersome.

The balance of advantage changed for the worse once the monsoon arrived in June, as visibility in the *khareef* was usually little more than twenty-five metres. This took the edge off a number of advantages that we enjoyed over the *adoo*. Air support from the much trusted Strikemasters could rarely be given, and long-range artillery engagements could be carried out only in fleeting moments when the cloud broke. Water collected in rock pools and vegetation suddenly began to flourish. The effect was to favour the *adoo*, who could now sustain themselves much longer on the *jebel*. They could move forward to the Hornbeam Line unobserved by day, which permitted mine-spotting, and their rapid-firing Kalashnikovs were far better at close quarters than our heavy single-shot FN rifles.

Patrolling had to continue, however, if the Northern Frontier Regiment was to maintain its grip on the Hornbeam Line – so clashes between patrols were inevitable. B Company's most serious such contact occurred in mid June 1974, in thick fog about five miles along the ridgeline west of Ashawq. It was fought partly in the dark, over and in a minefield.

131

In early June, Angus Ramsay had laid by moonlight a cluster of jumping mines and smaller anti-personnel mines at a narrow track junction. Mines laid at night were more easily spotted by the *adoo* by day and, one morning, the enemy attempted to lift them. In the process they set a mine off and the noise of the explosion was heard by sentries at Ashawq. Angus Ramsay passed a fire mission to the Mughsayl and Kumasi artillery, who immediately put down harassing fire on the area.

Information came through Regimental Headquarters that two *adoo* had been wounded, and a rapid follow-up might catch the enemy in disarray. Accordingly Angus gathered together a thirty-man fighting patrol, which included Charlie Daniel, and his senior Omani officer, the very experienced and courageous Lieutenant Salim Said. There was too little moon expected that night to work effectively in the minefield, so the B Company patrol set out from Ashawq in mid afternoon to make the most of the remaining daylight, trusting to the low *khareef* to shield them from view. They moved west steadily and without incident for two hours, reaching the little minefield just before last light. There was no one there, but the minefield had been disturbed, and a long piece of rope lay discarded on the ground. It seemed possible that enemy survivors may have been dragged off the ridgeline into small nearby wadis.

Lieutenant Salim Said arranged the patrol in the usual all-round defence, with a four-man picket or group on top of each of four surrounding low hills. Angus Ramsay and a small escort set off to look at the head of a *wadi* running down to the north, while Charlie Daniel and Staff Sergeant Ali Salim looked at the south. Visibility was grey and patchy in the low cloud and half-light.

Angus found nothing in the north, but as he was returning to the ridgeline, he heard a burst of firing from the south, where Charlie Daniel had encountered a group of about seven *adoo* at close quarters moving up the *wadi* towards him. This was just the sort of very close combat where the *adoo*'s light equipment, fast-firing assault weapons, initiative, and superb knowledge of the area gave them a marked advantage. Charlie and Ali Salim whirled and ran back up the *wadi* to the B Company patrol perimeter, with six men and one woman in hot pursuit.

Angus and Corporal Mohammed Sarhan ran down to meet them, threw themselves into firing positions, and engaged the onrushing *adoo*. Angus was carrying his preferred weapon, a captured Kalashnikov, and fired a long burst at the leading enemy soldiers, one of whom dropped. The remainder separated and ran like stags up the hill, jinking between the rocks and boulders. Charlie Daniel, Ali Salim, Mohammed

132

Sarhan and Angus Ramsay continued to fire at them, but they were breathless after running hard and the light was poor. The enemy gained the top of a small hill and began to return accurate fire. Ali Salim crouched motionless, pinned down behind a small boulder, quietly indicating enemy positions to Charlie Daniel who was in a better place to return fire, while Kalashnikov bullets splashed onto the rock in front of him.

Three more men appeared on top of a nearby hill to the south-east and began to shoot down into the *wadi* where the patrol headquarters was pinned down. This was a very nasty surprise as this hilltop had been occupied by one of the B Company four-man pickets and, for several moments, Angus could not believe that this new group were not B Company soldiers. In fact the four-man group from B Company had pulled back into dead ground when they saw the enemy coming, leaving the patrol headquarters dangerously exposed. One of the newcomers on the hill shot Corporal Mohammed Sarhan in the head, and another soldier was shot through the hand.

Finally accepting that the three men dimly seen on the nearby hilltop were enemy, Angus switched fire to engage them. There was very little cover and he hugged the ground so closely that his first four rounds hit the ground uselessly ten metres in front of him, but then, raising himself slightly, he shot the centre enemy in the stomach. Still not quite sure that he had not in fact killed one of his own men, Angus stopped firing, but Ali Salim and Charlie Daniel continued the firefight and the remaining enemy were hit or forced to run for cover.

There was a lull in the battle, and Charlie and Angus crawled over to Corporal Mohammed Sarhan, whose body was jerking intermittently – but he had suffered a mortal shot through the forehead and nothing could be done for him. Lieutenant Salim Said and two soldiers ran down the *wadi* and began to make arrangements to carry the body.

Salim suggested urgently to Angus that some artillery support might be helpful so he ran back up the *wadi* to the crest where his signaller, Private Abdul Rahim, was trying to make contact with base. As ever at night, and especially in the *khareef* fog, the radio was emitting a series of garbled squeals and a cacophonous blurred mush. Cursing it in the growing darkness, Angus muttered 'Come on, come on, come on!' until he realized the effect that his obvious frustration was having on the nearby soldiers, who were looking at him in alarm. '*Maa shay mushkila!*' – 'No problem' – he said to them with a forced smile; but there was indeed a serious and unforeseen problem.

Weak but workable communications were eventually established with the gun position officer at Kumasi, and Angus passed him the coordinates for a fire mission. 'Out of range', came the prompt answer.

Angus checked his map and verified the grid before passing the same mission. 'Negative, negative – you are out of range', came the answer again. This was impossible. The nearby minefield had been registered days earlier with the Kumasi gun troop, so Angus ordered the guns to fire on that. There was a further delay, the radio again began to wail uselessly, and the distant guns remained silent.

Unknown to Angus and Charlie, the Gun Position Officer at Kumasi had gone on leave two days earlier and had handed over to a Royal Artillery Warrant Officer, very newly arrived in Dhofar, and quite unfamiliar with what the guns at Kumasi could reach.

Suddenly more small-arms fire came from a new position in the west, where a fresh group of enemy had moved on to higher ground, and a B Company soldier was shot through the leg. Sergeant Saif Salim took the small man-portable mortar and, firing at a range far too close for accuracy, nevertheless managed to force the *adoo* to take cover.

It was clear that the patrol couldn't stay there. So Angus asked Charlie to withdraw the rear four-man pickets, the wounded and Corporal Sarhan's body, and set up a new position further to the east towards base. Groups of soldiers began struggling eastwards with the dead and wounded and their equipment, skirting the minefield and shuffling heavily-laden along the ridgeline, while Staff Sergeant Imam Bux and his western picket engaged the ridge line to the south west.

Then came several thunderous explosions – but it wasn't the longed-for artillery. The *adoo* had brought an RPG 7 rocket launcher onto the western ridgeline and fired several rockets into the *wadi* head where patrol headquarters had been minutes earlier. One of the B Company machine gunners was shot through the shoulder. Staff Sergeant Imam Bux seized the machine-gun and hose-piped fire onto the rocket firing position – but his tactical position was weak as the enemy could look down on him, and he began to withdraw his men, dashing in fifty-metre sprints back from rock to rock.

Things were going badly for the B Company patrol, which now had four wounded men and a dead body to carry. Arithmetic was beginning to count against them. They had started with thirty men. The five casualties each needed at least one person to help them. It would take four men to carry Mohammed Sarhan's body. The *adoo* were increasing in number and operating on their home ground. The *khareef* was thickening, the light was nearly gone, and the *adoo* seemed to be closing in. 'I think they may assault us' said Lieutenant Salim Said grimly to Charlie Daniel, as they struggled east towards a new position on a feature known as Land Rover Hill, so named because it was the furthest point a Land Rover could reach from Ashawq. Staff Sergeant Imam Bux was helping his wounded gunner, and his men were still keeping the enemy's heads down, but more *adoo* seemed to be arriving along the western hilltop.

Thirty metres behind them, Signaller Rahim Bux at last managed to contact the gun troop at Mughsayl. B Company headquarters at Ashawq and Viv Rowe at C Company headquarters on Reef helped to relay fire missions between Angus and the artillery. The first 25 pounder shell crumped down to the west behind the enemy, and communications held well enough for artillery corrections. 'Direction west, drop 200, two rounds fire for effect' shouted Angus into the handset – and the *adoo* heard him. Very accurate small arms fire immediately came down on the spot where he and his signaller, Abdul Rahim, were crouching. Abdul Rahim went down with a bullet through the face. As the artillery salvo smashed across the hilltop, Angus crawled to him and shook him '*Kayf a haal?*' – 'How are you?' he muttered urgently. '*Maa zayn*' – 'not so good' – moaned Abdul Rahim through a mouthful of blood from a shattered jaw.

Angus took the radio from him, but could not carry Abdul Rahim as well and he didn't know how badly he was hurt, so they crouched behind a rock. Angus whispered more artillery corrections to the Mughsayl guns, which began to zero in accurately and very close along the enemy ridgeline. He did not dare fire as he knew the muzzle flashes from his Kalashnikov would give away their position, so in desperation he considered bringing down the Mughsayl artillery on his own position where he and Abdul Rahim cowered together between the rocks.

They didn't realize it at the time, but at this darkest moment the tide of battle had already begun to swing in B Company's favour. Details of the action began to spread to Regimental Headquarters and Headquarters Dhofar Brigade. On the artillery radio net, the Oman Artillery Battery Commander got in touch with Kumasi from Mughsayl, and directed the Kumasi guns to join in, firing at the rear of the enemy position to deter reinforcements. Every off-duty gunner at Mughsayl ran to help the gun troop to load and fire with redoubled speed. Twenty miles to the east, at Salalah airfield, an RAF crew comprising Dick Forsythe and Brian Mansfield and John Mayes sprinted to the duty Wessex helicopter, which lumbered into the air to follow the white line of the coastal surf west to the lights at Mughsayl. There they waited circling to the east of Ashawq, holding until they were called into to land in the mountains. Back at Ashawq, the formidable Company Sergeant Major Ali loaded B Company's ancient but serviceable Land Rover with men and ammunition and roared off west cross-country to join the patrol. The track was barely passable for a vehicle, it was dark and he had no driving licence, but no one was checking.

135

Campowda Rasul Bux sprinted back to help Angus with Abdul Rahim, and the three of them dodged from cover to cover while repeated artillery salvos kept the *adoo*'s heads down. Joining up with Staff Sergeant Imam Bux, they broke contact with the *adoo* and moved east to join the rest of the patrol on Land Rover Hill.

Angus and two machine gunners brought up the rear while the rest of the group helped the wounded. Angus was much afraid that the enemy would pursue them along the ridgeline, so he and the machine gunners moved back in short bounds from ambush position to ambush position, correcting the artillery fire eastwards as they ran. It was an exhausting and nerve-wracking procession, with moves timed in between incoming artillery salvoes. The time of flight for a shell fired from Mughsayl was nearly half a minute – which meant a fifteen second dash in the dark to find whatever cover was available, and a cringing moment as the shells whistled in. The Mughsayl guns were handled with great expertise, but they were old and accurate only to 200 metres. But the screen worked – or perhaps it was unnecessary – for the *adoo* did not follow up. They might well have been deterred by the shells, or they might have been caring for their own dead and wounded.

On Land Rover Hill, Lieutenant Salim Said arranged the patrol in a tight defensive perimeter while Charlie Daniel gathered the body of Corporal Mohammed Sarhan and the six wounded – except for Abdul Rahim who had a *shemaagh* bound around his mutilated face and insisted on walking and carrying his rifle. From the east came a crashing grinding roaring, as Sergeant Major Ali hurled his battered old Land Rover (a vehicle rejoicing in the name of *Hamdi al Gammal* – Hamdi the Camel) along the ridgeline, and soon he and his men arrived to distribute fresh ammunition and strengthen the defence.

The *adoo* would have heard him coming, and were probably deterred even more by this evidence of reinforcements. Charlie called for the helicopter, which started its westwards descent from 500 feet above Ashawq, flying by stopwatch and the seat of the pilots' pants towards the patrol. Soon, Charlie heard it and sent a back-bearing, although communications being what they were, the pilots never heard him. Nevertheless, they started their cautious and courageous descent down into the black fog.

Angus and the machine gunners reached the rendezvous. They did not know where the nearest enemy might be, so Charlie at first dared only use torch lights to indicate the emergency landing site on the top of the hill. The pilots saw one of these but they lost sight of it at the critical moment and had to abort and try again. This time Charlie turned on the Land Rover sidelights. At the last moment on the second approach, Forsythe in the Wessex saw them and in a cloud of driven sand he successfully achieved an almost blind night landing. The moment he was firm on the ground, the lights went off and the dead and wounded were rushed into the cabin. Within three minutes, Forsythe, Mansfield and Mayes were gone, clawing upwards to the clear night sky above the *khareef* and, twenty-five minutes later, the six wounded soldiers were on the operating table of the superb British Field Surgical Team in Salalah. Freed of the burden of carrying casualties, the rest of the patrol returned to Ashawq in good order.

The following day, Nick Knollys went up in the left hand seat of a Strikemaster in the hope that the *adoo*, perhaps with casualties to carry, might not have moved very far from the scene of the action. But the rocky, stony valleys offered plenty of cover and protection and they saw nothing.

Later information indicated that the *adoo*'s casualties were one dead and three injured, so arguably they came off best in this encounter – but their domination of the western heights was shaken. This contact, which was illustrative of so many aspects of patrolling and fighting on the *jebel* in the mist, in the dark, with lousy radios, driven by the imperative of taking your casualties with you, nevertheless yet again constrained the *adoo*'s freedom of action west of the Hornbeam Line. It further increased their difficulties in breaching the Line in substantial numbers, which is what they would have to do if they wished to continue the war with any prospect of success.

B Company's wounded undoubtedly received the better treatment. With a 'bang-to-slab' time as short as two hours, the five wounded soldiers subsequently made a good recovery and, although one was invalided out of the Regiment, he was retained as a storeman. After lengthy surgery to repair his face, the brave signaller Abdul Rahim was later selected for officer training, and sent to the Royal Military Academy at Sandhurst before being commissioned a year later into the Northern Frontier Regiment. One of his Sandhurst instructors took an especially keen interest in him: it was Angus Ramsay.

I was on Kumasi during this contact. Viv Rowe was on Reef and Johnny was on Bole. We knew B Company had gone on patrol to the west, but it wasn't until we heard the artillery fire that we knew that there had been a contact. As the night came on, so radio communications became more and more difficult. I could hear Regimental Headquarters. I could hear the artillery radios, and I could hear B Company headquarters. I could hear the Wessex helicopter flying on hold waiting to be called in by Charlie. Very occasionally I could hear fragments coming from Angus and his patrol. Viv on the other hand could hear just enough to assist with relaying the fire control orders to the artillery. He de-conflicted the Kumasi battery from the one firing from Mughsayl, and from Angus's fragmentary transmissions and from the map, he moved the fire on the ground eastwards behind Angus. On more than one occasion, Regimental Headquarters, in its entirely natural wish to know what was going on, blocked out Angus's fragile transmissions. Viv spoke very forthrightly to them to shut them up while he tried desperately to hear what Angus was saying. Yet again, just as it was in the Wadi Sha'ath, Viv's cool professionalism was a shaft of light penetrating the fog of war.

Johnny told me to get myself and a party of men ready to stand by in case there was an opportunity to fly in reinforcements, in the same way that C Company had reinforced me in the Wadi Sha'ath. I knew only too well the process that Angus, Charlie and Salim were enduring as they became progressively more and more encumbered with each casualty they sustained.

It wasn't until well into the night that we ceased to be deeply anxious for our friends on the other side of the Jizalawt.

Salim Said, Imam Bux and Charlie Daniel were all decorated with the Omani Distinguished Service Medal for Gallantry. Private Abdul Rahim with the shattered face was awarded the Sultan's Commendation. For this action, and for eight months consistently valuable service in the air, Dick Forsythe received the Omani Distinguished Service Medal, and Brian Mansfield and John Mayes the Sultan's Commendation. Angus Ramsay received the Bravery Medal, the Omani equivalent of the Distinguished Service Order, for this action, and for his leadership of B Company over ten dangerous but highly successful months on the Hornbeam Line. Twenty years later, he was decorated with his second Distinguished Service Order, this time the British one, for his outstanding service in the Balkans as a brigadier.

At least one woman was involved in this contact. It was something of a surprise to find that women were fighting on the *jebel*, but I suppose it shouldn't have been. While Oman was indeed a Muslim country, and the position of women was limited and clearly defined, Ibadhism, the principle Muslim sect in Oman, allowed more leeway for women than in many other Muslim societies. And the Dhofaris were a little less assiduous in observing the conventions governing the female sex. In any case, the *adoo* was inspired by Communism which was anathema to Islam, and it would be only natural that women should take their place in the struggle for the liberation of the masses.

Another woman fighter had been killed by C Company in the eastern area of the *jebel* the year before. She was a member of an *adoo* group which had counter-attacked an ambush. She had been the sister of one *adoo* group leader and the wife of another. In the case of this woman, the two *adoo* groups – the Firqat Stalin and the Firqat Lenin – combined to conduct a revenge attack a couple of weeks later. It was an intense engagement with the *adoo* using a variety of mortars, but C Company took no casualties – although Viv Rowe took a piece of shrapnel through his hat directly above his forehead.

Chapter Nine

The Action:
South of the Line and at Sea

A Company manned the northern part of the line and tended to operate to the east. B Company was in the middle and operated to the west. Meanwhile, C Company, commanded by Viv Rowe with Mike Bourne and Chris Barnes and, later, with Said Nasser as his second-in-command, manned a complex of hills in the south around the Wadi Ashawq and Wadi Afal, including a peak named Whale, and a double peak called Pipe, and protected the Regimental Headquarters at Mughsayl. As a backstop, he also had troops at Adawnib ten kilometres to the east.

It can be easily understood that the wish to destroy the *adoo*'s mortar and Katyusha firing positions was something of a preoccupation, and some pretty imaginative operations were conceived and mounted to try and put them off their game. Viv Rowe was in the vanguard of this movement. Viv took over his positions from Iranian troops and, from what he could gather at his handover, they had been mortared on a regular basis. As has already been noted, the *adoo* could be creatures of habit, and Viv decided to see if there was any discernible pattern to the *adoo* attacks. It seemed that there was an interval of ten to fifteen days between them. Then on 7 December 1973, and fourteen days later on 21 December, there were two more attacks. Crater examination and terrain analysis indicated a mortar location over a thousand feet up on the cliffs across the Wadi Afal, and so an area ambush was planned for two weeks after the latest attack. Considerable coordination and negotiation were necessary to release enough troops from static tasks, and to ensure that the guns, aircraft and Jebali guides were all teed up. The armed dhow of the Sultan's Navy also had a part to play by covering any *adoo* movement that might be seen from the sea.

The devil is in the detail, even for relatively small operations such as this, and some important factors shaped the way it was conducted. The soldiers could only carry sufficient water for forty-eight hours. Resupply in position might compromise the ambush, so Viv had to choose carefully during which period of forty-eight hours he wanted to be *in situ*. He felt that it would be better to go late in the cycle rather than early. If they went too early, and they preceded the next attack, their tracks would compromise the possibility of doing a rerun. On the other hand, if they were too late, they could re-plan the operation with the additional intelligence gathered from the latest attack. He also had to take into account that the Jebali guides, the Firqat, insisted on being back in Mughsayl for a religious festival on the night of 4 January.

On the night of 2 January, four groups of C Company moved into position on the Afal Jebel overlooking the likely enemy mortar base plate position, accompanied by Tony Smith, an artillery forward observation officer. Not much happened on the first day, except that some heavy machine-gun ammunition was found in a cave. One armed man was seen briefly. Early on the second day some camels with carrying gear were seen, and more *adoo* appeared, apparently a reconnaissance party scouting out the area for the arrival of the mortar. In anticipation of the arrival of the main body and the mortar, Viv got the Strikemasters airborne ready for an immediate attack. Meanwhile the adoo lead scout came forward at one point to within twenty metres of Viv's position and continued to scan the area through his binoculars. After almost two hours, he withdrew and fired a shot in the air, an 'all clear' signal, at which seven more *adoo* emerged from a cave over one kilometre to the west and outside the ambush area. Through the afternoon, small groups of *adoo* appeared in different locations, but no mortar. Eventually as light was beginning to fail, knowing he would have to withdraw that night, Viv called in the strike on the largest group, assuming it would be most likely to have the mortar. After the air strike, C Company went forward to search the area and in the course of the night, found a cave with a warm meal for four people. Another cave contained twenty four mortar shells and an unarmed mine. Within the ambush area, another group found the well-used firing position of the *adoo* mortar. Throughout the searches and subsequent withdrawal, the dhow engaged potential target areas to confuse the *adoo*. All the evidence pointed to the intention of the mortar being brought up and fired the following day. The mortar itself was not found, but there were no more mortar attacks on C Company for the rest of their time at the southern end of the Hornbeam Line.

I listened to the progress of this operation on the radio. It was more exciting than any normal radio drama could be, and we shared

C Company's sense of anti-climax when it didn't quite come off as we had all hoped. But again, it all helped to unbalance the *adoo* and to discourage their attempts to break through our line.

While on this operation, Viv had noticed that the hill that he was on had been registered as a target by an *adoo* mortar. Again, from examination of craters and the tail fins that he found, he worked out the probable location of the firing position further to the west. The lie of the land seemed to protect the firing position from our artillery which would in any case have been firing at maximum range, and air strikes usually needed an observer on the ground. The *adoo* by now were pretty wary of ambushes in that area so any attempt at setting up an observation post in the vicinity would have been likely to be discovered, and another operation like the one he had just conducted was not going to be a runner.

Meanwhile, Gordon Gillies, the captain of the armed dhow, had been conducting his own research and had identified a small rocky outcrop in the sea about eight hundred metres offshore and about three kilometres west of the original ambush which might offer excellent views of the coastline. Viv and he got together and did a reconnaissance. The rock was tiny, about ten metres across, but was not covered at high tide. Could Viv possibly set up a covert observation post on this pimple? He was determined to try.

A small amphibious operation was devised whereby an observation post of two men would be put ashore from the dhow at night by silent rubber craft. They would stay on this tiny island for several days in the hope that they might spot *adoo* activity on the coast: the movement of a camel train, a mortar firebase, or perhaps a camp. Aircraft, and artillery if in range, would be used to strike anything observed, and the *adoo*'s freedom of action in this important area would be further constrained.

Our Commanding Officer, Bryan Ray, while recognising the inspired nature of this plan, saw that the risks were considerable. Amphibious insertion on a black night by rubber boat onto a sharp small rocky outcrop close by enemy country, allowed plenty of room for Murphy's Law to exert its dismal authority. Extraction would be no less fraught with imponderables. The outcrop offered little cover from the sun let alone enemy view and, should the observation party be seen, then their chances of survival would not be good. Emergency extraction, possibly under fire, would be near impossible. Extraction was weather dependent. Everything depended on the observation post not being discovered. The Commanding Officer resisted Viv's requests for some time. It was simply too dangerous.

But Viv persisted. This operation depended on good weather. It was now February. If it was ever going to go ahead, it would have to be done before the monsoon rollers appeared at the end of May.

Viv's plan envisaged Gordon Gillies and his pocket battleship standing offshore out of sight in support throughout. If the *adoo* twigged what was happening, they would be unlikely to be able to rustle up a boat with the capacity and speed to assault the rock before Gordon Gillies might be able to intervene. If there was to be a naval battle, Gordon was well placed to win it. So the *adoo* would probably mortar or machine gun the island. By day, this would force them to expose themselves to Strikemaster attack. Viv would brief the Strikemaster pilots fully on all aspects of the operation beforehand. By night, our artillery and the dhow could provide harassing fire, and extraction by night might be a possibility; just. As part of the strike direction procedure, the observer usually gives the pilot or the guns the direction – the bearing – between him and the target. To counter the possibility that his radio transmissions might be picked up by the *adoo*, Viv devised and agreed a code with the guns and the aircraft. The bearings that he would give would be a hundred and eighty degrees out, thus giving the impression that the observer was on land. Viv also planned to have part of C Company under command of Said Nasser, his second-in-command, in an observation position for two days roughly where they had been on the ambush operation. This too would constrain *adoo* counter movements if it came to that. Eventually Bryan Ray agreed that the operation could go ahead.

The first two attempts at landing Viv and an artillery officer, Tony Smith, were aborted because the swell was too great. The rock was surrounded by jagged smaller rocks which were potentially lethal for the small rubber boat. Nick Knollys and I joined Gordon Gillies in his battleship for the third attempt.

This time Viv was accompanied by Chris Barnes. They were inserted in millpond conditions in the rubber boat on the night of 28 February. The idea was to stay initially for three days, but they took supplies for a couple more in case resupply became difficult. The island was tiny and they felt very exposed. It was also covered in seabird dung – guano – and there was no way to avoid lying in it. Although it was a good observation point, the two men could not move a finger for risk of being seen.

On the first day they saw nothing and were thoroughly baked by the sun. They later found a small niche, just above sea level but facing the *adoo*, which they could squeeze into for some shade. However, to use it, they had to occupy it from before dawn until after dark. On the second day they saw four *adoo* with donkeys. On the second night, there was a considerable swell and Viv and Chris, although not in danger of being washed away, were frequently covered in spray. It would have been impossible to extract them or to resupply them under these conditions. Should the swell continue for several days, they might find themselves running short of supplies. Food, and especially water were important. But most critical of all were fresh radio batteries. Without decent communications, the whole operation would be a pointless, risky waste of time. They were not short of supplies but it seemed prudent to prepare for the possibility that they might not be resupplied or extracted for some days longer, so they asked for a resupply, if conditions permitted, on the third night. After three nights and two days close confinement, Chris felt that conversation was beginning to run a little dry too, so he asked for some reading material to be included in the resupply to relieve the tedium. That night conditions improved. The rubber boat sneaked in and dropped off the supplies, together with a damp copy of *Fisherman's Weekly*.

On the third day the two men had seen nothing and it was agreed they should stay for a fourth day. On the fourth day, there was considerable *adoo* movement on the beach. They saw men moving tactically and taking turns to swim. For nearly four days they had baked on the tiny rock and had kept very still for fear of being spotted themselves. Were the *adoo* now going to bring out a mortar or some other worthwhile target for them to strike? Viv scrambled the Strikemasters and kept them out of sight. Light was beginning to fade. Since this was their last chance to hit the *adoo* before they were extracted that night, they called in air strikes and guns anyway. By now the initial pair of Strikemasters had been replaced by a second pair. As luck would have it, one of the pilots of this pair had newly arrived in country and had not been briefed on Viv's code which had been designed to confuse any *adoo* trying to monitor the radio net and working out their position. Some of the adjusted strikes therefore went wide. Artillery fire was then directed in from Mughsayl.

It was difficult to say how effective the strikes were. At one stage Viv heard small arms fire which he assumed was the *adoo* shooting at likely observation positions – on land. That night, Gordon moved in with his dhow, and Nick and I blasted with machine-gun fire at possible targets on the shoreline which we had noted earlier. This provoked a robust response in the form of machine-gun fire. This firefight between dhow and shore continued for some minutes. Although not in danger, Viv and Chris felt they were piggies-in-the-middle.

In due course, the rubber boat went in and picked them up in flat calm conditions. We continued to shoot at shore targets and soon two tired and very warmly cooked officers were retrieved on board. When they arrived on deck, they noticed the crew quickly moved up-wind of them.

It was intended that this operation should be repeated but the availability of people, the dhow and other assets somehow conspired against it. We don't know what damage was inflicted on the *adoo*. But the uncertainty that these activities must have induced in an area where they had hitherto felt they had a free run added to their caution and hesitation, and thereby further enhanced the effectiveness of the Hornbeam Line. A year later, Gordon Gillies heard from the intelligence community that one of our shells had destroyed the base plate of the *adoo* mortar. Certainly, the Army positions at the south of the Hornbeam Line were not struck again during our tour.

For his leadership as second-in-command in the previous tour, and as commander of C Company in this tour; and for his skill and gallantry in conceiving, planning and leading so many operations which took the fight to the *adoo* over the better part of a year and a half, Viv was decorated with the Omani Distinguished Service Medal for Gallantry.

As in all wars, there were periods of inactivity and boredom. Life on the *jebel* was not always as exciting as it may sound, and there were times when one had to drive oneself and one's soldiers into vigilance. In spite of our efforts to the contrary, one did develop a routine. Our tour in the mountains was ten months long. Most of us took one month's leave during that time. For the remainder of the time, there was rarely a forty-eight hour period when we did not go out on a patrol, an ambush or another such operation, either by day or by night. There were quiet periods, and there were very busy periods, but one was usually the only English speaker, and the only British officer. While I only occasionally felt lonely, I almost always was conscious of the uniqueness of my position, and of the potential for things to develop very quickly from relative tranquillity into life-threatening crisis. Furthermore, there was always the usual background threat of incomers in the form of mortar shells ready to sharpen you up, or even an unannounced visitation from Wee Katie who might come and take you away. To quite a high degree, therefore, I lived on my nerves.

It was a hard routine, but a routine nevertheless. Complacency was the great enemy on the *jebel* as much as it is anywhere else. I too went on leave for a month after having been in the country for a year. When I came back I found that the positions on the Line had been reorganised, and C Company with Viv Rowe now was responsible for Reef. The *adoo* had probably worked out which areas I had not patrolled so assiduously, because one day a Jebali guide came to Viv and told him

145

of a scrape mark in the wire where it looked as if the *adoo* had been jacking up the bottom strands and wriggling underneath, pushing or pulling their equipment with them. In the same way as the sites of ancient hidden structures are not always obvious to the ground level observer, these scrape marks were first spotted from the air.

Viv accordingly beefed up this area with mines, trip flares and pre-arranged mortar targets. Sure enough, one night in early June, Chris Barnes was leading a patrol on the eastern side of the wire when they bumped into an *adoo* party crossing the obstacle. It is probable that the *adoo* saw part of the patrol first and was hurried into an incautious movement among the mines. There was a loud bang and the firefight started. Chris called down mortar fire, and Viv quickly came out in support with another patrol.

This was a confusing close-quarter battle in the dark, and at one stage Chris's patrol was brought under fire by our own troops from the A Company position at Kumasi further north in the line. When the fire subsided they found one dead *adoo* in the wire, killed by mortar fire and a mine. They surmised that some of the *adoo* had got through and dispersed to the east while others had withdrawn to the west. They were wrong on both counts.

It was decided to withdraw to Reef and follow up at first light. Chris and Mike Bourne went out again with a patrol the following morning. They found a second *adoo* body near the wire on the east side. While they were inspecting this, they heard a rustling sound from a long gully ten yards to their front. They were very exposed so they rushed into the gully firing into it as they went and killed two more armed *adoo* who were the only occupants.

Chris called a helicopter which removed the bodies. As the helicopter left, there was yet a further exchange of fire with two more *adoo*, this time to the west of the wire. Viv contemplated calling the helicopter back to shift Chris and his patrol to the other side of the wire, but then decided against it. Instead, he sent another patrol to the west. They found a blood trail which they followed until it disappeared. Viv then called off all further pursuit for fear of counter ambush.

It seems that the survivors had found themselves on opposite sides of the wire and had been unable to regroup before they were bumped again.

This was an unambiguously successful operation. For no casualties to C Company, at least four *adoo* had been killed and their weapons captured. At least one of the survivors was wounded and may have died subsequently. On the other hand, he may have survived to tell the tale, which doubtless would lose nothing in the telling, and would have its consequent effect on *adoo* morale. Either way, it all would serve to compound further the difficulties and uncertainties for the *adoo* trying to get men and supplies past the Hornbeam Line.

The dead were all young men who had apparently just completed their training and indoctrination in Hauf in the PDRY. The *adoo*'s complacency in their turn had been the death of these young men because, although these four may not have been there before, it was plain from the tracks that this had been a regular crossing point. Indeed, on a recent night operation in swirling mist, Viv had found his small patrol sandwiched between the scout group and the main body of between fifteen to twenty *adoo* approaching the same section of wire, this time from the east. Uncertainty over identification – there was another friendly patrol out nearby – meant that he dared not open fire too hastily. His patrol went to ground. The main *adoo* party withdrew back to the east, and the *adoo* scout group ran like hell. Not a shot was fired, although Viv engaged the adoo withdrawal route with mortars. However, the *adoo* had failed in their attempt to get through the wire.

There is always a balance to be struck between over activity and complacency. Maintaining an active aggressive programme of night patrols and ambushes requires enthusiastic, energetic leaders and well led and thoroughly trained troops. But one can overdo it, and routine will set in even with – perhaps especially with – the most experienced troops. And sheer fatigue always attends military operations. One way to counter this is to move troops around. What you lose in knowledge and experience of a particular piece of ground, you gain in freshness and curiosity.

Survival on either side often depended on the readiness to vary one's movements. Use the same track too often and the *adoo* might plant mines on it. They never marked their mines of course. Never use old *sangars* on the *jebel*: the *adoo* will mine them or boobytrap them. Pass the same way at the same time too often and the *adoo* might notice the pattern and fix you with mortars or an ambush. Patrol too much in one area and the *adoo* will notice and slip past you in another area. Vary your movements or someone will punish you for your laziness and your complacency. Routine and complacency I found to be great enemies of mine and I must admit I was not always their most valiant adversary.

Chapter Ten

The Action:
The Iranians and the Firqat

In late 1972, the Shah of Iran, encouraged by General Tim Creasey, took the generous but entirely logical step of offering practical military assistance. It was in his interest that Iranian oil was allowed to flow freely out of the Gulf to the industrial world. Oman, together with Iran, guards the gate to the Gulf, and an entrenched Communist state across the Strait of Hormuz was the last thing the Shah wanted, not least because the domino theory, which was received political wisdom at the time, indicated that once Oman fell, Iran would soon come under pressure too. So he came to the help of his neighbour.

His army was well armed and his air force had modern American machines: helicopters and fast jets. The airstrip at Thumrait, known to us as Midway, was given a 12,000 feet runway to accommodate these aircraft. An Iranian Special Forces Unit arrived first and was in place on part of the Hornbeam Line when the Northern Frontier Regiment arrived there in November 1973. Another substantial contingent of the Imperial Iranian Army and Air Force joined them in theatre shortly afterwards. The army unit was a battalion group about fifteen hundred strong.

On the face of it, this was a godsend. With the extra helicopter airlift, the Sultan's Army could be sustained safely on the *jebel* throughout the *khareef*, allowing our own helicopters to concentrate on the trickier operational tasks. When the Iranians first arrived, a number of their helicopters were armed, but because they tended to shoot at anything that moved, including us, they were soon disarmed.

With more soldiers, the possibility of more offensive operations presented itself. We had always tended to be rather reactive and defensive, chiefly because we didn't have the resources to do much

148

else. Among those resources we valued most highly was the morale of our men. We were always anxious to avoid a large butcher's bill; obviously for its own sake, but also for the effect on the morale of our soldiers. There would be little point in conducting a successful major offensive operation if it incurred substantial casualties unless one was in a position to follow it up with more successful offensive operations. The war would not be won by throwing people injudiciously into offensive operations before we were ready. In addition, about fifty percent of Oman's government spending went on defence as it was. Any more would have bankrupted the country.

Very soon after the Iranians arrived they conducted a successful operation to clear and hold the road from the coast to Thumrait, which then opened up the possibility of a road connection from Salalah to the north of Oman, a link which had long been broken by the *adoo*. So an air of optimism arrived with these new forces.

It didn't quite work out as well as we'd hoped. The problem was that the training of their people didn't match the task. The Iranian forces at that time had been trained by American teams to fight a conventional war. No doubt they were capable enough in that field but that wasn't the sort of war they were going to fight in Oman. In any case, while the Americans must have learned many lessons from Vietnam, it had probably been too early for those lessons to be applied to the training of these forces.

When training infantrymen – both officers and soldiers – you should start with the naked man, so to speak, and first teach him how to think and behave. He learns fieldcraft. He learns what gives you away when someone is looking for you: Shine; Shadow; Shape; Silhouette; Spacing; Movement. He learns how to look, observe and listen, even to smell, and how to move without being seen or heard. He learns to look at things from his adversary's point of view, both physically and mentally, because only by doing this will he understand how to surprise him, and avoid being surprised himself.

He learns how to survive, to endure and to remain effective in arduous conditions; like a wild animal in a wild environment. He learns to welcome darkness as a friend; a protector and an aid to his movement and his flexibility; to think of bad weather as something which offers possibilities rather than something which must be sheltered from. He learns to look after his 'oppo', his friend, and develops a two way trust in his fellows and in his superiors – teamwork. Then you introduce tools such as maps and compasses, so he can reliably navigate by night and day and you give him binoculars so he can extend his visual range.

Somewhere along this process, you start to introduce weapons and other equipment like radios and vehicles. You give him technical skills which add to his lethality, and extend his range to communicate and move. But these technical skills should always be built on the foundation of instinctive attitudes, values and behaviour. You equip the man. You don't man the equipment. It is all centred on the man, his attitudes, his values, and his personal skills; because wars are won by his endurance, his fortitude, his courage and his wits.

Every individual infantryman is a complete stand-alone weapons system. His feet are his mobility: his eyes, nose and ears are his sensors and his surveillance and target acquisition systems. In his rucksack he has his own logistics in the form of ammunition, food and water. But at the centre, serving all these is his computer; his brain. And the defining feature of any computer is the software. Only if the right software has been programmed will he be able to use the hardware and the tools and weapons to good effect. He operates within a wide framework of course, and rarely works on his own, but ultimately individual soldiers must make individual decisions which may affect the course of battles, or even wars.

This comes as something of a surprise to many non-military people. Even today, there are those who are still imbued with the notion of the lowest ranks being required only to obey orders and to be mindless cannon fodder. But soldiers at the lowest level make a thousand decisions daily upon which victory or defeat can swing. Few plans survive first contact with the enemy. Some plans don't even get that far, but if your people know why you are doing something, and how it fits into the bigger picture, they can use their brains and enterprise and make it work for you when the unforeseen happens; to help you to turn the CMFUs into SAMFUs and the SAMFUs into AMFUs (see glossary). To do that, they must be informed about what is going on, and trained and ready to use their initiative when the plan runs out – which it will.

The most junior person in the organization must know what it is you are trying to achieve and why, and be ready in every intellectual, spiritual and material way to make his individual contribution to success, otherwise defeat will be the default outcome. 'For want of a nail, a kingdom was lost.'

This is not to say that the quality and skill of the senior officer is of little account. Generals can still lose battles in spite of commanding the most stout hearted and enterprising of troops. But unless the general has engendered something of the character I have described above in his subordinates, his effort will be gravely handicapped.

In battle, officers and NCOs get wounded and killed, and men routinely find themselves taking the place of their superiors on a battlefield, and not just one level up. Two or even three levels are not unheard of. So while he usually operates within a large framework in concert with many other people, each individual human weapons system must have the skills, knowledge, training, confidence and self-reliance to make decisions and act upon them, in support of what he knows his bosses are trying to achieve. He should never 'not know what to do'. He should always be trained and equipped to be able to work out what he can do to make a contribution, however small, to the success of the whole endeavour.

This approach is based on the assumption that war is chaotic, and that the plethora of uncontrollable variables means that you cannot plan your battle in absolute detail beforehand. The temptation to plan in detailed totality is strong because the hope is, that by thinking of everything, you can rule out uncertainty. This is futile because war is the province of uncertainty. One must plan of course, and one may even plan in detail, but those plans must be made on the assumption that they will need to be adjusted, changed, or even abandoned and rewritten before the battle is over.

Planning before the battle must never become a substitute for taking decisions during it. That said, the difficulties in making decisions in the heat of a battle should not be underestimated either. Regimental histories, and the accounts of battles written by men anxious to preserve their reputations after the event, can give the impression that while things may not always have gone to plan, a logical consideration of the courses open was made, and the best course was selected. Reality is somewhat different. I often found that when events did not conform to my conception of how they should unfold, I felt stunned. There was a kind of detached surreal element to this too. I could almost step out of my body, stand to one side and see myself sitting there; stunned. Reviewing the situation, examining the courses open and selecting the best one does not come naturally when things are rapidly and dangerously getting out of control, and one's own life is under immediate threat. When I managed to make a decision, it was often either the first idea that jumped into my head, or it was someone else's idea that I snatched as it passed.

The good junior commanders are the ones who can control their fears – someone once said that courage is the art of being the only one who knows you're scared to death – and fight back the upwelling sense of panic that threatens to overcome them; make the necessary decisions based on imperfect, incomplete, or even plain wrong information; and give the appropriate orders to men who are able to carry them out. I don't believe anyone finds that easy. I certainly didn't.

Your chances of success, however, are greatly improved if, before the battle, you have a very clear idea of the effect that you are seeking to achieve, think through as many 'what ifs' as possible with your people, and plan what you can. But ultimately you have to trust and depend upon your subordinates to do what they can in support of your mission without reference to you. Tell them what to do and why you are asking them to do it, and give them the means to achieve it, but don't tell them how to do it. Let them have the freedom to decide the means in the light of the circumstances that confront them.

This implies good mutual understanding and great trust. Trust is the glue in all relationships. Trust is a two-way thing. The superior must trust his subordinates to make good decisions which support his overall mission. The subordinate must trust his boss to give realistic and necessary missions, with appropriate resources, and not to bite his head off if occasionally he makes a mistake. People who don't make mistakes don't make anything. Trust is at the very centre of success. Cannon fodder has no part in modern warfare of any kind.

That is how I was trained as a Royal Marine, and how I had trained my own Royal Marines and, in spite of the language and cultural barrier, it was the philosophy which we all tried to apply, however imperfectly, when training Omani soldiers. Apart from anything else, the medium/long term plan was to train Omani officers to take over from British ones – to Omanise the Army. Unless this philosophy was followed, what kind of officers would we breed to take over from us?

In his book, *The Rules of the Game,* Andrew Gordon says that Horatio Nelson's 'greatest gift of leadership was to raise his juniors above the need of supervision.' Second only to the need to fight and win the war, this was the most pressing task of the British officers in Oman. Indeed, it is probably one of the greatest duties of all leaders and commanders.

I had come across soldiers and marines of other nations while on NATO exercises in the Mediterranean. Some, like the French Foreign Legion, appeared to share this philosophy. Others like the Turks did not. With these Iranian troops, everything seemed to be centred on the machine not the man and, perhaps reflecting the influence of their American trainers, the importance of weight of numbers, technology and firepower was always emphasised. The philosophy described above depends on trust, and this was not a predominant feature in Iranian Army culture. So working with them was never going to be an easy or natural fit.

The Iranians took over a number of static positions on the *jebel.* They patrolled only reluctantly from these positions and in such large numbers that they could scarcely be called patrols. When in their static positions at night, one could watch the tracer arcing out from their defences, triggered by jumpy sentries. When one position started shooting, another often would follow suit. More often than not, they would start shooting each others' positions. It was not unusual therefore to observe a full blown fire fight with tracer at night on the *jebel* between two or more Iranian positions, initiated by nothing more than fertile imaginations. It was rumoured that the *adoo* used to fire at two positions simultaneously in order to start them off just for the fun of it. This was the stuff of cartoons. At least it would have been if it had been on celluloid.

I worked a good deal with Iranian helicopters as they built up our logistics supplies on the *jebel* prior to the *khareef* setting in – our monsoon stockpile. Once they got used to the terrain and the job, they could be relied upon to repeat routine tasks. But on at least one occasion helicopters were reported as lost: i.e. they didn't know where they were, almost as soon as they took off from Salalah. Their fast jets did not operate in Dhofar and I guess we didn't miss much.

The Iranians had some impressive officers who were articulate, able and tough. I had met one or two such warriors while they were undergoing British Special Boat Service training in UK. They were officers of the highest calibre and I would have happily marched to war alongside them. With the hard background that many of their soldiers came from they were mostly fit, tough, resilient troops. Neither did they lack for courage. But the gulf between the officers and their men was palpable. Officers seemed to treat their soldiers with contempt. Soldiers regarded their officers with fear.

I saw the same phenomenon again in the Argentinian forces that we captured at the end of the Falklands War. Argentinian officers whom I met seemed to be surprised that I spoke to my Marines in a normal fashion with courtesy, and that they spoke to us as normal people too. My officers, my NCOs and I didn't shout or bark at our people. We quietly, even politely, told them to do this and that, and even used the magic words 'please' and 'thank you' from time to time, and in every case they responded and obeyed immediately and willingly.

This did not appear to be the Argentinian way. In that army – and the Iranian one – the primary source of discipline for soldiers seemed to be the fear of their officers. When the fear of the approaching enemy eventually superseded their fear of their superiors, they broke and ran. Between officers and soldiers, fear is a brittle glue. Mutual respect, shared hardship, shared risk, trust and the imparting of hope form a more durable bond.

It was not an unknown sight to see an Iranian officer or NCO strike a soldier. It was even rumoured that the Iranians shot their soldiers occasionally. Whatever the truth of this may be, the rumour was believable. They seemed to treat their troops as cannon fodder. A glance at the list of Servicemen awarded medals for gallantry or otherwise outstanding service during the Dhofar War in AR Tinson's book *Orders, Decorations and Medals of the Sultanate of Oman* is illuminating. In the Sultan's Armed Forces, the ratio of awards to officers compared with those to other ranks is about 50/50. Of all awards made to all ranks, approximately ten percent were given to the lowest ranks; privates, gunners or seamen. Of the ninety or so Iranians so decorated, two were sergeants, one was a master sergeant, and there was one lonely private soldier. All the rest were officers.

The tactics of attrition and of mass attacks by soldiers in line which the Iranians employed in their subsequent war against Iraq from 1980 to 1988 did not come as a surprise to us.

The Iranian officers certainly shot their own soldiers by mistake from time to time. Ian Ventham commanded the Oman Artillery unit in support of the Iranian operation to clear the Thumrait/Salalah Road. During one contact with the *adoo*, he saw an Iranian soldier bleed to death, hit in the thigh by his own company commander's indiscriminate shooting. On a later occasion, at the urgent request of the Iranian commander, he arranged a night helicopter evacuation to be conducted by the Sultan of Oman's Air Force. Taking risks comparable to the ones described in the first chapter of this book, the pilots later found that they had evacuated a dead man who had been shot by his own side during the day. The Iranians had not wanted to pass the body through their own casualty evacuation chain. A night removal by SOAF was their way of avoiding censure from their masters.

It is only reasonable to expect troops operating in an unfamiliar environment to take time to adjust. There was much to learn about the country, the enemy, and the best way of operating. Perhaps we expected too much too soon. But although brave enough and aggressive, we saw little sign that they were willing to learn. The Iranian troops need not have been incompetent, but unlike the Omanis, you couldn't teach the Iranians anything; they knew it all. The sublime combination of arrogance and ignorance was a marvel to behold. One sympathized with the American teams who had trained them.

And yet, the Iranians could be appreciative. One could feel very isolated working in support of the Iranians as a liaison officer or a forward observation officer. Ian Ventham was deeply touched therefore, when the Iranian Brigade Commander took the trouble to seek him out on Christmas Day and present him with an orange. Under the circumstances, he felt this was more than a token gesture.

No doubt a number of Iranian officers did learn valuable lessons from their experience in this war. However, the Shah was deposed in

1979 and, given the propensity of the successor regime of Ayatollah Khomeini to kill anyone who had been loyal to the previous government, it seems unlikely that many of their experienced warriors would have lived much beyond the advent of his Islamic Republic. I often wonder how long my friends in the Iranian Special Boat Service survived.

Churchill once said that the only thing worse than fighting alongside allies is fighting without allies, and doubtless those with responsibility for trying to match scarce resources to the plethora of tasks that cried out to be done felt that the Iranians were a boon. Overall, there can be no doubt that the weight they lent to the wheel helped to shorten the war, and the political benefit for the Sultan in bringing the Iranians alongside as active allies was incalculable. However, the salient military contribution the Iranians made was the provision of helicopters. By early 1973, the Sultan's helicopter force had been overworked. It was in poor condition and was insufficient for the huge logistic tasks that confronted it. There was no money to buy any more machines, or to pay for more pilots. Something would have to give. The prospect of abandoning the position at Sarfait lay in front of us. Sarfait had limited military utility, and it was a notorious consumer of scarce supplies and precious helicopter hours, but sitting next to the border with the PDRY, it was demonstrable proof that the Sultan meant business in western Dhofar. Politically Sarfait was of cardinal importance. To abandon it would have sent entirely the wrong political message to our many friends, as well as to our enemies. The Commanding Officer of the Jebel Regiment holding Sarfait, Lieutenant Colonel Roger Jones, got as far as drawing up plans for withdrawal. He quite reasonably supposed that any situation that he drew up plans for was almost certainly not going to occur. He was right. The Shah's helicopters laid that particular spectre and, even for this alone, the Iranian contribution was pivotal.

But for us on the ground, trying to avoid being shot by the *adoo and* the Iranians was one risk more than we would have preferred.

The tour for the Northern Frontier Regiment in Dhofar on this occasion was ten months long. Towards the end of our Dhofar tour, in September 1973, Johnny handed command of A Company over to me. At the end of the tour, the Regiment returned to the relatively comfortable life in the north of Oman, training, and recruiting. Johnny meanwhile had been asked to join the Firqat Forces and stayed behind in Dhofar. He became the Firqat Officer for the *Firqat Al Tariq bin Zaid*, Tariq being the Arab warrior for whom Gibraltar – Jebel Tariq – is named. The Imperial Iranian Army had now arrived in strength in Dhofar and they needed local knowledge. He was to work with them. Mike Kingscote, our Regimental Intelligence Officer also stayed behind and started a new life as the Firqat Officer with the *Firqat Umr al Kitaab* – The Mother of The Book – the 'Book' of course being The Koran.

The word *firqat* means a military unit or group. The Firqat Forces units were made up of Dhofari Jebali tribesmen, many of who had been fighting on the other side but who had been persuaded to come over to the Sultan. These people were called Surrendered Enemy Personnel – SEPs – but it was a misnomer because it implied that they had been beaten. As soldiers, they were not beaten, but the political system which had recruited them was. Many of them had been trained by Russian or Chinese advisors. Indeed, Mike Kingscote came across one who had been trained as a doctor in Beijing and Odessa.

The means of persuading them to join the Sultan were various, but the money they received if they handed in their rifle or a mine or two, for which there was a set price list, certainly played a part. The Soviet AK47 which I used on the *jebel* came from this source. One was reminded of the remark someone once made about the Pathans from the North West Frontier of India: you cannot buy a Pathan, but you may be able to hire him for a time. Dhofaris had a similar attitude. They even looked like Pathans.

The *adoo* didn't always surrender just when one was expecting them to. Early one morning in 1974, Harry Wooley, an avuncular British quartermaster was driving in from outside Salalah on a road newly cleared of mines to attend a meeting at Brigade Headquarters. He was waved down for a lift by a Dhofari carrying an AK47. Harry naturally thought he was a member of Firqat Forces, of which he, Harry, was the Quartermaster. On arrival at the Headquarters, the Dhofari refused to get out of the vehicle. Not being much of an Arabic speaker, there was nothing Harry could say that would get him to move on. Eventually Harry called the Baluchi sentry over, who, after chatting to the hitch-hiker, explained that he was in fact an *adoo* who wanted to surrender, and could he please have a hundred *rials* reward for his AK47.

It must also be said that many Jebalis recognized the Sultan had won their hearts and minds by removing the causes of their original rebellion, and by meeting more closely their needs and aspirations. But perhaps the greatest incentive was that most human of instincts, the wish to be on the winning side when the war stopped. There could be no more unambiguous indicator that the Sultan was winning than the flow of these people to his side.

Regular soldiers could find the Firqat infuriating. The SAS, who themselves were somewhat irregular, and were trained to train irregular soldiers, were mostly pretty well adjusted to the task. However, the Firqat tended to be a law unto themselves. It was futile to try to get them to do what you wanted if they were at all unwilling. It was like herding cats. They were volatile, argumentative, unpredictable and grasping. But I daresay if I'd lived as hard a life as they did, I might be a tad grasping too.

Picking up the Scottish/Omani Highlander parallel again, one was reminded of a description of certain Highland and Irish regiments during the Great War. You couldn't be sure which way they would go – either towards the enemy or away from them – but whichever way they went, they would do it damned fast. In addition, there was always the likelihood that they had family and friends still serving on the *adoo* side, which inevitably meant that one hesitated to trust them with too much information, or indeed with anything else. Being ex-*adoo*, they looked like *adoo* and dressed like *adoo*, and often carried the same weapons as *adoo*, and this added to the likelihood of blue-on-blue engagements where one shoots up one's own side. Some felt that these were common enough in Oman without this added complication.

They were also expensive. They were supplied and paid like any other military formation. It was best not to be too rigorous with the arithmetic when counting them as there were always ghosts on the payroll and it was not easy to see what the Sultan was getting for his money. They were intensely tribal and would only work in their own particular tribal area and so, to the orderly military eye, they had limited utility. They had to believe in your ability to assist them, whether by rudimentary first aid, or by providing rations, ammunition, water, artillery or aircraft. Mike Kingscote became an expert at building roads, schools, mosques, houses and at sinking wells. He even found himself delivering a baby on one occasion.

Orders and Firqat did not go well together. Everything required negotiation and time. Mike's negotiations with the Firqat to participate in any specific operation tended to be lengthy and tortuous. Where was the operation? When do we leave? How many people do you want? How long are we going to be away? Reasonable enough questions perhaps, but often he suspected they were inspired by a wish to warn their 'cousins' that they were coming, or for some other agenda that he would never know. The trick was to keep the destination a secret for as long as possible, and then fly in rather than walk.

Mike Kingscote's description of one of the operations he conducted illustrates well the 'alternative' approach that the Firqat had to fighting. He and his Firqat were ambushing a water hole, supported by an Army company and an SAS detachment. They moved in and set up the ambush during the night. At dawn, Mike found he was on an exposed slope and in a complex of disused *sangars*. His *sangar* was overhung by

157

a tree, but he had a good view of the water hole. He was armed with a machine-gun.

As dawn broke, we scrutinised the area very carefully. While this was happening, I saw a member of the Firqat behind me lighting solid fuel blocks underneath an enormous kettle in the bottom of the *sangar*. I was very surprised and suggested that it might be better if he were to concentrate on the purpose at hand. He smiled and handed me a packet of sweet biscuits. At the same time Ahmed Ali, with whom I was sharing the *sangar*, and I saw at least ten *adoo*, possibly more, moving about in our killing area. The order to open fire was given.

I rattled my way through a couple of magazines, and received an RPG 7 rocket round into the base of my *sangar*, which showered Ahmed and me with dust and gravel. We continued firing and the next RPG round hit the tree above our heads, this time showering us with metal and branches. The SAS team, seeing that we were attracting the weight of the *adoo*'s fire, fired a rocket grenade into the enemy position and scored a direct hit. I was relieved, as having been bracketed with two rounds, I knew where the next one was going.

In the brief respite that followed, Ahmed Ali and I reloaded as fast as we could. I noticed that we were alone in the *sangar*. The other Firqat members had disappeared. I asked Ahmed where they were. He said, 'over the hill'. As the RPG rockets had started coming in, they had disappeared in the opposite direction. The firefight continued for another ten or fifteen minutes, and then the Army company started to move in from a flank. It was at this stage, the Firqat members started to emerge. There was no question of; 'how did it go?' or 'are you all right?' Merely; 'has the kettle boiled?'

Thereafter he resolved to keep the Firqat in front of him so that he could see what they were doing.

A group of Firqat lived and worked with me on my first position on the Hornbeam Line, Reef, for a while. I had a good knife which they spotted one day and it was made very clear they wanted it. (*Shoof- ureed* 'Look – I want!') I was reluctant to surrender there and then something which I might rely upon in the near future, but I agreed to buy a similar one for them during my imminent leave and bring it back for them. This I did, but when the question of payment was broached I received contemptuous hostility. 'But surely the knife is a gift? We certainly won't pay for it.' I was expecting them to drive a hard bargain, but I wasn't quite expecting this. I should have known better.

However, the concept of recruiting the Firqat and keeping them alongside was a courageous masterstroke, generally attributed to John Watts in 1970 when he was the Commanding Officer of the SAS. His officers in Oman made the first tentative moves to induce the tribes on the *jebel* to form groups to fight for the Sultan, and to open the door to members of those tribes on the *adoo* side to join them. It started with the placing of Civil Aid Teams with medics in the towns of Taqa and Mirbat. They treated all-comers but mostly the women and children. As the miracle of penicillin gradually banished hitherto chronic afflictions, the word began to spread to the men folk on the *jebel*. They too would then come in with their ailments, and so on; and thus the tide of war had imperceptibly but indubitably turned.

A small team of SAS soldiers would live with and train each Firqat group and, eventually, take them on operations. In time, these groups were put on a more formal footing – not that the word 'formal' really has any place in connection with the Firqat – and placed under their own headquarters. By the time I arrived in Dhofar, the Firqat were an established fact. But it must be acknowledged that their existence should never be taken for granted, and that all the work that was subsequently done by them was built on the fragile, innovative foundations created by Watts and his teams.

Hitherto, there had been virtually no Dhofaris in the Army, and the Sultan's forces in Dhofar had looked suspiciously like an army of occupation. By bringing the Jebalis on board in substantial numbers in the form of Firqats, that could no longer be said. This notion of giving your enemy a respectable means of coming across to your side – of amnesty and forgiveness – as we have already seen with the Gaelic Highlander, was not unprecedented, and it had its subsequent imitators in Rhodesia.

They were impressively tough, hardy, resilient men. As our former enemies they knew the ground and the tactics of their former friends intimately, and they were good at things that we were poor at, namely reconnaissance, gathering intelligence and communicating with the nomadic population. They were of that population after all. They were, therefore, extremely useful in retaining the peace in an area which had been cleared of *adoo*, thereby leaving conventional forces to get on with prosecuting the war elsewhere. For all their limitations, I do not believe we could have won the war without the Firqat.

It required a very special patience found in only a few British officers to win the faith of the Firqat. Mike Kingscote and Viv Rowe, who both worked extensively with them, had that patience. Viv even learned something of their language. Johnny had that patience in abundance. Johnny went to work with the Firqat in the reconnaissance role for the

159

Iranians. We feared that he was going to have a hard time of it. He would be the only man between the Iranians and the biggest CMFU of them all, but if any man had the patience and perseverance to handle it, it would be Johnny. He was going to return to the Northern Frontier Regiment in the New Year and take the Company back from me. I took some home leave over Christmas so that I could spend my last few months in Oman together with him.

At the end of my leave, on my way back to Oman through London, I called in at the Headquarters of the SAS in Sloane Square to catch up on the news. To my great sadness I learned that Johnny had been killed.

I was desolate. He had been my closest friend and mentor for fifteen months in peace and war. He had left the company towards the end of a Dhofar tour badly in need of a rest, but because he had been asked to help out in a difficult situation, he had stayed on. I had been looking forward to serving my last few months in Oman with him in cheerful, sociable circumstances, and now he was gone. The melancholy task of sorting and packing his clothes and personal possessions and sending them to his family fell to me when I got back to Oman, and this did nothing to ameliorate my sense of personal loss.

Johnny was killed trying to rescue his Firqat sergeant major under fire in an act not very different from the one I saw him perform in the Wadi Sha'ath. I regretted deeply that I or someone else had not been around to perform for him the service that he had so dependably been ready to perform for me and for many others: to help him out of trouble.

The Firqat were not without courage or commitment when well led. I was told they had done everything they could to support Johnny. I know they deeply appreciated what he was trying to do when he was killed. But it seemed to us that he had been asked to stay behind in Dhofar to help in a very difficult task because he was known to be someone who would never say no to a call to duty. Then again, war is war. He knew the risks, it was his choice, and he died doing the job he loved. His parents, whom I visited and corresponded with in subsequent years, never got over his loss.

He was awarded the Gallantry Medal, the highest Omani decoration for bravery and an equivalent of the Victoria Cross. He was one of only seventeen recipients. This makes it one of the rarest medals in the world. Only three British officers received this award and two of them died winning it.

I didn't see him in those last few months of his life, and I only know what happened to him from talking to people like Mike Lobb who were with him at this time, and from the citation for his Gallantry

Medal, written by his commanding officer, Colin McLean, which I draw on heavily here.

In early December 1974, it was planned that the Iranian forces would conduct a major operation to establish a new line west of the Hornbeam Line from the desert down to the sea at Raykhut – the Damavand Line. Two Iranian battalions would strike in a two pronged operation from north to south, the left prong being the main effort and the right prong a diversion. Johnny was to lead the Firqat guiding the right-hand western battalion.

The first phase of this operation was to establish a new position down off the escarpment below the tree line two kilometres away from the main position. Johnny was commanding his Firqat, personally leading the Iranian advance at the head of one of two columns of troops, when, on reaching the objective, it was discovered that the main body had become separated from the leading troops. Johnny then immediately returned and made contact with the missing troops, and rounded them up.

Later on the same day, 5 December, the *adoo* attacked the position with small arms fire and RPG 7 rockets killing ten Iranian soldiers and wounding an eleventh. As soon as sufficient fire was being returned, which no doubt he had organised, he personally went forward of the company perimeter and recovered the bodies of three other Iranian soldiers whom it had been thought the enemy had captured. Throughout this operation, he continued to assist the Iranian company commander, and he organised the evacuation of the casualties. His personal example and tireless vigilance enabled the company to withdraw later without further loss, despite more enemy attacks.

The following day, shortly before last light, the Iranian battalion sustained more casualties on one of their forward positions. The Iranians were unable to arrange an evacuation themselves, so Johnny took a jeep three kilometres forward of the main position along an undefended route in falling darkness to the troops in difficulty. On arrival, he arranged for a helicopter to come and lift out the wounded.

During the second of these actions, Johnny apparently heard or saw a pair of Strikemasters on their way back to Salalah from a reconnaissance action further west. He called them up and asked for help to cover his withdrawal to higher ground. The pilots had been told that the Iranians were self-sufficient for air support and under no circumstances were they to get involved in supporting Iranian forces on the ground. This order was inspired by perfectly sensible safety and airspace control considerations. The possibilities for misunderstandings and own goals with the Iranians were endless. The injunction included the Firqat Forces supporting the Iranians. Yet here was

Johnny, now a Firqat officer, plainly in trouble and calling for help. Bob Mason, who was leading the flight and who knew Johnny and the rest of us extremely well, did not hesitate to disobey his instructions. The pair of aircraft went straight into action directed by Johnny and provided the harassing and covering fire he needed to help him successfully extricate the Iranian casualties. Johnny thanked the pilots profusely.

On returning to Salalah, Bob Mason's feet didn't touch the ground. He was hauled into the Wing Commander's office and roundly reprimanded for disobeying an order. Bob, never one to hold back when he thought he should be going forward, made quite plain what he thought of such an order. He and his fellow pilots were professional enough to know when a situation was unacceptably dangerous. No one was going to order him to refuse a call for help from his close friends on the ground, who might be in danger of their lives. He was then put before the Brigade Commander to explain himself, which he again did. Brigadier John Akehurst arbitrated wisely and Bob and the Wing Commander went away reconciled. Bob was eventually decorated with the Distinguished Service Medal for Gallantry for his unfailing skilful and courageous support on this and many other occasions; an award which he, and many other pilots who were not decorated, roundly deserved.

The success of the overall operation was always going to depend upon speed and surprise. Move with speed and strength where the *adoo* were not expecting you and you had a good chance of success. Give the *adoo* time to react and they would do so in the most violent way with skill, bravery and persistence. However, following this discouraging start, it was decided to refocus the effort of this Iranian battalion more closely with the one on the left-hand eastern prong. The time involved in the re-planning and repositioning of the forces dissipated any advantage that surprise and speed might have offered. Among the reasons for the delay was the insistence by the Iranians that they change their camouflage clothing to something more appropriate when they descended below the tree line. It was over two weeks later before the operation was relaunched. For the experienced Dhofar officers like Mike Lobb and Johnny, it was clear that the delay could only increase the risk. Nobody was better acquainted with the ways of the *adoo* than the Firqat, many of them having been *adoo* themselves, and they did not want to continue with what they thought was now a very dodgy operation. Furthermore, Mike and Johnny knew that being at the forefront of the operation, they and their Firqats would be the first to make contact with the *adoo*, who by then would have had plenty of time to prepare. The Firqat stayed with it only because Mike and Johnny stayed. Johnny expressed these grave reservations to General Creasey whom he met on 24 December. However, under the circumstances, General Creasey, while he listened carefully, could only insist that the operation would go ahead. The operation finally recommenced early the following morning.

This time Johnny was again leading his Firqat, together with an Iranian patrol, down off the escarpment below the tree line. The leading troops of the patrol were ambushed by a group of *adoo* in thick trees who had been in position and waiting for some days for the Iranian advance. The Firqat sergeant major was killed in the opening burst of fire. A Firqat soldier picked up the sergeant major and attempted to carry him to the rear. Johnny, seeing that he was having great difficulty, handed his own weapon to another soldier and picked up the body. Shortly afterwards, Johnny was heard to cry out and fell to the ground mortally wounded. The enemy fire was such that it was impossible to recover his body, or that of the Firqat sergeant major. He was killed at eight o'clock on Christmas morning.

The citation for the Gallantry Medal says that, 'Major Braddell-Smith gave his life attempting to recover the body of one of his comrades while under intense fire from a ruthless and determined enemy. This action typifies the magnificent courage and complete disregard for his personal safety shown by Major Braddell-Smith during this and earlier actions. His gallantry and devotion to duty are beyond praise.' He was twenty-seven.

Johnny was not the last casualty of this operation. The *adoo* had indeed prepared well. The Commanding Officer of the Iranian Battalion and his entire headquarters, all eighteen of them, were wiped out in the same prolonged contact in which Johnny was killed. Mike Lobb, leading a second Firqat group on an axis parallel to Johnny's, was shot and wounded on Boxing Day, winning a Bravery Medal in the process. Nevertheless, the Iranians to their great credit pressed on and captured Raykhut on 5 January.

It was some six weeks before Johnny's body was recovered, and we buried him in the Christian cemetery near Muscat. His wake was held in one of the officers' messes in the north of Oman and I left it after a day and a half. For all I know, it is going on there still.

Chapter Eleven

The Curtain

I returned to Oman after my Christmas leave, saddened and demoralized at the loss of my closest friend. I only had a few months left to serve there and it would all be spent in the North, training and recruiting under a new commanding officer with whom I did not have the rapport that I had had with Bryan Ray.

Some time before, this commanding officer had quite reasonably given each company a training task to be carried out for the benefit of the whole regiment. A Company was to conduct a field seminar on the use of mortars. With Johnny dead, this now fell to me, and I had no appetite for it whatsoever. It seemed to me to be a time filling exercise and the bright idea of a peacetime British Army staff officer. I procrastinated on preparing for this until, the day before it was due to take place, I realized that I done nothing to translate what preparations were in my mind into reality on the ground. I spent the day preparing frantically, but by nightfall there was still much to do before success on the morrow could be assured. I planned to get up before dawn and complete preparations, but I would have to be pretty fleet of foot and mind if the mortar seminar was going to amount to much.

That night, it rained. Yes; in Oman, one of the hottest driest places on the planet, it rained. And it rained, and rained and rained and rained.

Much of Oman's distinctive topography with deep ravines and jagged mountains, has been formed by water in its more persistent and violent manifestations, but it had never happened to rain while I was there, apart from the unremitting drizzle of the *khareef* – until now. I had heard tales of rainstorms in arid places, and how fishes and frogs would appear within a few short days after the rains had come to even the most barren spot. Oman's annual rainfall is perhaps about four inches a year. We seemed to have had several years worth here in one night.

I got up early as planned and drove out to the scene of what was in danger of becoming a less-than-fully-baked exercise. I took a radio and a signaller, leaving orders for the mortar base plates to deploy to the positions I had arranged. I crossed the *wadi* in my Land Rover as usual. Having completed my preparations, I came back to the same *wadi* about an hour later, ready to meet the rest of the study group, and found what had been the usual barren dry channel of stones was now a raging torrent four feet deep and a hundred feet wide: an astonishing sight. I was cut off. More significantly, there was no possibility of my mortar seminar going ahead. No one at the barracks would be able to leave base until the waters subsided, which certainly would not be today, and probably not tomorrow either. I radioed base and it was agreed that the seminar was cancelled – with much regret, of course.

I sat with my signaller and driver on the wrong side of the torrent, waiting for it to subside, quietly nibbling the *khubbs* – the unleavened bread – and the onions we had brought, and smoking our cigarettes. As I puffed, I marvelled at my good fortune and my undeserved escape from the likely results of my own complacency and arrogance. This was yet another lesson on the dangers of complacency. How many more lessons would I have to learn? It was my twenty-fifth birthday.

I had intended to ride home from Oman on a motorcycle at the end of my time there. An officer in another regiment had agreed to come with me and we had started planning the acquisition of bikes and thinking about routes, but then he went on mid-tour leave and never returned. He had stopped off in Beirut on his way back out to Oman and been kidnapped by one of the many terrorist groups operating in Lebanon at the time and had been held for ransom. For a number of years, we had little idea of what had happened to him although we knew he had been released. I met him again ten years later and he was very cagey about it all. I believe he had been sworn to secrecy. It was rumoured that although he was a serving British officer, the British Government, in order not to be seen to be dealing with terrorists, had refused to pay any money. It was further rumoured that the Sultan had paid a million pounds to spring him. In any event, my plans for a motorcycle ride home were aborted and I decided to come home after a trip through Iran and India instead.

I arranged to sail in a dhow from Muttrah up the Gulf to Dubai, stay with friends, then cross the Gulf to Bandar Abbas in Iran. I would take a bus to Tehran, stay with more friends, and fly on to Calcutta from there. The medical officer in the Northern Frontier Regiment was a delightful Indian Army doctor, appropriately called Medhi, and he lived in Assam. He was on leave there at the time and urged me to come and see him. That is more or less how it all worked out, except that everything happened somewhat later than planned. On my final night in Oman, I was a passenger in a Land Rover that crashed into a dead camel lying on the road. I spent the first week of my leave in hospital.

A major road building programme was by then underway in Northern Oman, and many of the major routes were now hard topped tarmacadamed roads. In the evenings, the new tarmac road surface surrendered up its daytime heat more slowly than the surrounding desert, so these animals used to go to sleep on the highway in the dark. They would then be hit at night by the large road oil tankers that were now plying between the interior and the port. A ten thousand gallon road tanker travelling at 50 mph would barely feel the bump as it ran over a camel on the road. But they left several hundred pounds of camel flesh as a substantial hazard for lesser vehicles.

On this, my final night, I went to a farewell party at Rostaq on the seaward side of the Jebel Akhdar. After the party, I set off to the port of Muttrah where I was to board my dhow to sail away and up the Gulf to begin my journey to Iran and India. I fell asleep in the passenger seat. The driver didn't see the camel until it was too late. I woke up half way through the first roll, and we finished upright in a *wadi* after another. How we were not more badly damaged than we were, I will never understand. The large wooden box carrying my possessions in the back did not crush the head of Nick Franks, the officer sitting next to it, as it should have done. Instead it flew out on to the sand where it energetically and enthusiastically emptied itself. The driver broke his collarbone and was knocked unconscious. I got away with a torn ligament in my knee and Nick was dazed but unharmed. As we sat or lay by the side of the road, I wondered if we were going to be one of those accidents that lay undiscovered for hours, or even days. We weren't. A number of officers had been to the same party and within about half an hour, we were able to wave down the next homeward bound vehicle, without being run down, and warn them about the hazard that lay ahead.

So, supported by a stick and a couple of weeks late, I hobbled out of Oman. I had a leisurely journey in a dhow to Dubai, sharing my food with a friendly team of Omani sailors and sleeping on a pile of rope on the deck most of the way. My last sight of this fascinating country was from the sea. As we followed the Batinah Coast I tried to identify the villages where we had searched for, and Angus Ramsay had found, Communists trying to establish themselves in the North; past the Jebel Akhdar rising majestically in the mist up to 10,000 feet almost directly from the sea; past the Musandam Peninsula, that peculiar part of Oman detached from the main body; and through the Strait of Hormuz, the waterway which was so central to the strategy of the war. It was good to see it at last.

It was strange going to war as a British soldier while Britain was at peace. When he arrived in India after escaping from the Japanese invasion of Burma, my father was astonished and dismayed at the attitude of the British Indian civilian community. Condescending and complacent, they had no interest or comprehension that a struggle was taking place not so far away, the outcome of which could have momentous consequences for them and their way of life. With their solar topees and their spine pads and all their rigid conventions and social flummery, the appearance in their midst of a few men with only what they stood up in and bearing tales of disaster did nothing to move them. Admirable in some ways, I suppose, but today we might say they were in denial. Didn't they know there was a war on? Arriving in UK on leave, bearded and brimming over with tales of derring do, I began to understand how my father had felt. People did not know there was a war on.

The British Army in Burma called itself the Forgotten Army. Mountbatten told them they were not the Forgotten Army. 'Nobody has even heard of you' he said. Quite.

So, why did I go to Oman? I didn't have to go. I wasn't called to war by my country in danger in the same way as my father and grandfather, and all their brothers, cousins and brothers-in-law, were. In many ways it was a rather selfish impulse. I knew that my parents would worry, and would rather I had not gone, but, to their great credit, they never let me feel this. Only much later did I understand what great restraint they must have exercised. In many ways, it is the families who take the greatest strain in war. For the soldiers it may be dangerous and uncertain, but they are sharing the danger and uncertainty together with friends. For the parents, wives and children, the uncertainty continues until their soldier comes home. Yes, the soldier can lose his life; but the family risks losing him, and faces the prospect of living without him. In some ways, they may have more to lose.

There was a number of attractions to serving in Oman. It was something out of the ordinary, which appealed to me. Moreover, we Royal Marines lieutenants went up one rank and, if we commanded a company, we'd go up two ranks. In those days, Royal Marines ranks were one rank down from our equivalents in the Army, and so the awarding of local rank was common. It would be too confusing to try and explain to the Omanis why some of their company commanders were captains, and some majors, so we conformed with Army ranks

167

while we were there. On the other side of the balance was the inevitable reversion back to one's substantive rank on return to UK. But the prospect of swanking it briefly as a Major RM, a rank which, if one was lucky and passed an exam or two, one might – or might not – be promoted to in one's mid 30s, was part of the heady cocktail.

It was also financially lucrative. Loan service pay was generous and the opportunity to spend money was strictly limited. My salary nearly doubled when I went to Oman from about £2,000 to almost £4,000 per annum. It could be said that I was a mercenary of sorts. I spent next to nothing there. My father got excellent stockmarket advice for me and my money went on an oil company called Ultramar. There was an oil crisis in 1974, so, in spite of the stockmarket slump at the time, my money doubled twice in three years. With the miracle of compound interest and reinvested dividends, and the time allowed to youth, this investment formed the core for a number of other fortunate investments and therefore became an excellent financial foundation for the future.

We also got an Omani medal for serving on active service in Dhofar. You may think this an unworthy motivator, but it was another attraction in a culture where medals were parsimoniously given, and where opportunities to earn them were few and far between. I wear mine, and the Victory Medal that was subsequently issued, together with my Distinguished Service Medal for Gallantry, with great pride – even though nobody has a clue what they are. And because they are foreign medals, I am obliged to wear them after my British ones, even after the medal commemorating The Queen's Silver Jubilee for which I did absolutely nothing except be in the Armed Forces at the time and keep my nose clean. The prospect of booty and glory has motivated warriors since time immemorial. We were no different.

Furthermore, I hadn't been a very successful Royal Marine hitherto and I did feel the need to prove myself. Oman was regarded in the Royal Marines as a kind of officers finishing school. I wanted a place at that academy. It was 'cool' to go to Oman. I wanted some of that. I suppose in the same way as a businessman seeks wealth, or a politician seeks power, I felt the urge to go to the line and put my foot across. It wasn't war itself that I sought; it was a form of self-discovery. It was a trip to the wilderness to find oneself. Like any trip to the wilderness, it had its dangers and it did hurt. But I believe I was a far better man for having gone there. Not only had I gained in confidence because I had succeeded, but I had learned much about myself and other people. It helped to put things in perspective. Theodore Roosevelt once said; 'You've never lived until you've almost died. For those who've had to fight for it, life has truly a flavour the protected shall never know.'

I might not have put it quite so emphatically as that, but I think I know what he meant. I have never forgotten the surge of relief and gratitude I felt when I survived the battle in the Wadi Sha'ath, or the mined *sangar*. I said to myself then that every day I live hereafter is a bonus to be cherished; and when life has thrown the odd nettle or piece of broken glass in my path since then, and I have been tempted to feel sorry for myself, I have tried to remind myself; 'what's all this self pity? You should have died on 13 March 1974 and you're still here!' This has usually worked and, in consequence, I have had little difficulty remaining cheerful for most of my life.

I was not alone of course, but circumstances were such that one kept one's own company to a great degree on the *jebel*, so we had time to think. In addition, living in ascetic dangerous circumstances on top of a mountain in this beautiful barren place, under an open, pristine, star freckled night sky that is now almost entirely obscured in our light polluted hemisphere, it was not difficult to sense a spiritual side to our existence; another dimension to our being. Living at close quarters with devout Muslims sparked an interest in Islam and, at the same time I studied a small copy of the New Testament. I can't say that I answered any of the great questions of life, or developed a great faith, but I somehow ended up more at peace with myself.

I have already referred to Churchill and the relief one experiences having survived a battle. There is another post-battle feature which can be felt only by those who have fought. The placing of one's life in the hands of another man and, in turn, the receipt of a reciprocal trust; the shared hazard, the shared survival, and the shared loss; all conspire to develop a bond – an understanding – between soldiers which is like no other. Men who have not fought cannot feel this. And for the commander into whose hands many men may have placed their lives, the intensity of his feeling for those men is not easily to be described. It is both compassionate and possessive. They may not all be good men, and they may not all be nice men, but they are *his* men. Together with them, he risked everything, and won. On them his life and reputation rests. His commitment is a form of love, and long after the last shot has been fired, they will retain a preferential place in his heart.

And so, such men may not have seen each other for many decades, but on reacquaintance, the danger they shared makes their comradeship as fresh as if they had last met yesterday, and the years fall away. This unique bond transcends race, religion, rank, age, class and time. He fought alongside me. He understands.

There is a long list of British who have been captivated by Arabia. The culture, the language, the people, the desert, the mountains, the religion: all combine in a rich chemistry which casts a beguiling romantic spell. Among the better known of these devotees are Richard Burton, Gertrude Bell, Wilfred Thesiger, St John Philby, and T E Lawrence, but there are many others. We sometimes rather disparagingly and crudely describe this process as 'going native'. Yet we expect people from other cultures who come to live in our country to adopt our customs and wear our clothes so why we should look down our noses at our own people who do this in other countries is not clear to me. But we do. There were not many who 'went native' in Oman, but there were plenty who developed an understanding and an affection for the people and the country which made them want to stay there and work after their initial service. I felt the pull too, and I was tempted, but in the end I decided my future lay elsewhere. But whenever I hear the country mentioned, my heart quickens and my interest is stimulated, and warm memories of Oman and the Omanis come to the fore. And of course, the man who was my good friend lies there, together with other friends, British, Baluchi and Omani, and a part of me will always remain in that entrancing, fascinating, hauntingly beautiful country.

Conclusion

The Sultan's Armed Forces, having consolidated their position on the Central and Eastern Jebel, were now poised to dominate what had been the *adoo*'s territory and a no-go area for years: the Western Jebel – the area between the Hornbeam Line and Sarfait on the border with the PDRY. In December 1974 and during the months that followed, a series of aggressive and bold operations were mounted to take the Sheershitti Caves and the village of Raykhut, both of which I had glimpsed from Bob Mason's Strikemaster. Operations out of the Sarfait position down to the sea, so deceptively close on the big map, but in reality involving a 3,000 feet descent, were always going to be fraught with difficulty, but this was indeed finally achieved by the Muscat Regiment in November 1975.

As always, the *adoo* never gave up easily. There were some ferocious, lethal, confusing battles – AMFUs, SAMFUs and CMFUs – sometimes fought at long distance with artillery, sometimes at grenade throwing range; where aircraft were shot down, and brave men were wounded and killed, mostly in action, but also murdered in cold blood by the *adoo*. The Iranian operation in which Johnny Braddell-Smith was killed was ultimately successful and the Damavand Line further constrained the *adoo*'s ability to sustain operations in the more populated central and eastern areas. Some of the hardest fighting of the war took place in those last few months. Fresh, untried Iranian troops found themselves in over their heads. The Firqat, never short of courage, but always demanding a very special and rare persuasive leadership, predictably behaved unpredictably. An Omani rifle company mutinied against its British officers, and a British commanding officer was sacked and replaced in the course of a three day battle.

But the Sultan's Forces finally broke the *adoo*'s hold on Dhofar and in December 1975 the Sultan was able to declare Dhofar secure for civil

171

development. However no one told the *adoo* that they had lost the war. Even after the conflict was officially over, the helicopter from which Brigadier John Akehurst and Shirley, his wife, were dispensing good cheer around the *jebel* positions on Christmas Day 1975 was damaged by ground fire and forced down near Mirbat. No one was hurt, and they gamely carried on in another aircraft. There was a number of other incidents in the following months and years where government troops or civilians were killed when they thought that it was safe to move freely in areas where the *adoo* had held sway. And there were *adoo* in the central and eastern areas who, cut off from all sources of supply and support, simply did not know that they were beaten and who, like Japanese soldiers of the Second World War, had to be fought out to a man.

The last of the Sultan's soldiers to be killed in action was Donald Nairn, a New Zealander and an officer of the Frontier Force. Operating in the Eastern Area with his company of Baluchi soldiers, he engaged a group of four *adoo* in a fierce firefight and killed three of them. The fourth man fled and took refuge in a small cave, obscured by scrub and bushes. Nairn with his soldiers approached the area where the *adoo* had disappeared and called upon him to surrender. In response, the *adoo* fired one shot which killed Nairn, hitting him between the eyes. The *adoo* then immediately surrendered. This took place on 9 May 1979. Perhaps the most surprising aspect of this incident – apart from the fact that these *adoo* were still operating on the *jebel* over three years after the war had been declared over – is that the Baluchi soldiers accepted the *adoo*'s surrender and did not slaughter him out of hand then and there.

In 1984, John Akehurst wrote an account of the Dhofar War which remains the best overall history of the conflict to date. He called it *We Won a War*. The title was apposite. Soldiers of many nations all came together in common cause to help Oman rid herself of her virus. We were professionals who had been asked to come and do a job because of our expertise. Omanis had never been colonised and no one represented a past or present colonial power. We had all entered their world at their request, had learned their language, and respected their ways. All were invited guests, subject to Oman's laws. We were all part of that 'we'.

Moreover, the hint of surprise in his title also reflected how people felt at the time, even if only subconsciously. In the 1960s and 70s, the Cold War was still pretty chilly. True, Communism had been checked in Greece and Austria at the end of the Second World War, and it had been defeated in Malaya in the 50s and 60s. But in Cuba and Eastern Europe the Soviets were deeply entrenched, and in parts of Africa and the Far East, Communism seemed to be gathering new adherent states on a regular and inexorable basis. With the formation of the PDRY, Communism was now beginning to penetrate the Middle East. The Americans were in the process of losing Vietnam, and the spread of Euro-Communism looked like making the threatened Soviet invasion of Western Europe unnecessary. It is disingenuous to point now at the ramshackle empty shell that was revealed by the collapse of the Berlin Wall. In the 1960s and 70s, it looked as if Communism might achieve its self-professed goal of world domination without lifting a finger. Mao Tse Tung was still alive and the Cultural Revolution, driven by mobs of so-called students styling themselves Red Guards, had China in its grip. I had glimpsed something of this at first hand when I had been stationed on the border between British Hong Kong and Red China three years before. These crowds of thugs seemed able to communicate only very loudly in quotes from Mao's little Red Book, which was the bible of the 'progressive' left. Indeed it was said to have sold more copies than the Bible. I actually bought one out of curiosity myself. The Bible is the better read.

On the *jebel*, many of us kept in touch with the wider world by listening to the BBC World Service. Listening to British politics move to the left in the two General Elections that took place in 1974 was not encouraging. Listening to 'Radio Peace and Progress, the Voice of Soviet Public Opinion' while fighting an anti-Communist war wasn't much fun either. It all appeared to be of one piece and the tide was going in only one direction. We seemed to be surrounded by ideological enemies. Yet, we won a war.

John Akehurst's 'we' could also be said to embrace another group: the Dhofaris. Simplistically speaking, the Dhofari rebels were on the losing side. However, the achievements of the defeated should not be measured solely by their failure to attain their stated aims, in this case an independent Dhofari state. The real success of the 'losing side' lies in the extent to which, through their efforts and their sacrifice, they forced their opponents to adjust their own attitudes and approaches in order to beat them. By this yardstick, the Dhofaris were hugely successful. They forced the removal of a hated ruler and brought about the transformation of their country in a way which even the most farsighted of them could not have imagined in 1965. They also managed to avoid becoming a Communist state, a fate which befell a number of vulnerable peoples at that time. So, yes, their rebellion was suppressed; but the Dhofaris were winners too.

General Tim Creasey attributed victory to a number of factors. The leadership of Sultan Qaboos was critical. Without a sound political foundation, all our efforts were futile. With a good foundation, everything was possible. His accession allowed everything else to go ahead. It was important that everybody pulled in the same direction and this was achieved by setting up a National Defence Council, chaired by the Sultan, which addressed all political and military matters. After the flow of oil increased in 1972 and, especially after the oil crisis which followed the Arab-Israeli War of 1973 when the oil price quadrupled, Oman had new financial resources that at last made it possible to equip and pay the Forces properly. General Creasey also saw the active involvement of allies as very important, particularly Iran, Jordan and Britain, all of whom sent substantial forces and placed them at the disposal of the Omani Government. The air power we enjoyed also gave us the freedom to go anywhere we chose, and to strike anywhere we wanted, without notice. However, the emphasis on timely civil development which offered Dhofaris a better way of life than that which the Communists could offer, was a central enduring key. Meeting more precisely their expectations rather than forcing an unwanted regime upon them was war winning stuff.

All these things are true. What Creasey did not say, but what is also true, is that the wisdom, guidance, drive, leadership and confidence he himself provided was pivotal.

It may also be worth pointing out that while this was a low-tech, low-intensity war, the officers whom Britain sent to Oman, both contracted and regular, were highly trained volunteers. Most had the necessary commitment to stick it out and those who didn't left pretty soon. It is a strange irony that the low-tech war is no less demanding of the preparation and training that you give your people. Arguably even greater care is required in this sphere. The patience and tolerance to live harmoniously in an unfamiliar culture; the fortitude to be content with less than comfortable circumstances for prolonged periods; an understanding of and sympathy for a foreign history and religion; a willingness to learn a new language; the flexibility, imagination and humility necessary to climb into the head of people who live by a very different set of assumptions; none of these are found automatically in our modern developed Euro-Atlantic culture. These attributes, and the attitudes they imply, often need to be taught in addition to purely military skills. We seem to be able to churn out in large numbers officers who can manoeuvre around the high intensity battlefield in armoured vehicles by day and night. Finding and training people who have the necessary attitudes, skills and quality of character to live with, to be accepted by, and to lead successfully a group of Dhofari Firqat is another matter altogether.

One must also take great care to understand and respect one's enemy. In 1879, a powerful British force of 1,800 men was destroyed at

Isandlwana in South Africa by an army of Zulus armed chiefly with spears and knobkerries. By a series of manoeuvres little short of brilliant, the Zulu commander concentrated his force of some 20,000 men and moved it across country, unnoticed by the British. Through arrogance and over-confidence, the British allowed this force to approach unsuspected and unseen and to overwhelm them. In his book *Zulu*, Saul David draws our attention to a cartoon which appeared in *Punch* shortly after this *débâcle*. In it, John Bull is sitting on a stool in a classroom looking attentively at the blackboard. Standing at the blackboard is a Zulu warrior and he is writing 'Despise not your Enemy'. The British have not always hoisted in the lesson that the Zulus taught them, otherwise they might not have lost Gallipoli in 1915, or Singapore in 1942. But at least they didn't make the same mistake in Oman.

It will be clear now to the reader that the *adoo*, who were mostly Dhofaris, were clever, wily, hard, hugely brave and extremely determined: an enemy worthy of considerable respect as fighters. They were let down by internecine disputes, resentment of authority and an immoral political agenda that failed in the end to win popular support. As individual soldiers they were men – and women – of pretty high capability.

A new term, 'asymmetric warfare' has been invented to refer to the imbalances and the difficulties that arise when a technologically advanced force faces a relatively unsophisticated enemy. But this phenomenon is not new and has recurred many times in history. The basic skills and attitudes necessary to fight and beat the guerrilla are just as old. As Professor Richard Holmes has said, the real truth about asymmetric warfare is cultural asymmetry – those who can take it, and those who can't. It has been said by wise men that, in war, the side that wins is the side that is most motivated. By tacitly accepting this truth, the Sultan, by winning the hearts and minds of the Dhofaris, diverted their motivation so that his and theirs coincided. In the long run, there would have been no other way of beating them.

What were we British fighting for in another country's war? In the first place, the Omanis asked us to help them. But more importantly, no British Serviceman in Oman was in any doubt about the element of *realpolitik* in our presence there. It was very much in the British national interest that Oman should not become another Communist satellite. We were fighting for oil and we knew it. We weren't fighting for democracy. Democracy is a loaded word and means anything men want it to mean – even the East Germans called their republic a democratic one. It seems to be axiomatic that any country that has a derivative of the word 'democracy' in its title is almost certainly not one. The PDRY certainly wasn't. However, the goal of securing Dhofar for civil development and making it safe from Communism was one 'we' could all sign up to. We were fighting for oil, but in support of that goal, we were fighting so that Omanis could bring their country into the modern world in the way they wanted to – whichever way that was – without gross interference from Russia, China, Cuba and others. Conversely, one wonders how Oman would have fared if we had, with evangelical fervour, insisted upon our own values and system of government. Would that have constituted another form of gross interference?

Journalists are fond of asking the question: was it worth it? The answer is of course a highly personal one, because the burden of war is always unevenly borne. The family of a dead British or Iranian soldier cannot be expected to give the same answer as a commander or a politician, or even the family of a dead Omani soldier.

Speculating on the unhappened past is almost as great a folly as trying to foretell the future. But it is interesting to guess at what might have happened if the war had been lost. Whatever the American objectives were in going to war in Vietnam, it does not now seem that they were to protect her vital interests. Defeat had many significant effects but, with the benefit of hindsight, Vietnam was strategically insignificant. No vital resources were lost, no critical courses of action were closed by defeat, no important freedom of action was denied. Oman was different. It is difficult to imagine that the United States, Japan, or the European powers would have been comfortable with a Communist hold on the oil coming through the Strait of Hormuz. Much would have depended on how assertively the Communists wielded that influence. It might have served them well enough to let it flow. Simply being able to threaten to cut it might have been a sufficiently potent weapon for them. On the other hand, the Reagan/ Thatcher years were about to begin and, given their obdurate no-compromise approach to the Evil Empire, it is equally possible that a wider, far more damaging, conflict could have broken out. Fortunately we will never know.

The situation could only have been exacerbated by the fall of the Shah of Iran in 1979 and the installation of Ayatollah Khomeini's Islamic Republic. Thus the south side of the Strait would have been ruled by an atheistic Communist regime, while on the north side the deeply fundamentalist Shia Muslim Ayatollah would have sat scowling and fulminating with his uncompromising creed. The Ayatollah was, and the Communists would have been, deeply antagonistic to the West, as well as to each other. All sorts of fascinating possibilities emerge out of this scenario. It is thankfully an open question whether they would have gone to war against each other before the West felt the imperative to go to war against one, or the other, or both of them, to keep the Strait free for Western tankers. Or would the holy Ayatollah have struck an alliance with the infidel Communists, or even with the Great Satan itself in order to secure the position of his totalitarian regime? What would have happened to neighbouring Saudi Arabia and its massive oil fields is anybody's guess. What fun all this speculation is. Fortunately it is only fun, because it didn't happen. But it might have done.

Waging war can be compared to conducting invasive surgery without antiseptics or anaesthetic. One hopes that ultimately the result will be beneficial, but one can be sure that it will also be very painful, highly traumatic and will leave deep scars. Before one wields the knife one must also be mindful of the impossibility of prediction: that the risks are great, the outcome is uncertain, that there will be unexpected side effects, and that by operating one might even make things worse. Furthermore, it is a dismal fact that virtually every war in history has lasted longer than expected.

It is axiomatic therefore, that wars, like invasive surgery without antiseptics or anaesthetic, should be avoided if at all possible. But it seems certain that by fighting in Dhofar, we avoided something even more disruptive and destructive. By this token alone, the Dhofar War was worth fighting. What one can safely say is that although largely unknown and unseen, the war in the Frankincense Moutains was of momentous strategic importance. The world would certainly have heard about it if we had lost.

Hegel said that, 'What experience and history teach is this: that people and governments have never learned anything from history, or acted from principles deducted from it.' I am not sure that this is true, or even if true, why it should be so. It seems to me that there are lessons to be learned by politicians from historical precedents; and principles to be deduced and acted upon, if only they care to look.

Specifically, perhaps there are some lessons for politicians to learn – or rather re-learn – from the Oman experience. Harold Wilson's government, not an administration that immediately conjures up a portfolio of golden memories, nevertheless successfully resisted American pressure to get involved in the strategically irrelevant and ultimately disastrous Vietnam War. At the same time, Wilson and subsequently Edward Heath took low-key, effective, military and diplomatic measures to protect our vital interests which were threatened by developments in the Gulf. In the light of this and our experience from subsequent wars, perhaps the lesson was, and is, this: don't go to war unless by not fighting, you are faced with the near certain prospect of something even worse.

One should be mindful too of the maxim that the side that is most motivated tends to win, and that war is a clash of opposing wills. Therefore, before embarking on a war, politicians should judge whether there is sufficient political will, not only to start the war, but also to see it through to the bitter end in the face of all the setbacks and disasters that will almost certainly emerge. In other words, if you are a dog, don't fight a cat in a corner unless the death of that cat really, really matters to you. Otherwise you may find that the will of the cat to survive is greater than your will to sacrifice and to endure all the pain and damage that it will inflict upon you before you can kill it. Oman, Iran and Britain had more to lose than the Communists had to gain. Perhaps they were going to win one way or the other in the end.

The transformation started by Qaboos bin Said on that day in 1970, when Ray Kane passed him on the stairway of his father's palace in Salalah, has proceeded apace. Uncorrupt, forward looking and engaged, Qaboos represented the government that Omanis wanted. He was popular and widely respected. He gave good government. He may not have been democratic but he was accountable in an indirect way. The lesson of what happens when you are not responsive to your people's needs had been taken fully on board. Sultan Qaboos was a benevolent autocrat who, with the freedom of action that his victory allowed him, has gently but surely advanced his country on a liberalising course towards more directly accountable government. We were not expecting instant democracy to emerge out of the victory on the *jebel*. But we knew that Qaboos would slowly ease things forward at his own pace. It was an act of faith that the Oman that would emerge from our common endeavours would be something that we could all be proud of. That faith was not misplaced.

Beginning as she did from an educational standing start in 1970, it was inevitable that Oman would lean heavily on outside expert and technical help for a long time to come. But in the Army, Omanis very soon took over key command posts and the British stood back, first in an advisory or subordinate role, and then disappearing altogether. The relative ease with which this was done is yet another indication of the warm and mature relationship between the British and Omani officers. We were a partnership of equals. The Omanisation process has continued throughout the last thirty years and is now virtually complete. For anyone who knew Oman at that time, or before, the change is on the one hand astonishing, and yet on the other, somehow reassuring. Oman has travelled in a short thirty years a journey which other countries took a thousand years to complete. Indeed, the quantum changes took place in the first fifteen years. Subsequent change has been incremental. There are now motorways where once there were only tracks. There are highways on the *jebel* in Dhofar where we picked our way by day and night across the most inaccessible and inhospitable of mountain landscapes. The ancient trails where the traders of antiquity brought their frankincense from the trees in those mountains down to the sea are now modern roads. Indeed, just east of Mughsayl, where Viv Rowe, Said Nasser and Chris Barnes played cat and mouse with the *adoo*, there is now a fine road which at one point ascends the *jebel* side almost sheer for a thousand feet as if suspended in the air. Yet none of this is a surprise. Even while we sweated and laboured over that country then, we frequently amused ourselves by surmising that 'you'll be able to drive here in a car one day' and we weren't wrong. What is reassuring is that in spite of the immense tensions and pressures that such change must inevitably bring upon a society, the essential character of the people and the country does not seem to have suffered.

Of course it has changed. As the surge of Oman's renaissance matures into evolution, the memories of former times will fade. The aspirations and preoccupations of younger generations will have more in common with others of the developed world, and their parents and grandparents will, like parents and grandparents everywhere shake their heads and say, with perhaps better reason than most, 'it wasn't like that in my day'. But, perhaps because of the conservative but tolerant nature of Ibadhi Islam, Omanis remain substantially at peace with themselves and the increasingly numerous visitors to their country.

Oman today is a stable, peaceful, modern country with good relations with its neighbours and the wider world. Political power still remains substantially in the hands of Qaboos and he exercises it through an appointed State Council. All laws which have a bearing on the social and economic lives of the people go before an elected Consultative Council of eighty-three members for consideration and comment before they are enacted. Freedom of speech, freedom of association, freedom of religion and the equality of all citizens before the law are guaranteed by a Basic Statute. All men and women over the age of twenty-one have the vote. Television and radio are operated by the government, but the door to licensing of private stations has opened with recent legislation. Satellite dishes are allowed. There is a number of newspapers and other publications, although they are subject to censorship for political or cultural reasons.

Purist Western democrats may curl their lips at the retention of real power by one man and his appointees. However, when one considers what might have been, and when one looks at the norm for almost every other Islamic state in the Middle East, Omani citizens enjoy a remarkably high degree of accountability, transparency and representation.

Women play a full part in public life. There are women members of both the State and Consultative Councils, and there has been at least one female ambassador. There are female radio announcers and news broadcasters. They can also be found throughout the civil service and industry, many occupying senior positions. Taking this together with the many publicly funded schools which offer education to all boys and girls up to the age of sixteen, and the several universities and technical colleges that have been established, one could say that Oman sets the pace for political and social development for others in the region to follow. Religion plays an important part as it does in the politics of all Muslim countries, but the Ibadhi tradition of moderation stands good, and there is not the fundamentalist zeal that one encounters elsewhere.

There are shadows of course. The present relative prosperity depends on oil and gas. That will not last forever. Underground water aquifers, which have taken many hundreds of thousands of years to develop, are being perceptibly reduced and water levels in the Dhofar Mountains are getting lower as increased demands are made upon these finite reservoirs. Water is in effect being mined as a resource.

There are not yet enough suitable occupations to engage the increasingly large numbers of university graduates who are coming out of the fine education system. There remains the question of who will succeed Qaboos, who has no obvious heir, and what nature of government he will provide. But these difficulties are widely acknowledged and understood, and much is being done to address them, and to ensure long-term sustainability. Diversification into other industries is well under way and much emphasis is placed on developing a non-oil based private sector. There is a beach club and restaurant at our chosen spot at Mughsayl, although surprisingly no hotel at Mirbat. Doubtless it will come. But many others have been built, and Oman is rapidly becoming a sought after destination for the discriminating and discerning traveller. In any case, these uncertainties are trivial compared to the upheaval that would have smitten the country if the war had been lost.

I daresay Oman would have emerged out of her past whatever happened. But by not losing the Dhofar War, Oman retained the freedom to make choices and take steps without having to endure the destabilizing destructive tyranny that always seemed to be the concomitant of Communism. Her progress towards what we choose to call modernity has thus far been remarkably smooth. She needed time to do that, and that is what the war won for her. And, while Omanis won the war, they have also so far achieved that much more difficult feat: they are winning the peace.

Glossary

AB205	US designed, Italian built helicopter
adoo	an enemy, the enemy
AK 47	Kalashnikov 7.62 mm semi-automatic rifle
AMFU	Adjustable Military Fuck Up
base wallah	denizen of base camp, rather than the *jebel* or front line
bayt	house or home
bedu	nomadic Arab people who live in the desert
burmail	45 gallon oil drum, or anything similar
campowda	medical orderly
chai	tea
chargul	canvas bag for holding and chilling water
CMFU	Complete Military Fuck Up
dhobi wallah	man who washes clothes
dishdash	Arabian over-garment
djinn	a spirit
falaj	water course
firqat	military unit or group
FN	Fabrique Nationale, Belgian manufacturers of weapons
GPMG	General Purpose Machine Gun
halwa	sweet or dessert
jebali	a person from the *jebel*, of the *jebel*
jebel	a hill or mountain
Kalashnikov	Russian manufacturer of weapons
khunjar	curved Arabian dagger
khareef	mist resulting from SW monsoon
khubbs	unleavened bread, chapattis
khudaam	servants

Martini Henry	British Army rifle late 19th century
PDRY	Peoples Democratic Republic of Yemen
PFLOAG	Peoples Front for the Liberation of the Occupied Arab Gulf
RPG 7	Hand held anti-tank rocket propelled grenade launcher
SAMFU	Semi Adjustable Military Fuck Up
sangar	improvised stone breastwork to protect soldiers from enemy fire
SEP	Surrendered Enemy Personnel
shaiba	old man
shemaagh	Arabian headdress
SOAF	Sultan of Oman's Air Force
Sphaghin	Russian manufacturer of weapons
Strikemaster	British-made light jet bomber
suq	market
wadi	valley
wali	local governor
wizar	wrap-around kilt-like garment worn by Dhofari men

Index

185

187